U.S. War-culture, Sacrifice and Salvatio

Religion and Violence

Editors
Lisa Isherwood, University of Winchester, and Rosemary Radford Ruether,
Graduate Theological Union, Berkeley, California

Published

Reweaving the Relational Mat
A Christian Response to Violence against Women from Oceania
Joan Filemoni-Tofaeono and Lydia Johnson

Weep not for your Children
Essays on Religion and Violence
Edited by Lisa Isherwood and Rosemary Radford Ruether

In Search of Solutions
The Problem of Religion and Conflic
Clinton Bennett

America, Amerikkka
Elect Nation and Imperial Violence
Rosemary Radford Ruether

Shalom/Salaam/Peace
A Liberation Theology of Hope
Constance A. Hammond

Faith-Based War
From 9/11 to Catastrophic Success in Iraq
T. Walter Herbert

Crying for Dignity
Caste-based Violence against Dalit Women
Mary Grey

The Real Peace Process
Worship, Politics and the End of Sectarianism
Siobhán Garrigan

Forthcoming

Edith Stein and Regina Jonas
Religious Visionaries in the Time of the Death Camps
Emily Leah Silverman

U.S. War-culture, Sacrifice and Salvation

Kelly Denton-Borhaug

Routledge
Taylor & Francis Group

LONDON AND NEW YORK

First published 2011 by Equinox Publishing Ltd., an imprint of Acumen

Published 2014 by Routledge
2 Park Square, Milton Park, Abingdon, Oxon OX14 4RN
711 Third Avenue, New York, NY 10017, USA

Routledge is an imprint of the Taylor and Francis Group, an informa business

Notices
Practitioners and researchers must always rely on their own experience and
knowledge in evaluating and using any information, methods, compounds, or
experiments described herein. In using such information or methods they should be
mindful of their own safety and the safety of others, including parties for whom
they have a professional responsibility.

To the fullest extent of the law, neither the Publisher nor the authors,
contributors, or editors, assume any liability for any injury and/or damage to
persons or property as a matter of products liability, negligence or otherwise, or
from any use or operation of any methods, products, instructions, or ideas
contained in the material herein.

British Library Cataloguing-in-Publication Data
A catalogue record for this book is available from the British Library.

ISBN-13 978-184553-710-4   (hardback)
ISBN-13 978-184553-711-1   (paperback)

Library of Congress Cataloging-in-Publication Data

Denton-Borhaug, Kelly.
  U.S. War-culture, sacrifice, and salvation/Kelly Denton-Borhaug
     p. cm. — (Religion and violence)
  Includes bibliographical references and index.
  ISBN 978-1-84553-710-4 (hb) — ISBN 978-1-84553-711-1 (pb) 1.
Christianity and culture — United States. 2. War — Religious
aspects — Christianity. 3. Sacrifice — Christianity. 4. War an
society — United States. 5. Sacrifice — Social aspects — United States. 6
United States — Religious life and customs. I. Title. II. Title: United
States war-culture, sacrifice, and salvation.
  BR517.D43 2010
  261.8'730973 — dc22

                         2010012402

Typeset by S.J.I. Services, New Delhi

CONTENTS

ACKNOWLEDGEMENTS

Coleman Barks, 'Just this Once' *Winter Sky: New and Selected Poems, 1968–2008*, Athens, Georgia: University of Georgia Press, 2008. Reprinted with permission of the poet and the University of Georgia Press.

Some sections from Chapter One appeared in Kelly Denton-Borhaug, 'War-culture and Sacrifice', *Feminist Theology* 18(2): 175–91, Sage Publications, London, 2010. http://www.sagepub.co.uk/JournalsPermissions.nav. DOI: 10.1177/0966735009348552. Reprinted with the permission of SAGE Publications Ltd.

An earlier version of Chapter Two appeared in Kelly Denton-Borhaug, 'The Language of "Sacrifice" in the Buildup to War: A Feminist Rhetorical and Theological Analysis', *The Journal of Religion and Popular Culture* (Spring 2007). This version printed with the permission of the *Journal of Religion and Popular Culture*.

Parts of Chapter Three appeared in Kelly Denton-Borhaug, 'A Deadly Nexus: "Necessity," Christian Salvation and War Culture', *International Journal of the Humanities* 5.9 (Fall 2007): 161–68. Reprinted with the permission of Common Ground Publishing.

PREFACE

This book would not have come into being without the support, critique and wisdom of many generous good friends and colleagues. Peggy Rosana Preciado and Susan Stocker were there from the beginning, before I knew that I was writing a book, and along the way gave me so much encouragement, in addition to the gift of their insightful and intelligent response to my work. I sincerely thank them, especially for the speed with which they are able to turn around a draft and send it back with precise and helpful comments!

Moravian College was generous with a number of small grants to assist research, enable travel, and use the summer months for research and writing. It has been very meaningful to have the strong support of faculty at my teaching institution. After Clarke Chapman read an early draft of the entire book, and responded with copious and detailed notes, we had a wonderfully memorable and for me, helpful theological conversation over lunch, discussing and debating many issues and questions. Don St. John is a genius when it comes to editing; also, both he and Clarke were unfailingly encouraging with examples of war-culture they found and shared with me. Don, Carol Moeller, Daniel Jasper and Khristina Haddad led me to additional thinkers whose writings helped me make important connections and deepened my own critical thought. On one glorious fall day Khristina and I had a three-hour walk along the river in Bethlehem, while we talked fast and furiously about liberalism, sovereignty, the nation-state and sacrifice. The Peace and Justice Studies Faculty group at Moravian College and the Institute for Jewish and Christian Understanding at Muhlenberg College (led by Peter Pettit) both invited me to develop presentations on this material, and I'm grateful to them for these opportunities. My student, Naiomi Gonzalez, provided much-needed assistance with the bibliography.

As the book began to come together in earnest, I discovered the Britain and Ireland Feminist School of Theology, and in the summer of 2008, was given the opportunity to present a seminar for the school based on research for this book. I'm truly appreciative that Lisa Isherwood included me, making it possible for me to experience a few days with this wonderful international group of women academics, clergy and activists. It was a joy and privilege at the summer school to hear Rosemary Radford Ruether give the keynote address based on her book in this series. My participation in that event led to consideration of my book for the *Religion and Violence* series, and I'm deeply grateful to Rosemary and Lisa for their support of this work.

Along the way other colleagues have read chapters and provided invaluable feedback. I'm especially indebted to Sharon Thornton, Pamela Brubaker, Denny Weaver, Mary Condren and Joerg Rieger for the benefit of their time, experience and intelligence. Thanks also must go to my dear friend Nita Gilson who created a website for the book: www.KellyDentonBorhaug.com

Though I mention my family last, their love, forbearance and fortitude really come first and I thank them all, especially my beloved Gunnar.

Garth, Thomas and Laura, living with me you've been exposed to my growing hope regarding the possibilities for constructing a less violent world. I had you so much in my heart and mind as I worked on this project. In comparison with so many other young people around the world, your lives have been relatively free from the devastation of war, but you have breathed the atmosphere of war-culture from your very beginnings. This book is for you, with hope that you and your generation will discover tools for resistance, and the capacity to reconsider and reform our way of living in the United States.

Kelly Denton-Borhaug

INTRODUCTION

How are we involved, I want to know, in the traumas of others? And as a theologian, I want to know whether and how our spiritual commitments involve us in violence.

Tom Beaudoin[1]

The purpose of this book is to expose and analyze the enduring and destructive relationship between U.S. War-culture, and frameworks and practices of sacrifice. No doubt readers are very familiar with the emphasis on sacrifice in U.S. Christianity; popularly understood, Jesus' sacred sacrific is the necessary act that paves the way for the salvation of humankind. But generally speaking, we have not given much thought to the equally dominant presence of sacrificial images, rhetoric and understandings in common discourse about politics, economics, and especially, with regard to the military and the use of armed force, nor do we question the interplay of sacrificial constructions between these different contexts and the consequences that result. However, as I will argue, the rhetoric and practices of sacrifice animate U.S. War-culture, and we must understand this relationship more clearly if we are to develop resistance to the dynamics of increasing militarization in the United States.

Theologian Tom Beaudoin suggests that American Christianity most accurately is assessed not by what it professes, but by what it fails to see, challenge and contest. And with respect to the sacrificia - ism of U.S. War-culture, there is much that remains to be seen and understood, much less challenged. After the attacks on the World Trade Center's twin towers and Pentagon on Sept. 11 2001, a new refrain entered the common American vocabulary: 'The world will never be the same.' However, looking back, did we really have any

1. Tom Beaudoin, *Witness to Dispossession: The Vocation of a Post-modern Theologian* (Maryknoll, NY: Orbis Books, 2008), p. 34.

idea about the scope of the changes that would be wrought as a result of these events?

Economists tell us that the military budget of the United States increased by 73 percent between 2001 and 2008. In 2008 alone the government spent an estimated $624 bn on the military, or about $2,000 for every resident of the country.[2] Approximately 5m U.S. citizens work either directly for the military or for the thousands of civilian industries directly connected to the military.[3] By the time this book goes to print, the wars in Afghanistan and Iraq will have endured for close to ten years. At the beginning of 2010, President Obama intimated that the 'War on Terror' comprised no fewer than five different fronts throughout the world. Not only Iraq and Afghanistan, and those 'unfinished wars,' but news reports described covert U.S. military activity against Al Qaeda also occurring and escalating in Pakistan, Yemen and Somalia.[4] At the beginning of the second decade of this new century, we in the U.S. live in the midst of a 'military-industrial-technological-entertainment-academic-scientific-media-intelligence-homelan security-surveillance-national-security-corporate complex.'[5]

While U.S. War-culture predates the terrorist events of the first decade of this new century, 9/11 provided an opportunity for U.S.

2. Robert Pollin and Heidi Garrett-Peltier, 'The U.S. Employment Effects of Military and Domestic Spending Priorities: An Updated Analysis,' *Political Economy Research Institute*, University of Massachusetts Amherst, October 2009, p. 1.

3. Pollin and Garrett-Peltier, 'The U.S. Employment Effects of Military and Domestic Spending Priorities', p. 1. In addition to the millions who are directly employed by defense contractors, it would be difficult to assess how many additional millions of U.S. citizens earn their livelihood through sub-contracting corporations with lucrative military contracts. Chapter One addresses this aspect of the militarization of contemporary U.S. culture and economics.

4. 'The Transcript of Obama's Remarks on Airline Security and Terror Watch Lists,' *Washington Post*, 28 December 2009, http://voices.washingtonpost.com/44/2009/12/obama-remarks-on-airline-secur.html, accessed 31 December 2009. President Obama remarked, 'We will continue to use every element of our national power to disrupt, to dismantle and defeat the violent extremists who threaten us, whether they are from Afghanistan or Pakistan, Yemen or Somalia, or anywhere where they are plotting attacks against the U.S. homeland.' Also see Eric Schmitt and Robert F. Worth, 'U.S. Widens Terror War to Yemen, a Qaeda Bastion', *The New York Times*, 27 December 2009.

5. Nick Turse, *The Complex: How The Military Invades Our Everyday Lives* (New York: Metropolitan Books, 2008), p. 16.

militarism's exponential increase. How is it that U.S. citizens could be living in the middle of the largest war-culture the world has ever known, and have so little consciousness of it? Why do so few Christian leaders and churches raise their voices against U.S. War-culture? Along the lines of Beaudoin's theological challenge above, what do we need to understand in order to accurately assess our own context in the United States?

Theologians have spoken in the strongest possible terms about the urgent need for penetrating self-examination, religious, political, economic, social and otherwise, in Western nations such as the U.S. For example, Douglas John Hall writes, 'the association of the Christian religion with white Western/Northern economic, military, and cultural imperialism constitutes possibly the single most insidious cause of global peril.'[6] He urges more profound self-interrogation in the United States regarding the links between religious practices, assumptions and values, and the overarching social, political/military and economic structures that determine so much of our lives (and the world outside our borders). Yet in the post-9/11 period we in the United States have been fixated primarily on the perceived dangers from outside, instead of looking inward to our own national character, history and actions, and their connection to religious ideas and commitments. 'Why do terrorists do what they do?' 'What motivates suicide bombers?' 'How can we stop them?' Questions such as these have dominated the national conversation in the United States, questions that assume that our biggest problems are 'out there.'

In fact, even stronger language may be used to describe our situation in the United States. For not only is our tendency not to look inward, we in fact resist the invitation to do so. American exceptionalism, that is, our deep-seated belief in an America as 'innocent and good, chosen by God to defend freedom and democracy around the world,' makes it excruciatingly difficult to 'see through the ideological smokescreen' that hides a history of imperialism and widespread destruction of lands and peoples in the name of our own self-interest.[7]

6. Douglas John Hall, *The Cross in Our Context: Jesus and the Suffering World* (Minneapolis, MN: Fortress Press, 2003), p. 4.
7. Rosemary Radford Ruether, *America, Amerikkka: Elect Nation And Imperial Violence* (London: Equinox Publishing, 2007), pp. 1–2.

Nowhere is this self-delusion as intense as at the intersection of U.S. militarism and popular Christianity. In the post-9/11 period there was growing ineffectiveness of protest in the United States against militarism and war. The millions around the world who protested the planned Iraq War in 2002 were easily sidestepped and condescendingly dismissed, while increasing religiosity connected to U.S. War-culture made it harder to critically penetrate the growth and consequences of U.S. militarism. At the end of 2009, despite the dismal shape of the U.S. economy, and despite intense debate regarding the economic cost of passing a universal health care bill, both the U.S. House and Senate, overwhelmingly and with little protest, passed the 2010 military budget proposal from the Obama Administration for $636 bn – billions more than President Bush's final defense bill [8]

This book addresses an important piece of the puzzle with respect to the incongruity of the growth of militarism and war-culture in the United States, and its increasing imperviousness to protest. The dominance and impenetrable nature of U.S. War-culture depend upon the discourse of sacrifice. And while a wide variety of thinkers have examined the growth of war-culture as one example of 'U.S. Empire,' what has been missing is a deeper excavation of sacrificial images and understandings that slip easily between nationalism and Christianity, and that lie at war-culture's base and energize its operations.

As William T. Cavanaugh rightly points out, 'the myth of religious violence' is one important cause of lack of awareness regarding the structural forms of violence that shape us in United States war-culture. In this era, 'victimage rhetoric' resurfaced through the polarized and binary classifications of 'us' and 'the enemy.' Simplistic and reductionist stereotypes involved U.S. citizens and leaders identifying themselves as rational, peace-making and secular, over against the dangerous 'others' whose religion predisposed them to fanaticism and violence, and whose more 'primitive' societies had not yet developed into liberal and secular forms of government. This has 'legitimated the marginalization of certain types of practices and groups labeled religious, while underwriting the nation-state's monopoly on its citizens' willingness to sacrifice and

8. Robert Taylor, 'Senate Puts the Finishing Touches on Obama's $636 Billion "Defense Budget"', *Philadelphia Examiner*, 20 December 2009.

kill.'[9] Focus on the religious violence of 'the other' blinded American citizens with respect to our 'secular violence.' In fact, Cavanaugh concludes, such distinctions between 'religious' and 'secular' finally are misleading and mystifying. These labels rationalize the armed force of the United States as the only possible response to the 'irrational religious violence' of others, and create the mechanism for shielding and justifying the nature, causes and consequences of our own violent character and actions.

But Cavanaugh's argument may be taken one step further. Investigation of the rhetoric and practices of sacrific in the U.S. context demonstrates that U.S. political and civil society at the beginning of the twenty-first century is in fact deeply religious in its own way. In fact, this book's examination reveals an even more dangerous element in the U.S. context absent in certain Islamic contexts in which religious and governmental structures are closely aligned. In contrast to societies that openly espouse religious governance, people of the United States are largely heedless to the deep intertwining of sacrificial practices that unite popular Christian understandings with militaristic, supposedly 'secular' civil, political and governmental values and functions.

Thus, we march quite confidently ahead with the assurance that we are 'free' in our liberal democracy from the radical religious fundamentalism that 'infects' other societies and nations and that contributes to 'irrational violence.' Nevertheless, analysis of the dominance of sacrificial discourse and practices of exchange in the post-9/11 era reveals the elision of religious ideas and practices with deeply nationalistic values in U.S. citizens' self-identity.[10] The bond

9. William T. Cavanaugh, *The Myth of Religious Violence: Secular Ideology and the Roots of Modern Conflic* (Oxford: Oxford University Press, 2009), p. 4.

10. I find Jon Pahl's description of the 'violence iceberg' a helpful typology. He defines violence as 'any harm to or destruction to life, whether intended by individuals or enacted by systems of language, policy and practice.' The bottom level of the 'iceberg' involves cultural, religious or verbal violence, including discourses and images of domination and revenge; the next level involves systemic/social/community violence, such as community-based inequities in housing, healthcare, education, the environment, etc. The most obvious institutions of violence include prisons, military, the legal system, etc. Finally, at the top of the iceberg is criminal violence. One of the outcomes of the iceberg typology, therefore, is the conclusion that though criminal violence at the top of the iceberg may be foremost in our consciousness/sight, in reality the greatest depth and breadth of violence are to be found on the lower levels of

between nation and religion created through sacrificial constructions has placed a sacred canopy over the reality of U.S. War-culture
and plays an active and forceful role that shields war-culture from
criticism and sanctifies its actions.

During the last decades of the twentieth century a new body
of theological literature theorized a critique of sacrificial norms in
Christian doctrine, history and ecclesial practice. These theologians
and ethicists began with deep concern regarding the consequences
of sacrificial mandates and structures for women's lives, and their
body of work profoundly informs this book's cultural critique of
sacrificial exchange structures at the heart of U.S. political and military culture. Over time, women's writing on the dangers of sacrifice
has grown to include an ever wider frame of reference. For instance,
Grace M. Jantzen surveyed the whole of canonical biblical literature, both the Hebrew Scriptures and the New Testament, to demonstrate 'the significance of sacrifice in the genealogy of violence in
the West.'[11] The religious ideal of covenant is powerfully connected
both to holy war and sacrifice in the West to shape 'a constellation
of gendered violence.' She writes:

> My point is that the representation of a patriarchal god requir-
> ing sacrifice is part of the same constellation of ideas in which
> God's demands for holy war also find a place, ideas which recur
> in Christendom's notions of Jesus as "Lamb of God" and endless
> warfare, spiritual and literal, against ungodly Others.[12]

Jantzen encourages us to hold ideologies of sacrifice up for serious
analysis and criticism. And in the theological world, this process
has most definitely begun; in fact, moral investigation of sacrificial
formulations in Christianity is well advanced. However, there remains almost a complete dearth of suspicion in the U.S. with regard
to the rhetoric and practice of sacrifice in the political realm, and

---

the iceberg. See Jon Pahl, *Empire of Sacrifice: The Religious Origins of American
Violence* (New York: New York University Press, 2010). As Bruce B. Lawrence
and Aisha Karim note with respect to violence, 'context matters' in terms of
what is remembered, how variables are highlighted (or not), what is celebrated or mourned. See Bruce B. Lawrence and Aisha Karim (eds), *On Violence: A
Reader* (Durham, NC: Duke University Press, 2007), p. 1.

11. Grace M. Jantzen, *Violence to Eternity*, eds, Jeremy Carette and Morny Joy
(London: Routledge, 2009), p. 118.

12. Jantzen, *Violence to Eternity*, p. 137.

much less recognition of the links between *this* articulation of sacrifice and its relatedness to religious formulations. For instance, compare Jantzen's words with those from President Barack Obama in his acceptance of the Nobel Peace Prize. Though President Obama called himself a 'living testimony to the moral force of non-violence' exemplified in the lives of Martin Luther King, Jr. and Gandhi, he went on to say that his role as Commander-in-Chief did not permit him to be guided by their examples:

> Peace entails sacrifice... The United States of America has helped underwrite global security for more than six decades with the blood of our citizens and the strength of our arms. The service and sacrifice of our men and women in uniform has promoted peace and prosperity.[13]

President Obama is only the most recent in a long line of U.S. presidents and other leaders who have depended upon the ideology of 'the necessity of war-as-sacrifice' to justify and normalize U.S. armed force and militarism. And by and large, this logic goes unquestioned, even though, amazingly, this precisely is the rationale on which the unquestioned nature of U.S. War-culture rests. This book investigates the incongruous but substantive connections between religious and nationalistic/militaristic understandings and practices of sacrifice in the U.S. context, as an exercise in deepening self-awareness, introspection, and self-criticism on the part of U.S. citizens *and* followers of Christianity.

While I acknowledge and celebrate the growing pervasiveness of religious diversity within the United States, I focus here on the dominance of Christian understandings and practices as they have collided with political, military and social patterns and practices in American life. I hope that readers of this book will include those who most definitely count themselves as committed Christians, *and* those who do not hold Christian convictions, but care about the nature and ethics of citizenship in the United States. Traci C. West has defined the major purpose of social ethics in the following way: 'Social ethics is a normative project... not only to analyze existing practices that inhibit and assault the social and spiritual well-being

13. 'Remarks by the President at the Acceptance of the Nobel Peace Prize,' 12 October 2009, *The Whitehouse.gov*, http://www.whitehouse.gov/the-press-office/remarks-president-acceptance-nobel-peace-prize, accessed 14 January 2010.

of persons, but also to specify how those practices should be transformed to provide or support socially just and spiritually nurturing
relations among us.'[14] All U.S. citizens have reason to understand
more deeply the dynamics of war-culture intertwined with Christian
narratives, metaphors and practices, because these dynamics affect all of us (and many people around the world), regardless of
our religious orientation. In addition, Christians themselves have a
particular ethical responsibility to think seriously about the social
consequences of their proclamation, system of symbolism and doctrine with respect to sacrifice, and to consider what their awareness
requires of them, particularly in a war-culture such as the United
States.

Chapter One introduces and defines 'U.S. War-culture.' Clearly,
many, perhaps most U.S. citizens simply do not believe that there
is anything to be concerned about in the United States with regard
to the size of our military, the increase of the military budget, the
propensity with which we resort to armed force, the growth of our
business as weapons salespersons to the world, or the number of
military bases we operate across the globe. U.S. citizens generally
support these measures, while knowing relatively little about them.
Our 'oblivion' protects us from more deeply understanding our troubling reality. I define war-culture as the normalized interpenetration
of the institutions, ethos and practices of war with ever-increasing
facets of daily human life, economy, institutions and imagination
in the United States, and explore the extent of U.S. War-culture by
tracing some of its most powerful tentacles in the everyday life of
U.S. citizens. The 'military-industrial complex' President Dwight
Eisenhower worried about at the beginning of the 1960s pales before the reality of what economists now describe as 'a permanent
war economy.' Once we begin to see U.S. War-culture more clearly,
questions inevitably arise in our minds. I analyze causes behind
American attitudes of 'obliviousness' to U.S. War-culture and discuss the practices of legitimation that naturalize it. Lastly, Chapter
One includes investigation of a case study to introduce how the
rhetoric of sacrifice plays a significant role in American 'obliviousness' through masking and sacramentalizing war-culture.

---

14. Traci C. West, *Disruptive Christian Ethics: When Racism and Women's Lives
Matter* (Louisville, KY: Westminster John Knox, 2006), p. 38.

Over the years that I have been exploring and analyzing war-culture, I have compiled a collection of diverse examples of its inter-penetration with a wide variety of cultural sites in the United States. Readers are invited to peruse my website for additional material to accompany study and discussion of Chapter One's investigation of war-culture.

Chapter Two looks back to the beginning of the post-9/11 era in order to work through a case study of the political/religious rhetoric of sacrifice that was used in the United States to promote and maintain war in Afghanistan and Iraq. Political speeches and proclamations from the Administration of George W. Bush provide ideal material for analysis of the way that the language of sacrifice played a central role in building and protecting the drive to war following the attacks on the Trade Towers. Communication stud-ies analyses of 'victimage rhetoric' and 'framing' are useful tools to demonstrate how sacrificial rhetoric drives common sense thinking *toward* war as the one and necessary option in the face of conflict. I additionally draw upon theorized critiques of sacrific from femi-nist theological thinkers to address American war-culture and its dependence on sacrificial rhetoric and values. I encourage deeper awareness regarding the strong ties between political, supposedly 'secular' speech, and religious language and understandings based on sacrificial images, theories and narratives. In the wake of 9/11, and the public reactions in the U.S. of incredulity, fear and anger, familiar sacrificial Christian constructions merged with political and military rhetoric, and created a frame with deep emotional resonance that encouraged quietistic support for war, manipulated self-sacrificial identity inculcation in the American military, and enabled a comforting interpretation of utterly unexpected events.

The naturalization of war-culture in the United States is sup-ported by an ideology of 'necessity.' What underlies the assumption that violence is masterful, effective and determinative – in a word, 'necessary'? Chapter Three explores 'the logic of masculine protec-tion' in contemporary U.S. culture investigated by political theo-rist Iris Marion Young. This provides a starting point for thinking through the religious and secular values that are the precondition for assumptions about 'the necessity of war-as-sacrifi e.' Chapter Three exposes the strong links between patriarchal 'necessity,' sac-rifice, and the Just War tradition. Just War discourse is strongly tied to patriarchal protective schemes, and is influenced by Christian understandings of sacrifice as the mechanism through which the Just War operates and through which the losses and damages associated with war are justified and given transcendent meaning. The research of cognitive linguists regarding the functions of sacrificial cognitive frameworks further helps to explain both the ubiquity of sacrificialism and its absence from alert consciousness. Chapter Three also outlines methods to reveal, investigate and critique the dynamics and outcomes of this deadly nexus, 'the necessity of war-as-sacrifice.' One of these ways forward involves more stringently scrutinizing the theological operations of the cognitive metaphor of sacrifice itself. This leads to the project of Chapter Four

Once we begin to see and understand more deeply the destructive nature of the relationship between sacrifice and war-culture, we are faced with the theological conundrum: are there articulations of sacrifice in Christianity that can provide *resistance* to the sacred canopy over war-culture provided by sacrificial metaphors, understandings and practices? Do various theological reconstructions of sacrifice help us in this respect? Do they go far enough? Chapter Four explores three different theological responses to the problem of sacrificialis . First, I evaluate the theologies of Mark Heim and Bruce Chilton, who are alert to the problems of sacrificialism and scapegoating, and who attempt to reinscribe more fruitful and less harmful sacrificial understandings. Second, I turn to the current impasse in Womanist theological understandings of soteriology and sacrifice as represented by Delores S. Williams and JoAnne Marie Terrell. The third trajectory I explore is Western sacrificialism in neoliberal economics as investigated by Brazilian theologian Jung Mo Sung. Chapter Four also includes methods to address the social and theological dangers associated with sacrificial assumptions, and suggests possibilities for finding resources outside the conundrum of sacrificialism.

What would we think and say about the deaths of U.S. soldiers killed in the Iraq and Afghanistan wars, and the deaths of so many Afghan and Iraqi men, women and children, if we distanced ourselves from the sacrificial constructions that leap so readily to mind? If previous chapters have argued for and demonstrated a critical analytical method to reveal the underside of sacrificiali m, Chapter Five's purpose is to 'detranscendentalize war,' that is, develop alternatives for thinking, seeing and valuing less captive to the discursive frameworks that underlie 'the necessity of the ultimate sacrifice.' The first part of the chapter returns to the plurality of images of Christian redemption, and the plethora of interpretations regarding Jesus' death from the first century onwards, as resources for destabilization of the univocal emphasis on the substitutionary sacrifice of Jesus as the archetype for the 'necessary sacrifices' of war and war-culture. The second part of the chapter focuses on detranscendentalizing the ways we conceive of the military, beginning with the question of how to interpret soldiers' deaths outside of sacrificial frameworks. One way to de-center theologies of sacrifice is through a shift to a theology of *work*. Lastly, I return to the question of detranscendentalizing the nation, and draw on the work of various political theorists to analyze the idolatry of the nation seen in the 'submerged sovereignty' of national sacrificial logic and practice.

If we agree that U.S. War-culture must be resisted, we also must question the use and abuse of sacrifice that has electrified war-culture's growth, especially in the post-9/11 era. Moreover, if we are to understand the meaning of our post-9/11 religious and political moment in the United States, we must promote wiser and more life-giving ways forward as communities of faith and as a nation. Our awareness must grow, so that we more insistently question the energetic impulses between Christian notions of salvation and sacrifice, and our political, economic, cultural and military sacrificial frameworks and practices. This book is one step toward the development of such an ethic.

Finally, in this introduction, I acknowledge the difficulty associated with defining the very word, 'sacrifice.' As I note in various places throughout this book, it is a great challenge to investigate sacrifice because it has been understood differently and practiced in widely diverse ways throughout both chronological time and multiple contexts. Making matters more complex, sacrific is referred to in many spheres of human existence, often simultaneously, with its operations in one sphere frequently impacting others. In other words, sacrifice functions not only religiously, but socially, politically, economically, militarily. This book explores the links between these spheres, and raises questions regarding sacrificial frameworks, values and practices in our midst, and the way they shape American self-identity, allegiance and moral vision.

Etymological clues to understanding the word, 'sacrifice,' underscore various connotations associated with this word: 'making

sacred,' 'gift-giving,' and 'exchange.' In addition, sacrificial phenomena tend to involve three participants, objects, or domains: one
who initiates the exchange/giving, one that is exchanged, and one
that receives or reciprocates. Sacrificial rituals frequently involve
forfeiting through bloodletting, decapitation, dismemberment, suf-
focation, drowning, cremation and other forms of destruction or killing; and often include the obligation to eat the thing which has been
sacrificed. Sacrificial reflexes unite community members together in
an atmosphere of sanctity *and* separate them from evil, frequently
working along both lines simultaneously. As Jeffrey Carter further
explains, 'religious sacrifice is any sacrifice where one or more of the
central parties involved is believed to be, or to represent, an agent of
the superhuman realm.'[15]

I align myself with contemporary theological and anthropological theorists who are wary of constructing a universal theory of sacrifice, such as Bruce Chilton, Nancy Jay and Grace Jantzen. Chilton's
open-ended description of sacrifice includes three elements, so that
sacrifice entails:

1. Affective human interactions;
2. The use of pragmatic material elements; and
3. Sacrificial dynamics resulting in some sort of ideological (or
   other form of) exchange.[16]

Additionally, while some theologians argue for one particular
meaning of 'authentic Christian sacrifice,' I am more interested in
understanding the actual operations and engine of sacrificial rhetoric, practices and dynamics themselves.[17] Even Chapter Four's analysis of Christian articulations of sacrifice is undertaken to provide

15. Jeffrey Carter, *Understanding Religious Sacrifice. A Reader* (New York:
Continuum, 2003), p. 4.

16. See Chapter Two for further analysis of Chilton with respect to understanding and defining sacrifice, and Chapter Four for theological and anthropological analyses of sacrifice.

17. For example, see Robert J. Daly, *Sacrifice Unveiled: The True Meaning of
Sacrific* (London: T & T Clark International, 2009). While Daly acknowledges
that there are many diverse meanings of the word, 'sacrifice,' including secular
meanings and general religious meanings, he argues for an 'authentic Christian
sacrifice' that involves three 'moments' – 1. The self-offering of God the Father
in the gift of the Son; 2. The self-offering 'response' of the Son; and 3. Human
action empowered by the same Spirit that was in Jesus to enter into the life of
the Trinity. See Daly, *Sacrifice Unveile* , p. 5.

theological grist for resistance to the sacrificial dynamics of U.S. War-culture and wider imaginative space beyond the confines of current sacrificially-maintained dynamics in our common life. The prevalence of sacrificial constructions and practices in human existence has the consequence of rendering them normalized, and thus largely invisible. In this study, the sacrificial dynamics in the relationship between Christian understandings of salvation and U.S. War-culture are thrown into greater relief for the purpose of moral deliberation. Religiously, socially, economically and politically, the dominant sacrificial frameworks within which we live and frame meaning in the United States are contributing to death, destruction, and waste. I am impatient not only to increase awareness and critique, but to find a way beyond and outside of these constructions.

Chapter One

War-culture and Sacrifice

Introduction

On the eve of the 2008 Democratic Convention in Denver, Colorado, more than 1,000 anti-war protesters took to the streets, led by Ron Kovic, the paralyzed Vietnam Veteran made famous by the Hollywood film, *Born on the Fourth of July*, and Cindy Sheehan, anti-war activist and mother of Casey Sheehan, a soldier killed in the Iraq War. Carrying signs decrying the use of torture and calling for an end to the war in Iraq, along the way of their march they encountered about 50 counter-protesters. Among them was Nancy Hecker of Colorado Springs, mother of yet another young man killed in Iraq, Maj. Bill Hecker. When asked about her reasons for participating in this counter-protest, Mrs. Hecker replied, 'I'm here to honor our son and the sacrifice he made for our country and to support the troops and the families who give so much.'[1]

What would we say about the losses associated with war if we did not describe them as sacrifices? Moreover, in a nation still dominantly shaped by Christian religious understandings and practices, how is sacrificial language such as Mrs. Hecker's influenced by religious frameworks emphasizing Jesus' sacrificia self-giving life and death? In the United States, language about 'the necessity of sacrifice' operates as an electrical conduit between the institutionalization of 'war-culture' and the understandings and practices of popular Christianity. At the same time, this conduit is entirely naturalized and mostly unquestioned in U.S. culture at large. As a result, the hinge of sacrific between nationalism and Christianity

---

1. Judith Kohler and Colleen Slevin, 'Will War Protesters "Recreate 68"?' *Associated Press*, 25 August 2008, http://www.mcall.com/news/local/all-a1_cvnprotests.6560317aug25,0,1932893.story, accessed 28 August 2008.

remains largely invisible to many if not most U.S. citizens, and the sacred sheen to war-culture contributed by sacrificial language and understandings goes unchallenged. The purpose of this book is to thrust this same relationship between Christianity, sacrifice and war-culture into visibility so that we may see it in operation, examine it, think about it and make judgments about what our awareness requires of us. The depth, breadth and intensity of war-culture as a dominant facet of the post-9/11 United States renders our clear thinking all the more urgent and timely.

What do I mean by 'U.S. War-culture'? Defined, this refers to the normalized interpenetration of the institutions, ethos and practices of war with ever-increasing facets of daily human life in the United States, including the economy, education, diverse cultural sites, patterns of labor and consumption, and even the capacity for imagination. If 'militarism' is a traditional term that refers to the dominance of military over civilian authority, and the prevalence of war-like values in society, contemporary scholars now utilize the terminology of 'militarization' to refer to much the same reality described here as 'war-culture.' Catherine Lutz's definition is particularly apt:

> Militarization is a discursive process, involving a shift in general societal beliefs and values in ways necessary to legitimate the use of force, the organization of large standing armies and their leaders, and the higher taxes or tribute used to pay for them...[it is] an intensification of the labor and resources allocated to military purposes including *the shaping of other institutions in synchrony with military goals* (italics mine).[2]

Lutz's insight regarding the way militarization *shapes* other institutions, perceptions and identities is important. Militarization does not stand apart as an isolated element in U.S. culture. On the contrary, in the post-9/11 world of the United States, militarization is a powerful force that shapes the dynamics of collective power, identity, memory and daily experience. 'War-culture' describes how this force has become a driving influence in U.S. culture at large. As Andrew Bacevich says, 'the global military supremacy that the

---

2. As quoted in Henry A. Giroux, *University in Chains: Confronting the Military-Industrial-Academic Complex* (Boulder, CO: Paradigm Publishers, 2007), p. 31. See Catherine Lutz, 'Making War at Home in the United States: Militarization and the Current Crisis,' *American Anthropologist* 104.3 (September 2002), p. 723.

United States presently enjoys – and is bent on perpetuating – has become central to our national identity.' He continues,

> More than America's matchless material abundance or even the effusions of its pop culture, the nation's arsenal of high tech weaponry and the soldiers who employ that arsenal have come to signify who we are and what we stand for…Americans in our own time have fallen prey to militarization, manifesting in a romanticized view of soldiers, a tendency to see military power as the truest measure of national greatness, and outsized expectations regarding the efficacy of force [3]

Though some citizens are aware and worried about the bloated U.S. military budget and alarming level of arms production, understanding war-culture involves becoming aware of the tentacles of militarization that reach into the entire realm of culture, resulting in 'the quasi-militarization of everyday life.' The educational process of our entire social and cultural experience, our institutions and all relationships that teach, define and illuminate (i.e., our 'public pedagogy') are permeated more and more by militarized values, aesthetics, experiences, goals and culture.[4]

Many analysts of militarization or war-culture utilize the descriptive phrase first used by President Dwight Eisenhower in his farewell speech to the American people on 17 January 1961, when he coined the term, 'the U.S. military-industrial complex' to begin to outline the dangerous interpenetrations of the defense industry, congress and the military in the United States.[5] But in the intervening 50 or so years, 'the complex' has morphed beyond Eisenhower's wildest imagination, assisted by a powerful rhetorical schematic that spreads its influence in the lives of people in the U.S. (and the world). The growth of the complex since his time makes this analysis all the more imperative.

3. Quoted in Giroux, *University in Chains*, p. 36. See Andrew Bacevich, *The New American Militarism* (New York: Oxford University Press, 2005), p. 14.

4. Giroux, *University in Chains*, pp. 39–40, 42. In 2008 the U.S. agreed to sell or transfer more than $32 bn in weapons and military equipment, in comparison with $12 bn just three years earlier, in 2005. See 'U.S. Arms Sales Increase,' *UPI*, 14 September 2008, http://www.upi.com/Top_News/2008/09/14/US-arms-sales-increase/UPI-70641221429321/, accessed 20 September 2008.

5. 'Eisenhower's Farewell Address to the Nation,' 17 January 1961, *Eisenhower Archives*, http://www.eisenhower.archives.gov/speeches/farewell_address.html, accessed 16 August 2008.

While many scholars and activists have explored and condemned the growth of war-culture and empire in the post-9/11 United States, less attention has been paid to the significance of the rhetoric and cognitive framework of sacrifice that undergirds war-culture, and that simultaneously is tightly interwoven with experiences and practices of Christianity in the U.S. Sacrificial constructions, I argue, electrically draw together Christianity and war-culture, and enliven and inform each by way of the other. At the same time, however, not only does the cognitive framework of sacrifice act as an internal engine, it also places a sacred canopy over the institutions, culture and practices of war and thus is one important element through which the reality of war-culture is thrust out of conscious view; in other words, not only does the framework of sacrifice energize war-culture, it also plays a decisive role in the normalization of war-culture to the extent that it becomes invisible, simply part of the expected fabric of life in the U.S. Christianity is a usable pawn in this chess game, even at times a willing partner to the machinery and culture of destruction, idolization of security, and death. Moreover, when we explore this dynamic more deeply, we see that the flow of electricity moves in more than one way. If Christianity enables the operations of war-culture, then at the same time, the symbols, understandings, rhetoric and practices of war also seep through into Christianity via the same hinge of sacrifice. Thus, not only must we examine the dynamics of sacrifice in war-culture, such investigation reveals a certain vulnerability in Christianity to the influence of war-culture through this same relationship. Ultimately this book raises questions about any continuing ethically viable role of sacrificial constructs in a responsible Christianity that is conscious of the hinge of sacrifice that connects war-culture with Christian doctrine, understanding and practice.

Let us return to that final speech given by President Dwight Eisenhower in 1961, and his coining of the term, 'the military-industrial complex,' to describe the new 'conjunction of an immense military establishment and a large arms industry.' The influence of this complex, he warned, had economic, political and even spiritual impact, and while Eisenhower acknowledged that the need for this development was unarguable, nevertheless, he emphasized, it was imperative that Americans 'not fail to comprehend its grave implications.'

Among those implications, Eisenhower specifically outlined four inherent dangers as a consequence of the growing military-industrial complex: 1) the intrusion of unwarranted influence into government by the complex; 2) the potential dangers to liberties and democratic process; 3) the danger to the free university if government contracts 'substitute for intellectual curiosity' and the nations' scholars become dominated by Federal employment and allocations and the power of money; and 4) the potential for public policy to become captive to a scientific-technological elite. He closed by warning, 'We should take nothing for granted. Only an alert and knowledgeable citizenry can compel the proper meshing of the huge industrial and military machinery of defense with our peaceful methods and goals, so that security and liberty may prosper together.'

Eisenhower's initial description of the military-industrial complex and his concerns about it may be compared to the proverbial pebble dropped into a pond. Since his time, the depth and breadth of the ripples of war-culture extending out into the water of U.S. culture have grown exponentially and been analyzed by many scholars. What follows is a brief foray into some of the major facets comprising these connected waves.

Military Buildups and Decreasing Boundaries

Between 1950 and 2003, the U.S. experienced four periods of 'intense military mobilization' and concomitant increases in weapons purchases, including the Korean War, the buildups during the Vietnam War and under Ronald Reagan, and the boon overseen by the second Bush Administration following the attacks of 9/11.[6] Militarism is characterized by at least three indicators: 1) the growth of a professional military class and the glorification of its ideals; 2) the infiltration of military officers and/or representatives of the arms industry into elevated government positions; and 3) an increasing embrace of policies that emphasize military preparedness as the highest priority of the state.[7] If Eisenhower was concerned about the influence of increasingly permeable boundaries between Congress, the arms industry and the military, a fourth institution

---

6. Chalmers Johnson, *Sorrows of Empire* (New York: Metropolitan Books, 2004), pp. 55–56.

7. Johnson, *Sorrows*, p. 63.

now plays an influential role in the spread of militarism: think tanks, 'modern patriotic monasteries.' But this is only the beginning of the story of the increase and permutations of war-culture in the United States. Beginning with the Korean War, huge defense expenditures became institutionalized in the U.S., altering the entire economy of the nation. Indeed, such spending became 'a normal feature of civilian life,' an expected characteristic of the United States and a naturalized aspect of the work of Congress, as more and more of its members sought lucrative defense contracts for their districts. 'Americans are by now used to hearing their political leaders say or do anything to promote local military spending.' The 'circulation of elites,' with high ranking retiring defense contractors receiving appointments as officials in the Pentagon, undercuts attempts by the Congress to enforce accountability with respect to military spending. It has become common for vast sums of money in this system to disappear, such as occurred in 2001 when the Pentagon's Deputy Inspector General admitted that $1.1 trillion 'was simply gone and no one can be sure of when, where or to whom the money went.' Political scientist Chalmers Johnson remarks, 'the fact that no one seems to care is also evidence of militarism.'[8]

The Manhattan Project to build the atomic bomb was the beginning of the development of so-called 'black budgets' enabling the Department of Defense to protect itself from public scrutiny. 'Special Access Programs,' including weapons research and acquisition, operations and support (including funds for Special Forces), and intelligence, all are 'black budget' programs whose expenses are only shared with a few members of Congress. Increasingly, secrecy and disinformation have become the hallmarks of war-culture even as Pentagon pressure grows to ever increase its size and functions. In addition, the Iraq and Afghanistan wars utilized sub-contracting corporations to an extent never seen before in the history of war. For instance, private military companies, such as Vinnell Corporation of Fairfax, Virginia, a subsidiary of the defense conglomerate Northrop Grumman, are authorized and paid by the U.S. government to train both U.S. and foreign armies.[9] By 2010 the revenue of subcontracting companies exceeded $202 bn. However, according to the bipartisan Legislative Commission on Wartime Contracting in Iraq and

8. Johnson, *Sorrows*, pp. 26, 57, 58.
9. Johnson, *Sorrows*, p. 135.

Afghanistan, the heavy use of contractors in the field of war created as many problems as temporary solutions:

> More than 240,000 contractor employees, about 80 percent of them foreign nationals, are working in Iraq and Afghanistan to support operations and projects of the U.S. military, the Department of State, and the U.S. Agency for International Development. Contractor employees outnumber U.S. troops in the region. While contractors provide vital services, the Commission believes their use has also entailed billions of dollars lost to waste, fraud, and abuse due to inadequate planning, poor contract drafting, limited competition, understaffed oversight functions, and other problems.[10]

Nevertheless, the use of contractors for the business of war has been growing for well over a decade. Among other services, the military more and more contracts out base construction, maintenance and security. Kellogg Brown and Root, one such military maintenance contractor, was purchased by Halliburton in 1962 and authorized to begin supplying logistical services to the army while Dick Cheney was Secretary of Defense. Between the years of Cheney's role as CEO of Halliburton, 1995 and 2000, Brown and Root was the beneficiary of $2.3 billion in government contracts, advancing from 73 to 18 on the Pentagon's list of top contractors.[11] Moreover, following the drawdown of troops in Iraq to 50,000 in 2010, reports from the Commission on Wartime Contracting suggested that increased reliance on military contractors will continue to grow. The biggest difference is that while these contractors once were employed by the Department of Defense in Iraq, they increasingly also operate through the State Department. In Iraq, from convoy security to explosive ordnance disposal, and from recovering killed and wounded

10. 'Official Commission Press Release,' *Commission on Wartime Contracting in Afghanistan and Iraq,* 5 June 2009, http://www.wartimecontracting.gov/nr4-wartime-contracting-concerns.htm, accessed 15 June 2009.

11. Johnson, *Sorrows,* p. 144. In May 2009, it was reported that the Pentagon had failed to collect over $100 m in overcharges from Defense Contractor Kellogg Brown and Root, though over two years had passed since officials of the contracting company admitted wrongdoing related to overcharges. According to news reports, this failure 'is likely to revive allegations that the Pentagon has become so close to KBR, and relies so heavily on it, that there is little inclination or incentive to discipline the company, in response to either Congress or critics outside the government.' See James Glanz, 'Senators Accuse Pentagon of Delay in Recovering Millions,' *The New York Times,* 4 May 2009.

personnel to dispatching of armed response teams, contractors will fill the gaps left by departing troops, but their authority and responsibility in these same functions remains unclear at best. The report asks, 'What if the assailants are firing from an inhabited village or a hospital? Who weighs the risks of innocent casualties, directs the action, and applies the rules for the use of force?'[12]

Eisenhower was concerned about maintaining appropriate boundaries between military, governmental and civilian institutions for proper governance and balance of powers. But diminishment and slipperiness of the boundaries between the four components of the military-industrial-congressional-think-tank complex were augmented by a weakening in constitutional government, especially in the post-9/11 period. Chalmers Johnson writes, 'When it comes to the deliberate dismantling of the Constitution, the events that followed the Supreme Court's intervention in the election of 2000 that named George W. Bush the 43rd president have proved unprecedented.'[13] For instance, in 2001, President Bush issued an executive order that enabled him and future presidents the power to veto requests to see presidential records, effectively overturning the Freedom of Information Act. Second, the infamous 'torture memo' from 1 August 2002, claimed that Commander-in-Chief power in a time of war could override U.S. law on the prohibition of torture. Third, the Foreign Intelligence Surveillance Act (FISA) was consistently ignored in the post-9/11 period. President Bush authorized wiretapping of telecommunications systems without legal warrants, sidelining the FISA requirements, and justifying his decision as in keeping with executive war powers. With the approval of a democratically controlled congress, FISA was effectively legislatively eviscerated in 2008.[14] Finally, fourth, the proclivity of attaching 'signing statements' to legislation (over 505 extra constitutional challenges to provisions of legislation were written in Bush's first term) amounts to presidential power over and above any attempts

12. 'Better Planning for Defense-to-State Transition in Iraq Needed to Avoid Mistakes and Waste', *Commission on Wartime Contracting in Afghanistan and Iraq*, 12 July 2010, http://www.wartimecontracting.gov/docs/CWC_SR2010-07-12.pdf, accessed 10 October 2010, p. 6.

13. Chalmers Johnson, *Nemesis: The Last Days of the American Republic* (New York: Metropolitan Books, 2006), p. 244.

14. Eric Lictblau and James Risen, 'Officials Say U.S. Wiretaps Exceeded Law', *The New York Times*, 15 April 2009.

by congress to pass law and override presidential vetoes.[15] While some of these abuses began to be rolled back with the change of presidential administrations, many citizens have been dismayed by President Obama's refusal to openly condemn and prosecute various war-related policies, especially those related to practices of torture inaugurated in the Bush Administration.

In addition to everything above, war-culture is expressed in the unfettered growth of U.S. military bases around the world. By 2009, it was estimated that at least 909 U.S. military facilities existed outside of the United States on foreign lands, employing more than 190,000 troops and 115,000 civilian workers. The bases were on land owned or rented by the U.S., amounting to over 795,000 acres of land and 26,000 buildings and structures valued at $146 bn.[16] While the Pentagon inventories the number of overseas bases at 716, scholars have demonstrated that the total number perhaps rises to over 1,000, especially if one includes so-called 'black sites' such as the Al-Udeid Air Base, a billion-dollar location in Qatar that is secretly operated by the U.S. Air Force for the use of unmanned drone wars.[17] Many Americans, if they think about these bases at all, generalize hazy assumptions to rationalize their existence. Some Americans may assume that military bases are an economic boon to countries outside of the U.S., or that foreign nations have invited the presence of these bases. Or Americans may think that any presence of the most 'advanced and civilized' military in the world is bound to be beneficial and welcome. Lastly, Americans justify the presence of the bases as a necessary security measure given the reality of 'global

15. Johnson, *Sorrows*, pp. 253–55. See also Eric Lictblau, 'Senate Approves Bill to Widen Wiretap Powers,' *The New York Times*, 10 July 2008.

16. Catherine Lutz, 'Introduction: Bases, Empire and Global Response,' in Catherine Lutz (ed.), *The Bases of Empire: The Global Struggle Against U.S. Military Posts* (New York: New York University Press, 2009), p. 1.

17. This higher number of bases includes the nearly 400 U.S. and coalition bases in Afghanistan, according to Colonel Wayne Shanks, a spokesperson for the U.S.-led International Security Assistance Force. While some of the bases are very small, others, such as the made-over Bagram Air Base in Afghanistan, serve more than 20,000 troops and include fast-food outlets such as Burger King and Popeyes, miniature golf centers and other amenities. See Nick Turse, 'The 700 Military Bases of Afghanistan: Black Sites in the Empire of Bases,' *TomDispatch.com*, 9 February 2010, http://www.tomdispatch.com/dialogs/print/?id=175204, accessed 13 February 2010.

terror.'[18] In contrast, Chalmers Johnson asserts five post-Cold War missions that serve as the rationale for the existence of these bases: maintaining 'military preponderance' over the rest of the world; gathering communications intelligence of citizens, allies and enemies alike; controlling as many sources of petroleum as possible; providing work and income for members of the military-industrial complex; and supplying a comfortable life and entertainment for military abroad.[19] He writes,

> The only truly common elements in the totality of America's foreign bases are imperialism and militarism – an impulse on the part of our elites to dominate other peoples largely because we have the power to do so, followed by the strategic reasoning that, in order to defend these newly acquired outposts and control the regions they are in, we must expand the areas under our control with still more bases.[20]

All in all, on the hundreds of U.S. military bases spread throughout the globe, over 500,000 U.S. troops, spies, contractors, family members and others are stationed in over 130 countries. Their mission is 'force projection,' defined as 'the maintenance of American military hegemony over the rest of the world.'[21] In contrast, there are no foreign military bases within the United States.

The Cost of War-culture

Of all the statistics about the economics of war-culture, two stark facts especially deserve attention. First, in June, 2009, the Stockholm International Peace Research Institute reported that in the previous ten years alone, global military expenditures rose by 45 percent to the staggering sum of $1.46 trillion per year. Military expenditures of United States accounted for more than one-half of this increase.[22]

18. Cynthia Enloe, 'Foreward,' in Catherine Lutz (ed.), *The Bases of Empire*, pp. x–xii.

19. Johnson, *Sorrows*, pp. 151–52. For Johnson's updated count on the number of U.S. military bases abroad, see Chalmers Johnson, 'America's Unwelcome Advances,' *Mother Jones*, 22 August 22 2008, http://www.motherjones.com/print/15574, accessed 15 June 2009.

20. Johnson, *Sorrows*, p. 152.

21. Johnson, *Nemesis*, p. 6.

22. See 'Recent Trends in Military Expenditure,' *Stockholm International Peace Research Institute Report*, 21 October 2009, http://www.sipri.org/research/armaments/milex/resultoutput/trends, accessed 21 October 2009.

Second, the United States is far and above the leading supplier of weapons to the rest of the world. In 2008, the U.S. sold $37.8 bn in weapons to the rest of the world, representing 68.4 percent of all the world's sales in the international arms bazaar.[23]

When all is said and done, Nobel Prize winning economist Joseph E. Stiglitz and economist Linda J. Bilmes conservatively estimate that the financial cost of the Afghanistan and Iraq wars will amount to at least $3 trillion. In 2007, the two wars combined cost the U.S. approximately $16 bn per month, or what amounted to the *entire annual budget* of the United Nations. Moreover, as these two economists emphasize, this amount per month *did not* include the $500-plus billion per year that the U.S. already spent on 'regular expenses' of the Defense Department.[24] Despite the change in presidential administrations in 2009, these numbers are only increasing overall. What does this mean in terms of defining the reality of war-culture in the United States? Analysts concluded that by 2008, the U.S. spent approximately 60 percent of its 'discretionary income' on war-related expenses.[25] In any given year during the first decade of the twenty-first century, in the United States between 3.5 and 5.3 percent of the total National Gross Domestic Product funneled toward military expenses.[26] Of course, all these figures are in stark contrast to what the highest officials of the U.S. government claimed at the outset of the Iraq and Afghanistan wars, such as Office of Management and Budget director Mitch Daniels and Secretary of Defense Donald Rumsfeld, who estimated the total costs of the Iraq and Afghanistan wars in the range of $50–$60 billion.[27]

23. Thom Shanker, 'Despite Slump, U.S. Role as Top Arms Supplier Grows,' *The New York Times*, 6 September 2009.

24. Johnson, *Nemesis*, p. 9.

25. See Robert Scheer, *The Pornography of Power: How Defense Hawks Hijacked 9/11 and Weakened America* (New York: Twelve, 2008). Scheer spoke about these expenditures on *National Public Radio's* 'Radio Times,' 5 June. See *WHYY RadioTimes*, http://www.whyy.org/91FM/radiotimes.html, accessed 5 June 2008.

26. 'Military Expenditure as a Share of GDP, 2001–2007,' *Stockholm International Peace Research Institute Report*, 21 October 2009, http://www.sipri. org/research/armaments/milex/resultoutput/trends, accessed 21 October 2009.

27. Linda Bilmes and Joseph E. Stiglitz, *The Three Trillion Dollar War: The True Cost of the Iraq Conflict* (New York, NY: W.W. Norton and Company, 2008), p. 7.

Post-9/11 changes in the way war is organized and operated have contributed significantly to much higher costs, such as the already mentioned increase in private contractors, whose number in the Afghanistan and Iraq wars mushroomed to ten times that of the use of private contractors during the Gulf War in 1991. For instance, in 2003, Blackwater Security was given a $27 bn no-bid contract to guard the Administrator of the Coalition Provisional Authority, L. Paul Bremer III; but by 2007 the amount of Blackwater's contract increased to $1.2 bn.[28] Also, because the U.S. government uses 'cash accounting,' that is, only accounting for what is actually spent today, and ignoring future obligations and costs, the full expenditures for war are hidden from view. Faulty accounting practices of the Department of Defense (DoD) further shield or muddle war-culture's true costs. The year 2007 was the tenth *in a row* that the DoD 'flunked its financial audit.'[29] In order to obtain a more accurate accounting for the war, four categories must be considered: 1) the amount of money already spent to conduct the wars; 2) future costs for waging these wars; 3) 'hidden costs,' such as increases in the core defense budget and expanding the size of the military; and 4) the interest costs on borrowed money.[30]

Notwithstanding these enormous increases in military budgets in recent years, the story of the growth of war-culture spans a much longer time frame than the Iraq and Afghanistan wars. Following every major war until the post-WWII era, the United States demobilized its military to its pre-war size. This corresponded with the use of the U.S. military as a means for economic and geopolitical

28. In January 2009, Blackwater Worldwide was barred altogether from Iraq, following 'improper conduct and excessive use of force,' that resulted in the deaths of 17 civilians in 2007, according to Iraq's Interior Minister. See Sinan Salaheddin, 'Iraq Bars Blackwater, Tarnished by Civilian Deaths,' Associated Press, 29 January 2009, *Common Dreams.org*, http://www.commondreams.org/headline/2009/01/29, accessed 29 January 2009. In response to negative press, Blackwater rebranded itself as 'Xe Services.' Before the company went out of business, Blackwater successfully contracted with the U.S. government for over $1.5 bn between 2001–2009. See Adam Ciralsky, 'Tycoon, Contractor, Soldier, Spy,' *Vanity Fair*, January 2010, http://www.vanityfair.com/politics/features/2010/01/blackwater-201001, accessed 16 December 2009.

29. Bilmes and Stiglitz, *The Three Trillion Dollar War*, p. 19.

30. Bilmes and Stiglitz, *The Three Trillion Dollar War*, p. 34. Also see Jeremy Scahill, *Blackwater: The Rise of the World's Most Powerful Mercenary Army* (New York, NY: Nation Books, 2007).

gain. In the 1940s and 50s, all this changed as prolonged military buildup became the rule and the military-industrial complex came into being. According to economist Ismael Hossein-Zadeh, we must search out the economic beneficiaries of war dividends in order to more clearly understand the overriding forces behind historical U.S. military expansion. More than anything else, the most significant driver behind increased militarism is all those who are 'vested in the business of war.' This is 'parasitic militarism,' that exists as an end in itself. Who are these beneficiaries? 'The Iron Triangle' includes 1) the civilian agencies such as the Office of the President, the National Security Council, the Senate and House Armed Services Committees, the CIA and NASA; 2) the military institutions, including the Joint Chiefs of Staff, The Pentagon, top officials from the Air Force, Army, Marines and Navy; Veterans organizations, and 3) the corporate and manufacturing base, including the 85,000 private firms that profit from this system and encourage millions of workers within it to push for unending growth in the military budget.[31]

A revolving employment door moves individuals from one influential position within the Iron Triangle to another; it was reported that at least 32 major Bush policy makers had significant ties to the arms industry; five of the top six donors to the House Armed Services Committee were nuclear weapons and missile defense contractors in 2001.[32] The revolving door also moves influential players between industry and positions within 'think tanks' that draw up policy for ever increasing war, and dividing war spoils. In his role as a corporate lobbyist called upon to help draw up post-conquest economic strategy in Iraq, Grover Norquist 'boasted of moving freely at the Treasury, Defense and State Departments.' 'Moving the Iraqi Economy from Recovery to Growth,' a State Department document he helped to draft, included 'calls for Iraqis to sell off to international oil companies the nation's 'downstream' assets – that is, the refineries, pipelines and ports.'[33] In 2008, *The New York Times* reported on the use of retired military officers involved in a symbiotic

---

31. Ismael Hossein-Zadeh, *The Political Economy of U.S. Militarism* (New York: Palgrave, 2006), p. 13.

32. Hossein-Zadeh, *The Political Economy*, pp. 16–17. See also the sub-section in Chapter Seven of his book, 'The "Revolving Door" Syndrome and the Spoils of Military Spending', pp. 187–99.

33. Hossein-Zadeh, *The Political Economy*, p. 21.

relationship with the Pentagon, in which they were courted by leaders in the DoD and coached on 'talking points' to buttress a positive view of Iraq in media outlets. Referred to by the DoD as 'message force multipliers,' these same retired officers in large numbers also held board positions connected to various military contracting corporations. One such corporation, Omnitec Solutions, was paid hundreds of thousands of dollars by the Pentagon to monitor databases for any appearance of these same 'analysts' in the media in order to evaluate their effectiveness as 'branding experts.'[34] The interpenetration of war-culture involving government officials, business, the media, and military leaders amounts to an unassailable social structure almost impervious to critique.

Hossein-Zadeh contends that what sets the U.S. military empire apart from older examples of empire is its market-driven, capitalist foundation and machinery. Whereas, in earlier empires, arms manufacturers were not beholden to market imperatives, today,

> the combination of private ownership and the market-driven character of the United States' arms industries has drastically modified the conventional relationship between war and the means of warfare: it is now often the supply or profit imperatives of weapons production that drive the demand for arms, hence the need for war...It is this built-in propensity to war that makes the U.S. military-industrial complex a menace to world peace and stability, a force of death and destruction.[35]

Hossein-Zadeh further argues that the proponents of increased militarization are extremely effective in their strategies against those who would restrain the military budget. In addition to lobbying politicians and manipulating media sources, more subtle tactics include commissioning 'disinterested civilian groups of experts,' to study issues of 'national security,' 'strategic directions,' or 'military capabilities.' For example, the reconstitution of 'The Committee on the Present Danger' in the 1950s was organized to oppose talks that might have defused tension with the Soviets under President Truman. Opposition to this diplomacy resulted in the effective continuation of higher military spending.[36]

34. David Barstow, 'Behind TV's Analysts, Pentagon's Hidden Hand,' *The New York Times*, 20 April 2008.

35. Hossein-Zadeh, *The Political Economy*, p. 200.

36. Hossein-Zadeh, *The Political Economy*, pp. 69–70.

In addition, victimage rhetoric that exaggerates the danger of the enemy to demonic levels, is also a very effective tool, whether it be used against 'the Communist threat,' 'the evil empire,' 'rogue states,' or 'militant Islam.'[37] This last tactic was utilized successfully when in 1980 President Reagan, stoking fear regarding 'the evil empire' of the Soviet Union, increased the Pentagon budget from 5 to nearly 7 percent of the Gross National Product (or about one-third of the federal budget), a decision that increased the Pentagon's prime contract awards 35 percent over the previous year. Though the Soviet Union began to unravel later in the Reagan presidency, so that the specter of 'the evil empire' lost traction in the American consciousness, the beneficiaries of war and militarism maintained the momentum of increased militarism by shifting the description of the role of the U.S. military from 'Soviet containment' to 'maintaining stability in all areas of conflict in the world. [38]

Lastly, proponents of 'military Keynesianism' suggest that military expansion is a useful stimulant to the economy as a whole, and leads to 'spinoff' in high technology arms production that eventually reaches the civilian sector. Examples of such technological development include microchips, radar, lasers, satellite communications, cell phones, GPS and the Internet.[39] Economist Martin Feldstein, Harvard professor and former Chair of the Council of Economic Advisors, advised President Obama to 'increase government military spending in the Department of Homeland Security, FBI and other parts of the national intelligence community' to respond to the 2007–2009 recession.[40] While other economists agree that the vast sums of money involved in militarization do provide economic stimulus and have led to technological developments, a closer look at the military budget increases in U.S. federal budgets in the post-WWII period shows that increases in military spending,

37. See Chapter Two for analysis of victimage rhetoric in the George W. Bush Administration.

38. Hossein-Zadeh, *The Political Economy*, pp. 73, 210. Once again, a panel of experts was called upon to study and rewrite U.S. military doctrine, and released a report in 1988 that focused on 'discriminate deterrence,' a military strategy to respond to third-world conflicts 'before they get out of hand.'

39. Hossein-Zadeh, *The Political Economy*, p. 211.

40. Robert Higgs, 'Military Keynesianism to the Rescue?' *The Independent Institute*, 2 January 2009, http://www.independent.org/newsroom/article.asp?id=2399, accessed 9 December 2009.

especially since the 1980s, have been accompanied to a large degree by cutting nonmilitary public spending, drawing down the Social Security Trust Fund, and through increased national deficits [41] In other words, what gets 'crowded out' are the needs of physical capital (education and health) and physical infrastructure such as roads, bridges, mass transit, schools, alternative energy, etc. Both the Reagan and George W. Bush Administrations combined increases in military spending with drastically lowered tax rates on higher incomes.[42] Overall, the 'permanent war economy,' has played a significant role in the decline of the nation's infrastructure in the last 30 or more years.[43] Ultimately, these dynamics may be described as a kind of 'redistributive militarism,' a way of transferring national resources in a way that benefits the most affluent and hurts those at the bottom of the economic ladder. As Hossein-Zadeh concludes,

> soldiers are obviously not winners, nor are persons in the reserves and National Guard who are called to protracted active duty overseas. The real winners are war industries, their CEOs, and their lobbyists, who are bilking the American taxpayers.[44]

U.S. spending on militarism grew exponentially following the attacks of 9/11. Between 2002 and 2008, the U.S. military budget swelled by $500 bn, a 'significantly faster' rate than over the previous 40 years.[45] However, at the beginning of the Obama Administration, though much media attention was paid to the elimination of a few over-the-top weapons programs, such as the F-22 fighter jet, the change in presidential administrations in 2009 did not involve any decrease of the budget numbers overall.[46] In fact, the military plans to increase its numbers by 92,000 by 2012.[47] These increased

41. Hossein-Zadeh, *The Political Economy*, pp. 219, 221. For instance, the 29 percent increase in real military spending from 1978 to 1983 was accompanied by a decline of 25 percent in federal grants to state and local governments, a major source for investment in public works projects.

42. Hossein-Zadeh, *The Political Economy*, p. 220.

43. Hossein-Zadeh, *The Political Economy*, p. 222.

44. Hossein-Zadeh, *The Political Economy*, p. 227.

45. Bilmes and Stiglitz, *The Three Trillion Dollar War*, p. 20.

46. Christopher Drew, 'Obama Wins Crucial Senate Vote on F-22,' *The New York Times*, 21 July 2009, http://www.nytimes.com/2009/07/22/business/22defense.html, accessed 10 December 2009.

47. Bilmes and Stiglitz, *The Three Trillion Dollar War*, p. 48.

numbers correlate with the military strategy enacted by Secretary of Defense Rumsfeld in 2002, called 'the 1-4-2-1 Defense Strategy' that intends to enable military defense of the United States while at the same time deterring aggression and coercion in four additional regions (Europe, Northeast Asia, East Asia and the Middle East). The goal of this plan is to enable the U.S. to defeat combatants in at least two regions simultaneously and 'win decisively' in at least one additional region.[48]

Why aren't more U.S. citizens alarmed about this rate of militarized expenditure? Economists Jurgen Brauer and John Tepper Marlin claim that the obscene reality of war-culture's economic costs is muted through various threats or grievances, by which leaders make the case for unending growth of resources dedicated to war. In addition, though most businesses actually have a much greater economic stake in an environment that is nonviolent, the 'myopic profit opportunities' involved in the business of war prevent meaningful change:

> The strong interest of a minority of businesses and sometimes of political leaders that benefit from increasing levels of internal or external violence can obscure the broader interest by businesses, suppliers, employees, customers, and investors in living and working in peaceful environments.[49]

In addition to the characteristics of secrecy and disinformation as a growing facet of militarism in the U.S., an examination of the cost of caring for veterans reveals a particularly heart-wrenching snapshot of the most direct of war-culture's consequences, economic and otherwise. By 2008, more than 263,000 returning veterans from Iraq and Afghanistan had been treated at veterans' medical facilities, one in four returning veterans applying for compensation for more than

---

48. Frida Berrigan, 'Entrenched, Embedded and Here to Stay: The Pentagon's Expansion Will be Bush's Lasting Legacy,' *Tomdispatch.com*, 27 May 2008, http://www.tomdispatch.com/post/174936/frida_berrigan_the_pentagon_takes_over, accessed 29 May 2008.

49. Jurgen Brauer and John Tepper Marlin, 'Defining Peace Industries and Calculating the Potential Size of a Peace Gross World Product by Country and by Economic Sector: Confidential Report for Economists for Peace and Security,' *Vision of Humanity: The Global 2010 Peace Index*, April, 2009, http://www.visionofhumanity.org/, accessed 11 June 06/11/2010, p. 28.

eight separate disabling conditions.[50] In 2005, the U.S. paid $34.5 bn in annual disability entitlement pay to veterans from previous wars. Not only the Veterans Administration, but other health care institutions and Social Security will be called upon to cover costs associated with Iraq and Afghanistan veterans' health care, social security and disability needs. These costs will run somewhere between $422 bn (in a best case scenario) and $717 bn (in a realistic-moderately conceived scenario).[51] Yet such monetary expenditures don't begin to account for many other grievances incurred, such as the economic value of the loss of a productive young life, difficulties and deficits due to mental health disabilities such as Post-Traumatic Stress Disorder and traumatic brain injury, the costs of 'quality of life' impairments to veterans, their family, friends and communities, and more.

War-Culture, Consumerism and Everyday Life

A multitude of various facets make up today's military-industrial complex. 'The Complex' has become deeply embedded in American existence, everyday life and even imagination. Not only is it 'an entity light-years beyond the size, scale and scope of Dwight Eisenhower's military-industrial complex,' making matters more pernicious is the fact that frequently, it hardly looks 'military' at all.[52] We are securely connected to the complex in ways that are completely invisible to us on a daily basis, through vast arrays of products we rely on in our everyday life, the realities in our workplaces and schools, the production and consumption of our entertainment, in unending cultural sites and activities and more. In fact, what Eisenhower called 'the military-industrial complex' is today more appropriately described by sociologist Nick Turse as, 'this new military-industrial-technological-entertainment-academic-scientific- edia-intelligence-homeland security-surveillance-national security-corporate complex.'[53] He writes,

---

50. Bilmes and Stiglitz, *The Three Trillion Dollar War*, p. 66.
51. Bilmes and Stiglitz, *The Three Trillion Dollar War*, p. 87.
52. Nick Turse, *The Complex: How The Military Invades Our Everyday Lives* (New York, NY: Metropolitan Books, 2008), p. 271.
53. Turse, *The Complex*, p. 16.

> The high level of military-civilian interpenetration in a heavily
> consumer-driven society means that almost every American is,
> at least passively, supporting the Complex every time he or she
> shops for groceries, sends a package, drives a car, or watches TV...
> The Complex is connected to everything you would expect, from
> the top arms manufacturers to big oil corporations – as well as nu-
> merous government agencies connected to the U.S. Department of
> Defense and allied entities such as the Central Intelligence Agency
> and the Department of Homeland Security. But it is also connected
> to the entertainment industry and the world's largest media con-
> glomerates. It is in league with the nation's largest food suppliers
> and beverage companies. It supports the most prestigious univer-
> sities in America and is tied to the leading automakers.[54]

Huge defense industry corporations continue to profoundly influence the military-industrial complex in the contemporary U.S.
However, in comparison with 1970, when 22,000 prime contractors
worked for the U.S. Department of Defense, today over 47,000 contractors and over 100,000 subcontractors have business ties with the
military. As a result, all kinds of products we rely upon from the
minute we awake through our night-time sleeping hours are made
by corporations with lucrative military contracts. From Cheerios to
Dawn dishwashing liquid, Nature Valley Granola Bars to Wolfgang
Puck's gourmet pizza, household appliances, home computers, video games, car manufacturers, sunglasses, clothing, the list of items
produced by defense-related mega corporations and manufacturers
goes on and on.[55] The result is a symbiotic relationship in which
each side feeds, profits and ultimately is dependent on the other

War-culture penetrates into ever increasing cultural and social
areas of human life, institutions and imagination in the United
States. Scholars analyze entertainment, telecommunications, youth
culture, the oil industry, mega corporations, the regime of military
bases, consumerism, and food production, to name only some facets
of interpenetration. One troubling example is the interpenetration
of the Complex in youth culture, especially video gaming and internet sites infiltrated by the military, such as *Myspace.com*. In addition
to video games such as *America's Army*, that have been produced by
the military and provided free of charge to youths for the purpose

54. Turse, *The Complex*, pp. 16–18.
55. Turse, *The Complex*, pp. 5–7, and Section II, 'Today's Corporate Bedfellows',
pp. 61–82.

of military brand enhancement and recruitment, a revolving employment door operates between the video game industry, potential and/or actual soldiers and military advisors in a kind of mutual dependency. The military uses war video games to train soldiers, and has come to rely on the skills children build through hours at the video game controls for high-tech military functions in the fields of war. The *America's Army Official Website* not only makes it possible for gamers to download the war video game for free, it has chat rooms, links to pictures and statements of currently deployed soldiers. The video-war-game highlights in its game play exactly the same weapons these warriors use on current battlefields, though it is rated 'T,' for 'teen', meaning that youngsters from 12 years and up are not likely to encounter any resistance when they ask their parents' approval to join the ranks. Its recruitment intentions are clear, as this centrally placed statement on the webpage indicates:

> From recruitment to retirement, the U.S. Army provides a unique and diverse lifestyle. Soldiers are given every opportunity to grow. With expert training in one of more than 150 different jobs for Soldiers on Active Duty and more than 120 in the Army Reserve, you'll gain a foundation of confidence, discipline, and leadership – and an experience that will give you an edge over those in the civilian world.[56]

Turse writes,

> The day is not far off when most potential U.S. troops will have grown up playing commercial video games that were created by the military as training simulators; will be recruited, at least in part, through video games; will be tested, post-enlistment, on advanced video game systems; will be trained using simulators, which will later be turned into video games, or on reconfigured versions of the very same games used to recruit them or that they played as kids; will be taught to pilot vehicles using devices resembling commercial video game controllers; and then, after a long day of real-life *war-gaming* head back to their quarters to kick back and play the latest PlayStation or Xbox games created with or sponsored by their own, or another, branch of the military.[57]

---

56. *America's Army.com*, http://www.americasarmy.com/usarmy/, accessed 10 January 2010.
57. Turse, *The Complex*, p. 140.

Along just these lines, the Institute for Creative Technologies at University of Southern California was funded in 1999 with $45 m from the Department of Defense to create a research center to develop advanced military simulations. Here we have the military-academic complex conjoined with both film studios and video game designers not only to develop simulators for a military application, but technological advances for 'more compelling video games and theme park rides.'[58] Typically such efforts involve personnel in that revolving employment door from the halls of the academy, to the military to the defense industry to the gaming/Hollywood film industry and back.

For example, Steven Woodcock, the lead software engineer for Gameware Development at Lockheed-Martin Real3D, also worked for Martin Marietta Information Group on weapons code development and Advanced Real-time Gaming Universal Simulation (ARGUS). Among other applications, ARGUS involves interactive command-and-control simulation for ballistic missile defense. At the same time, when defense contractor Martin Marietta contracted with Sega (the videogame manufacturer), Woodcock shifted from working on strict military applications to oversee the game development on an arcade game for Sega called *Behind Enemy Lines*. He noted that his earlier defense work proved invaluable in designing the multi-player environment of video games.[59] If the video gamers' virtual world has been utterly colonized by such collusion with military purposes, culture and applications, the opposite also is true. General Charles C. Krulak, in his 1996 directive, 'Military Thinking and Decision Making Exercises,' mandated that all marines make use of PC war games on a daily basis 'to develop decision making skills, particularly when live training and opportunities are limited.' He further *ordered* that the Marine Combat Development Command develop and disseminate such games, resulting in the *PC-based Wargames Catalog* on the Internet.[60]

---

58. Tim Lenoir, 'All But War Is Simulation: The Military-Entertainment Complex,' *Configuration* vol. 8, no. 3 (Fall 2000):, pp. 289–335, ICT was awarded additional money in 2004 to continue their work for an additional five years. See the 'Background' link on their website for additional information. *USC Institute for Creative Technologies* http://ict.usc.edu/background, accessed 27 June 2008.

59. Lenoir, 'All But War Is Simulation', pp. 321–22.

60. Lenoir, 'All But War Is Simulation', p. 323.

From 2008 to 2010, at the Franklin Mills Mall near Philadelphia, the Army developed and operated 'The Army Experience Center.' Accompanying the news article from Army.Mil/News, a photograph of the center showed teenage boys in shorts and T-shirts in a Humvee simulator, their arms wrapped around military artillery rifles or machine guns. Located near a popular entertainment complex in the suburban mall, The Army Experience Center was next door to an indoor skate park, a favorite gathering place for youth looking for something exciting and entertaining to do. According to the army's own news website, the more than 20 soldiers who operated the site were 'not recruiters' (though the article does admit that these soldiers are 'trained recruiters'), but were there to facilitate the site as 'an attraction tool.' Ignited Corporation (a marketing company) and the makers of the video game *Halo* partnered with the army to build the $12 m interactive site (funded through tax dollars). In its own promotional video for the center, the marketing company clearly stated the need for high-tech, hyper-realistic and sensory-filled experiences to mitigate against 'unpopular wars and falling recruitment numbers.' In addition to dozens of computer terminals where young people could log on and play video war-games, and simulators that enabled youth to 'act out' fighting the bad guys, the Army Experience Center featured an interactive video 'career center' highlighting the variety of career options in the military, and private conference rooms where military personnel were available to meet with young people. At least 40,000 people visited the center during the two years, and 236 enlisted specifically as a result of their encounter. As one blogger sarcastically summed it up,

> while the potential recruits are coming off their adrenaline high of shooting up an Iraqi village, a friendly, shiny-faced soldier in khaki and a polo shirt can guide them over to the interactive, state-of-the-art Career Navigator kiosks so that they can learn all about the 170 fantastic Army career opportunities.[61]

The Army Experience Center is only one example of intensified recruiting and marketing efforts developed through the Department

61. Carrey McLeroy, 'Army Center Experience Opens in Philadelphia,' Army. mil/News, 2 September 2008, www.army.mil/-news/2008/09/02/12072, accessed 5 May 2009. See also '*The Army Center Experience: The Future of Recruiting*,' 20 February 2009, Redpill.8.blogspot.com, http://redpill8.blogspot. com/2009/02/army-experience-center-marketing.html, accessed 5 May 2009.

of Defense during the Iraq War. If, by the middle of 2005, military recruiters estimated that they needed to speak with 150 young people
to successfully enlist one individual, by 2008–2009, given the economics of the Great Recession in the U.S., and rising levels of unem-
ployment, the 'poverty draft' meant that recruitment goals for the
wars could be met much more easily. In 2010 the Army Experience
Center was closed, with military officials declaring that 'it was a
success'. In Philadelphia, which in 2008 had 'the lowest propensity
toward military service' in the nation, the numbers of recruited individuals rose by at least 15 percent over the course of the two years
of economic fallout in the nation. Meanwhile, the Army planned to
move the various high-tech elements from the center to other recruiting stations around the country. The center had met its goal: to
'determine the most effective tools for public outreach'.[62]

War-Culture and Education

Another disturbing facet of war-culture is its interpenetration with
public and higher education. If the very idea of the university con-
jures the notion of open space for critical thinking and learning,
dialogue and debate, public service, cultural appreciation and expression, and socially responsible research, Eisenhower's earlier
fears about the state setting the agenda for university research, and
the value of open curiosity constrained by Federal money are, in
the post-9/11 world, only the tip of the iceberg. Not only do 150
military-educational institutions operate to inculcate 'a youthful
corps of tomorrow's military officers' in the values, militarized sets
of knowledge and skills of the warfare state; in addition, hundreds
of colleges and universities rely on Pentagon-funded research, resulting in 'the militarized civilian university.'[63]

During WWII, ten top universities involved in weapons development received at that time the enormous amounts of $10 m

62. Edward Colimore and Nicole Lockley, 'Army Experience Center in
Northeast Will Close,' *The Philadelphia Inquirer*, 10 June 2010, http://www.
philly.com/inquirer/local/pa/20100610_Army_Experience_Center_in_
Northeast_will_close.html, accessed 12 October 2010. Also see Cynthia Enloe,
Nimo's War, Emma's War: Making Feminist Sense of the Iraq War (Berkeley, CA:
University of California Press, 2010), p. 138.

63. Turse, *The Complex*, p. 32.

each. By 2002, according to a report by the Association of American Universities, almost 350 colleges and universities conducted Pentagon-funded research. After the National Institute of Health and the National Science Foundation, the Department of Defense ranks as the third-largest funder of university research.[64] In addition, Congressional earmarks funding college and university research reached an all-time high in 2008, representing a 25 percent increase from 2003. Over 920 institutions of higher education were granted these funds that are dispersed outside of any traditional process of open competition and peer review. Moreover, during this same time period, 2003–2008, the two other principal federal sources for academic research money, the National Institute of Health and the National Science Foundation, saw their budgets decline so much that each agency in 2008 expected to approve only one in five grant applications, in comparison with funding one in three in 2001. A total of 41 percent of earmarks in 2008 came from the Department of Defense, 'a favorite spot for lawmakers to tuck in academic earmarks,' resulting in a total of $2.25 bn dollars.[65]

What kind of impact does all this have on colleges and universities? Are they adversely affected? Ethically compromised? What impact does such a Department of Defense presence have on the value of academic freedom? Surely the documented decline in competitive and peer-reviewed grant funding is one reason for concern. But leaders in higher education list additional reasons we should be worried. First, and exactly along the lines of Eisenhower's concern, the interpenetration of war-culture with the academy leads to research that is not the result of objective decisions, freely arrived at in the spirit of an enlightened quest for knowledge; rather,

64. Turse, *The Complex*, pp. 34–35.

65. Jeffrey Brainard and J.J. Hermes, 'Colleges' Earmarks Grow, Amid Criticism,' *Chronicle of Higher Education*, 28 March 2008, http://chronicle.com/free/v54/i29/29a00101.htm, accessed 12 June 2008 . In 2009 the DoD requested a 4.0 percent increase to $1.7 billion for its basic research ('6.1') portfolio, the majority of which is performed in universities. 'The Department of Defense (DoD) R&D investment continues to grow, with a proposed increase of $2.9 billion or 3.7 percent to $80.7 billion in fiscal year (FY) 2009 but both the 2008 and 2009 totals will grow by billions later this year when war-related supplementals are added,' says researcher Kei Koizumi. See Koizumi, 'R&D in the FY 2009 Department of Defense Budget,' *AAAS Report XXXIII*, http://www.aaas.org/spp/rd/09pch5.htm, accessed 10 October 2009.

'"these scientists" agendas are determined by the architects of military strategy.'[66] Second, not only is the area of research impacted, research results also may be challenged or silenced if they are in disagreement with Pentagon Policy. Third, 'secret research of any kind is …the antithesis of free and open inquiry' upon which the entire system of higher education is founded; it circumvents open debate, and is not open as an area of learning and inquiry to students without sufficient security clearances. Fourth, related to the issue of secrecy is the experience of increased pressure many academics experience to obtain grants for research in order to achieve tenure. Especially in the fields of science and engineering, the 'multi-billion pot of military Research and Development funding constitutes a powerful magnet for faculty in pursuit of research money.'[67]

But not only does the lure of big money from military research and development impact decision-making in university research. Heavily military-oriented research at top tier educational institutions also is a powerful incentive for graduate students to follow in the steps of their professors and advisors; and many find that the highest paying and most prestigious jobs also will lie in the same military-oriented environments. Moreover, given that military research and development (R&D) is the nation's most crucial technology-developing resource, and given that at least 30 percent of the nation's engineers and scientists are engaged in such activity, some economics scholars argue that as a result, the growth of civilian-oriented technology has been retarded. Over against those who would argue that a 'spinoff' or 'spillover' effect means that military-oriented technological development 'spills over' into civilian areas of technological advancement, some economists underscore the serious erosion of U.S. predominance in science and technology in recent decades. The number of patents awarded in the U.S. fell by about 30 percent beginning in the 1960s at the same time that many other countries saw their own number of patents rise. One

66. Jay Reed, 'Toward a 21st Century Peace Movement,' 12 Sept. 2001, *UTWatch.org*, http://utwatch.org/war/ut_military.html, accessed 12 June 2008.

67. Lloyd J. Dumas, 'University Research, Industrial Innovation, and the Pentagon,' in John Tirman (ed.), *The Militarization of High Technology* (Cambridge, MA: Balinger Publishing Company, 1984). See http://utwatch. org/war/militarizeduniveresearch.html, accessed 27 June 2008.

economics scholar remarks, 'As the technological brain drain gener-
ated by the military sector led to deterioration in the rate of civilian
technological development, productivity rates began to collapse.'[68]

But even greater issues are at stake than concerns for academic
freedom and levels of economic production. Ultimately, educators
must struggle with the question: can the contribution of such research to death and destruction around the world be aligned with
the mission of higher education? In the 1960s, across university
campuses in the United States, open debate took place regarding
the appropriateness of military research and development as a
part of the agenda of higher education. Does the college or university have any responsibility regarding the kinds of teaching and
research activities that take place?

Military recruitment represents yet another facet of war-
culture's interpenetration with educational institutions. After the
U.S. Congress ended the male draft in 1973, and realizing that white
and middle-class men would have wider career options open to
them, the U.S. Army began to focus on other recruitment options for
an all-volunteer army, specifically soliciting people in lower socio-
economic classes, people of color, and women. As the Iraq War began, African American women constituted 13 percent of American
women, but 34.3 percent of active-duty women in the Army.[69] In addition, in the post-9/11 period the United States increased intense
recruiting of ever younger actual and would-be citizens for participation in the military-industrial-academic complex. The *No Child
Left Behind Act* includes provisions that require all public schools
receiving federal funding to allow military recruitment on their
campuses. The Junior Reserve Officer Training Corps (JROTC) was
founded in the mid 1990s and established on high school campuses
across the country. Participating students dressed in military uni-
forms, had military veterans as teachers, and took part in various
military activities – all intended to naturalize and promote military
enlistment following high school.[70] Students have been recruited as
young as 14 years-old for the 'Delayed Entry Program' (DEP), that
involves them in pre-military training, testing and culture while in

68. Dumas, 'University Research.'
69. Cynthia Enloe, *Nimo's War, Emma's War*, pp. 159, 166.
70. Cynthia Enloe, *Nimo's War, Emma's War*, pp. 151–152.

high school for preparation to enter active duty.[71] Some high school guidance counselors use the military's own career aptitude test in order to test their students – and share the results of testing with the Department of Defense.[72] In addition, recruiters' promises of citizenship through enlistment have proven to be especially powerful in a political climate with growing pressures on undocumented people, and have been criticized by immigrants' rights activists as a form of 'blatant exploitation of a vulnerable population.'[73] At the same time, the Pentagon, using a marketing company called BeNOW, compiled one of the largest private databases ever created on young people in the U.S., 30 million 16 to 25 year-olds, their names, addresses, email addresses, cell phone numbers, ethnicity, social security numbers and areas of study.[74] While the DEP originally was created after the Vietnam draft ended, students who now sign up to become a part of the program

> are targeted, tested, gifted, video-gamed, recruitment-faired and career-counseled into enlisting before they turn 18. They are also paid $2,000 for every friend they talk into signing up with them and, until recently, were paid $50 for every name they brought in to a recruiter.[75]

Without a college education, most of the DEP students will go on to combat duty to fill this greatest area of need for the military. They can earn extra pay in active duty if their friends also sign up, or if they volunteer for 'hazardous duty,' dismantling explosives or dealing with toxic chemicals. The concern of public educators was so high with regard to such recruiting tactics and their incursion into what educators hoped would be the safe, open and nurturing space of the public middle or high school, especially on the part of those who educate students in largely Latino communities, a key recruiting site for soldiers sent to Iraq, that the California Federation of Teachers passed a resolution in March of 2007, calling for the elimination of the reauthorization of the *No Child Left Behind Act.*

---

71. Deborah David, 'Yo Soy El Army: If You're an Immigrant, at Least Uncle Sam Wants You,' *Metroactive*, 19 September 2007. See http://www.metroactive.com/metro/09.19.07/news-0738.html, accessed 5 June 2008.

72. Cynthia Enloe, *Nimo's War, Emma's War*, p. 133.

73. David, 'Yo Soy El Army.'

74. Giroux, *University in Chains*, p. 45.

75. David, 'Yo Soy El Army.'

The resolution 1) describes the infringement of student privacy and rights created by the recruitment statute of *No Child Left Behind,* 2) insists that 'military recruitment does not belong in any federal statute on public education,' 3) criticizes the 'deceitful and high pressure sales tactics' of military recruiters, and 4) decries the huge funding deficit for public education as funds are diverted for war [76]

The increasing invisibility of any boundaries between war-culture and the academy raises questions regarding the mission of higher education. What is its purpose? What if any boundaries should be respected and preserved between the institutions and practices of war-culture and the college/university? What are the ethics of educational institutional involvement with the Pentagon and intelligence agencies of the U.S.? Responses to the above questions vary substantially. On the one hand, some academics have suggested that all boundaries should be lowered between education and the intelligence community, such as Elizabeth Rindskopf Parker, Dean of the McGeorge School of Law and the University of the Pacific: 'It is time to close the cultural divide between academe and the intelligence community... the United States must have the commitment and cooperation of its scholars and its national-security experts.'[77] Of course Rindskopf Parker, like Secretary of Defense Robert Gates (who formerly held positions as the Director of the CIA and President of Texas A&M University), is the product of the revolving employment door between academe and institutions of the military, having served as former legal counsel for the CIA and National Security Agency. Those with similar views argue for a natural and seamless relationship between the mission of higher education and the needs of the U.S. military and homeland security apparatus. On this view, creating careful boundaries between military and educational institutions is not only unpatriotic, but undemocratic and unpragmatic.

On the other hand, and in contrast to dismissal of ethical concerns about the interpenetration of the military and higher education, the ongoing debates about social sciences research and training for the purposes of war, intelligence-gathering and the military, illustrate the complexity and importance of questions about the purpose of

76. 'California Federation of Teachers Resolution 27,' *The Coalition against Militarism in Our Schools,* http://www.militaryfreeschools.org/, accessed 29 May 2008.

77. Giroux, *University in Chains,* p. 64.

the academy in light of war-culture. What impact does the acceptance and reliance on Department of Defense funding have on the academy? The DoD supplies 60 percent of all electrical engineering research funding; 55 percent of computer sciences, 41 percent of metallurgy/materials engineering and 33 percent for oceanography.[78] How does this relationship shape the research agendas that may be taken on (or those abandoned or inadequately funded)? Does the academy and/or do individual academics bear any responsibility for thinking about how their research may be used?

The DoD's incursions into the fields of applied science are well-worn and many decades old by this point, but relatively few U.S. citizens are aware of the debate that took place within the American Psychological Association beginning in 2006 regarding psychologists' role in 'enhanced interrogation' procedures at so-called 'black sites' operated by the CIA.[79] In addition, though little public attention has been given to the controversy, the Pentagon's attempts in recent years to plow new ground in the discipline of anthropology have not met with unqualified appreciation from the community of anthropologists in colleges and universities. These Pentagon programs include (but are not limited to):

The Pat Roberts Intelligence Scholars Program, PRISP – a program funded by an initial $4 m grant from the CIA, that gives participating students up to $50,000 over two years. Students are directed to language, political science, international affairs and national security studies in areas of concern to the Directorate of Intelligence, mostly in Asia and the Middle East. Students must do an internship with an intelligence organization and have demonstrated an interest in an intelligence analysis career. They undergo security clearances as a part of their application and are required to keep

---

78. Giroux, *University in Chains*, p. 53.

79. David Glenn, 'A Policy on Torture Roils Psychologists' Annual Meeting,' *Chronicle of Higher Education*, 7 September 2007. In August 2008, the APA passed a ballot referendum prohibiting such activity. The key statement reads, 'Be it resolved that psychologists may not work in settings where persons are held outside of, or in violation of, either International Law (e.g., the UN Convention Against Torture and the Geneva Conventions) or the U.S. Constitution (where appropriate), unless they are working directly for the persons being detained or for an independent third party working to protect human rights.' See the *Psychologists for Social Responsibility* website for the full-text referendum. http://www.psysr.org/voteyes, accessed 25 August 2008.

their participation in the program secret from friends and family, the university, etc.[80]

The National Security Education Program (NSEP) Scholarships – awards scholarships to American students for study of world regions critical to U.S. interests (including Africa, Asia, Eastern Europe, Eurasia, Latin America and the Caribbean, and the Middle East). Students are required following their study to work in the federal government in positions with national security responsibilities.[81]

The Human Terrain System – was initiated in September 2007 with a grant of $40 m authorized by Robert Gates, Defense Secretary, to assign teams of anthropologists and social sciences in each of the 26 American combat brigades in Iraq and Afghanistan. The senior social science advisor to the program, Dr. Montgomery McFate, said: 'I'm frequently accused of militarizing anthropology...but we're really anthropologizing the military.'[82]

The Minerva Consortium – also announced by Robert Gates in 2008, is a new program of university-based, national-security-oriented social science research. 'The changes in the type of warfare we're fighting and the situations our soldiers are finding themselves in necessitate this type of research,' said Representative Brian Baird, Democrat of Washington and Chair of the Congressional Subcommittee on Research and Science Education. Initially $150 m has been allotted for the first year of this program [83]

The Obama Administration Intelligence Officer Training Program was announced in June 2009, authorizing colleges and universities for grants to introduce courses of study to 'meet the emerging needs of the intelligence community.' Student participation in the program is kept secret, as in other programs, and participants need to pass security clearance procedures in order to procure grant money to

80. As detailed on the PRISP website, *Pat Roberts Intelligence Scholars Program*, https://www.cia.gov/careers/jobs/view-all-jobs/pat-roberts-intelligence-scholars-program-p, accessed 30 May 2008.

81. As detailed on the NSEP website, *National Security Education Program*, http://www.nsep.gov, accessed 17 January 2010.

82. David Rohde, 'Army Enlists Anthropology in War Zones,' *The New York Times*, 5 October 2007, http://query.nytimes.com/gst/fullpage.html, accessed 30 May 2008.

83. David Glenn, 'Congressional Panel Weighs Social Science's Role in Warfare,' *Chronicle of Higher Education*, 25 April 2008, http://chronicle.com/daily/2008/04/2633n.htm, accessed 25 April 2008.

cover tuition and provide a stipend while they are in college. The intelligence community already has a Centers of Academic Excellence Program that funds programs in national security studies at more than 14 colleges and universities, with a goal of having 20 participating schools by 2015. The programs receive between $500,000 and $750,000 a year.[84]

In response to such developments, a group called, 'Concerned Anthropologists,' protested what they see as 'the exploitation of anthropology, the science that studies peoples' origin, history and culture, in the war on terror.'[85] Academics who have joined the group sign a pledge claiming that covert work, or work that contributes to the harm and death of other human beings, or work that breaches trust with research participants, is labor that anthropologists should not undertake. As one professor described the ethical dilemmas such programs create, 'What safeguards exist to impede the transfer of data collected by anthropologists to commanders planning offensive military campaigns?'

Such concerns notwithstanding, at a teleconference roundtable of 'Department of Defense bloggers' convened by Thomas Mahnken, the Deputy Assistant Secretary of Defense for Policy Planning, participants were invited to make comments and raise questions about the Minerva Consortium.[86] Mr. Mahnken noted that while the DoD has a long history of funding research in the physical sciences, this foray into social science, while not entirely new, is much less of an established relationship. The transcript of the defense bloggers reveals their assumption that a perceived seamless and permeable relationship between the DoD and applied sciences in university research eventually will be equally achieved between the DoD and

84. Walter Pincus, 'Obama Administration Looks to Colleges for Future Spies,' *Washington Post*, 20 June 2009, http://www.washingtonpost.com/wp-dyn/content/article/2009/06/19/AR2009061903501.html?referrer=emailarticle, accessed 24 June 2009.

85. Dina Rabie, 'Militarizing Anthropology,' *Islamonline.net*, http://www.islamonline.net/, 18 October 2007, accessed Sept. 20, 2008. Also See *Network of Concerned Anthropologists*, http://concerned.anthropologists.googlepages.com/home, accessed 17 January 2010.

86. David Glenn, 'New Details of "Minerva Project" Emerge, as Social Scientists Weigh Pentagon Ties,' *Chronicle of Higher Education*, 12 May 2008, http://chronicle.com/news/article/4467/new-details-of-minerva-project-emerge-as-social-scientists-weigh-pentagon-ties, accessed 11 June 2008.

the social sciences. Any concerns are dismissed through comparison with the relative ease with which the DoD seeks support and participation from academics in physical and applied sciences: 'if you're in, you know, oceanography or if you're in a lot of other fields of science, government contracts and government funding is just part of what you do,' said Mahnken. 'You know, we're able to call upon the full talents of the nation when it comes to, you know, physical science or engineering. We're not able to do that when it comes to some of these vitally important topics.' When asked about possible perception of the Pentagon encroaching on what should be funded by the State Department or Department of Education, Mahnken replied, 'Look, we would certainly welcome other parts of the government funding this research as well...But I don't see that that is an argument against our doing it.' He concluded,

> I've met with a lot of university presidents and provosts and chancellors...You know, many of these folks are people for which this is uncontroversial. I mean, they come from the physical sciences, they come from engineering, and government funding is part of the way they do business.

However, some anthropologists have described a 'far darker' cast with regard to the nature of anthropological cooperation with military purposes. One pointed to an unclassified statement by Assistant Deputy Under Secretary of Defense John Wilcox, who described the benefits of anthropological human-terrain mapping in the following way, as 'enabling the entire kill chain.' Anthropologist David Vine responded,

> Providing cultural-sensitivity training in a classroom or briefing peacekeepers charged with preventing violence and protecting civilians is one thing. But when an anthropologist steps onto the battlefield to assist soldiers at war, occupying another nation, engaged in regular, active lethal combat operations, a line has been crossed.[87]

Along the same lines, recalling a 'fraught history' of anthropology assisting U.S. military purposes in conflicts stretching from Vietnam as far back as WWII, Roberto J. Gonzalez, Professor of Anthropology at San Jose State University, had this to say:

87. David Vine, 'Enabling the Kill Chain,' *Chronicle of Higher Education* 54.14 (30 November 2007): B9–B10.

> We are deeply concerned that the war on terror threatens to militarize anthropology in a way that undermines the integrity of the discipline and returns anthropology to its sad roots as a tool of colonial occupation, oppression and violence.[88]

By 2009, the Annual Report of the American Anthropological Association articulated the following official position regarding members' participation in DoD-sponsored collaborations such as the Human Terrain Systems Program:

> ...when ethnographic investigation is determined by military missions, is not subject to external review, data is collected in the context of war, in a potential coercive environment, and results are integrated into the goals of counterinsurgency – all characteristic factors of the Human Terrain System concept and its application – it can no longer be considered a legitimate professional exercise of anthropology.[89]

To conclude, if at least some of the results of the 'militarized civilian university' include, as listed by Giroux, the production of weapons, increase in the arms race, collusion with forces of secrecy and domination, subversion of or inadequate resources dedicated to scientific knowledge that could be peaceful and/or non-militarized, and the imposition of the assumption that using civilian institutions to suit military desires and pursuits is the normal way of doing things – then key questions must be articulated by those whose commitment is to shape a different ethos in higher education. 'What role do intellectuals play in the conditions that allow theory and knowledge to be appropriated by the military; and what can they do politically to prevent theory, knowledge and information from being militarized in the first place?[90]

Seeking Civilian Legitimation and Obliviousness

War-culture involves the interpenetration of the culture and institutions of the military and war into ever increasing areas of human

88. Rabie, 'Militarizing Anthropology.'

89. '"2009 Annual Report: American Anthropological Association: Anthropology, Democracy, Inclusiveness, Transparency," American Anthropological Association,' http://www.aaanet.org/about/Annual_Reports/upload/AAA-2009-Annual-Report.pdf, accessed 7 June 06/07/2010.

90. Giroux, *University in Chains*, p. 57.

life, community, institutions and imagination in the United States. In a 'hyper-modern' globalized world, boundaries between all sorts of institutions and practices that once were taken for granted are increasingly permeable.[91] Defense industries reach out to American students in the earliest grades with lures such as robotics teams, offers to tutor students, and invitations to shadow defense industry employees in their workplaces, not to mention lucrative tuition reimbursement programs for those who enter the field [92] These efforts not only bring new blood into the field but have the added benefit of attaching a philanthropic gloss to such corporations. In this 'quasi-militarization of everyday life,' the military appropriates the culture, lifestyles and aesthetics of people being marketed as potential recruits, while the military's own deeply masculinized, heroic, and 'high-adventure,' aesthetic simultaneously is marketed and appropriated by a wide variety of cultural realms.[93]

Yet another angle to this diminishment of the boundaries has to do with the increasing interpenetration of virtual and actual realities – any boundary separating these is thinning as Hollywood films, news programs and virtual video game reality take on a more seamless relationship with the actual reality of life in the military, military culture and actions of war. In addition to the example of the Institute for Creative Technologies at University of Southern California, the video magazine *Wired* reported that the 'Project Office for Gaming, or TPO Gaming' had been installed in the Army's Kansas-based National Simulation Center, focusing on 'using videogame graphics to make those dull military simulations more realistic, and better-looking.'[94] The boundaries between war-

91. John Armitage defines 'hypermodernity' as 'an escalation of faith in militarized knowledge factories' within 'a heightened level of modern intensification and acceleration.' See 'Beyond Hypermodern Militarized Knowledge Factories,' *Review of Education, Pedagogy, and Cultural Studies* 27 (2005): 219–39, see p. 220.

92. See, 'Inside Aero08 Report: Working Together to Build the Aerospace Workforce of Tomorrow,' 13 May 2008, http://www.aiaa.org/pdf/public/Inside_Aero08_Report_and_Recommendations.pdf, accessed 20 September 2008.

93. Giroux, *University in Chains*, p. 40.

94. Noah Schachtman, 'Army Sets Up New Office of Videogames,' *Wired*, 12 December 2007, http://blog.wired.com/defense/2007/12/armys-new-offic html, accessed 12 June 2008. See ICT's website, http://ict.usc.edu/, accessed

culture and non-militaristic facets of life diminish as the institutions of war-culture assume more and more responsibility for ever-increasing domains of life and work that in the past were civilian, diplomatic, or within the responsibility of educational institutions. The 'leap and creep' of Pentagon expansion in the post-9/11 period '… dwarfs other institutions of government' as the military encroaches more and more into areas that were formerly civilian, diplomatic, educational, and cultural.[95]

Eisenhower's speech may seem almost quaint to contemporary ears with its concern about the 'economic, political, even spiritual – influence of the military-industrial complex felt in every city, State house, every office of Federal government.' And while many scholars criticize abuses of power and conflicts of interest represented by inner dynamics of the complex, even more significant is the observation from Nick Turse regarding the 'obliviousness of the civilian population.' Many if not most U.S. citizens generally are unconcerned and unaware about the depth and breadth of the growth of the military-industrial complex; in Turse's words, they are 'oblivious.' Why? Such lack of awareness may be traced to a number of different causes.

First, because the complex is everywhere, we don't pay it much attention; it has become as naturalized to us as any other everyday aspect of life. Why shouldn't it be everywhere? Why should it be of any concern to me that Starbucks, Oakley, Disney and Coca-Cola, just to name a few mega corporations, have ongoing huge contracts with the military? Should it matter that the hybrid car I am looking to buy is made by a corporation that also builds vehicles for the army? One key component of war-culture and militarization is the way legitimacy for all sorts of projects, products, and processes is pursued through association with military goals.[96] This process of legitimation deeply impacts the manufacture, consumption and cultural impact of products in the U.S. such as toys, clothing,

12 June 2008. The ICT initially began with a grant of $45 m to USC to 'create a research center to develop advanced military simulations.' See Lenoir, 'All but War Is Simulation', p. 328.

95. Frida Berrigan, 'Entrenched, Embedded, and Here to Stay,' *Tomdispatch. com*, http://www.tomdispatch.com/post/174936/frida_berrigan_the_pentagon_takes_over, 27 May 2008, accessed 11 June 2008.

96. Giroux, *University in Chains*, p. 50.

automobiles, movies, etc. At the same time, as legitimation occurs, attention moves away from the center of critical consciousness; in other words, it becomes a normalized process that is less and less acknowledged, much less critically analyzed.

We can see legitimation at work in an example such as the Ford 'concept vehicle', called 'Synus,' that was premiered at the 2005 North American International Auto Show. The description of the vehicle provided by Ford demonstrates the penetration of the culture of war into that all-important American cultural symbol, the automobile:

> As the population shifts back to big cities, you'll need a rolling urban command center. Enter the Synus concept vehicle, a mobile techno sanctuary sculpted in urban armor... When parked and placed in secure mode, Synus deploys protective shutters...the flanks and roof are non-opening and bullet resistant...plus, you can monitor your surroundings in real time as seen by the rear-mounted cameras.[97]

The militarized language is enough to make one wonder whether one is buying a car to commute to work, or for self-protection in a field of war! But the conflation of the two environments is exactly the point: Ford's description of this concept vehicle is a perfect example of the way 'a kind of pathologized militarization has become sutured into everyday life.' Moreover, the same militarization is 'tamed' through the language and culture of consumerism. Turse's awareness regarding U.S. citizens' 'oblivion' is related to Jonathan Schell's observation regarding what he calls 'the extremism of the center' in the post-9/11 period. The concentrations of diverse forms of power, political, financial, military and media into 'huge combines' became a naturalized characteristic of national life. These combines are extremely difficult for citizens to penetrate with resistant awareness and action. Moreover, such concentrations of power are not a result of extreme right-wing or left-wing ideology or activism, but 'grow quietly out of business as usual.'[98]

Civilian obliviousness results from normalization of the complex as war-culture penetrates into more and more facets of life in the United States. But in addition, second, civilian lack of concern and

97. As quoted in Giroux, *University in Chains*, p. 51.
98. Jonathan Schell and Robert S. Boynton, 'People's Power vs. Nuclear Power: a Conversation,' *Daedalus* (Winter 2007): 28–29.

awareness of the complex also may be traced to the military's sophisticated and largely successful efforts to portray itself especially in contemporary times as hip, attractive, technologically savvy, powerful and fun. Who wouldn't want to be connected? Contemporary military recruiting tactics involve flashy Hummer 2s trotted about in Latino communities (especially in places where youths are likely to gather), painted with the words 'Yo Soy El Army' on the side and the latest video and sound technology on the interior combined with plush leather seating. Special Operations troops and 'armchair warriors' alike use Oakley high-end footwear, 'the Elite Special Forces Standard-Issue Assault Boot' (at prices that start at $225). Whereas in 1994, the army issued protective eyewear to troops that failed to be used by many soldiers, in 2005 the army embarked on a 'culture change,' to contract with Oakley for sunglasses that the enlisted would find hip and attractive. But not only is Oakley considered 'cool' by soldiers out in the field

> at home, Oakley trades on a *badas* rep, cool-looking gear, and tough sounding products like the "Killswitch" and "Crosshair" (men's footwear), the "Bullet" jacket and pants, the "Stomped" hoodie, [and more]. Behind all the civilian martial and macho hype lies a deepening relationship with the military.[99]

These insights about the reality and causes of U.S. 'obliviousness' are a contemporary counterpart to Eisenhower's concern about the 'spiritual influence' of the complex on U.S. civilians and culture. But third, other scholars have suggested that American 'obliviousness' results from our very way of life, especially in terms of the dominance of consumerism and insistent dependence on an oil economy despite the resulting dire consequences. This situation presents an inherent crisis in the American republic that citizens are discouraged from acknowledging. Instead of looking within the nation and examining our own culture, government leaders (with citizens' tacit encouragement) direct our focus to external problems as the real source of any trouble we face. Instead of seriously addressing a failed U.S. energy policy, and instead of facing a history of trade deficits in the U.S. that began in the 1960s, citizens' seemingly limitless lust for inexpensive consumer goods, based on cheap overseas labor, only has grown. All of this is characterized as 'the American

99. Turse, *The Complex*, pp. 142, 67–70.

way of life' we deserve, and any inherent problems or contradictions are mystified by a belief that all our problems are external, international issues that can and will be solved by a dominant, omnipotent American military.[100] Chalmers Johnson concludes,

> In fact, the purpose of our overseas bases is to maintain U.S. dominance in the world, and to reinforce what military analyst Charles Maier calls our "empire of consumption." The United States possesses less than 5 percent of global population but consumes about one-quarter of all global resources, including petroleum. Our empire exists so we can exploit a much greater share of the world's wealth than we are entitled to, and to prevent other nations from combining against us to take their rightful share.[101]

All these reasons help us to understand how this '800 pound gorilla' exists in the American living room without anyone really seeming to notice. But explaining American obliviousness about the reality of U.S. War-culture is even more complex. In addition to all the foregoing explanations, one more area demands further attention and exploration. Rhetoric and practices of sacrifice, running like an electrical current between nationalistic, militaristic institutions, culture and values *and* religious institutions, traditions, culture and practices, also play a deeply important yet almost unrecognized role in the maintenance, pervasiveness and seemingly sacred nature of war-culture in the United States.

'Chinook-gate': A Liberal Arts Case Study

At first glance, a small liberal arts college on the east coast, such as the one where I teach, might seem to be far-removed from many of the interpenetrations of war-culture described above. Yet a college incident at the end of spring semester revealed that even these educational institutions are not disaffected by these complexities. As professors were teaching final classes, collecting end-of semester projects and giving exams, an unexpected email from the Office of Public Communication lit up our computer screens: 'Chinook

---

100. See Andrew Bacevich, *The Limits of Power: The End to American Exceptionalism* (New York, NY: Metropolitan Books, 2008).

101. Chalmers Johnson, 'America's Unwelcome Advances,' *Mother Jones*, 22 August 2008, http://www.motherjones.com/print/15574, accessed 15 June 2009.

helicopter to land in Quad.'[102] An ROTC cadet who attends the college requested that the administration permit the military helicopter to land in the college's Central Quad while classes were still in session, to pick him up and ferry him to a ROTC training event to be held elsewhere in Pennsylvania. The college community was given this information about 24 hours in advance of the landing itself, though the leaders comprising the President's Staff had known and were planning with the city for the helicopter landing for much longer.

An Army Chinook helicopter is a serious piece of military machinery, as the same public notice advertised, 'a twin-engine, tandem rotor, cargo helicopter used for movement of supplies and ammunition, repair parts, petroleum and tactical movement of artillery, troops, and special weapons on the battlefield.' In short, it is most definitely a war-machine. On the liberal arts campus of approximately 1600 students, about 200 people were present in the Quad that day to witness the event. After landing on the grass, the helicopter remained stationary in the Quad for perhaps one hour while army personnel in camouflage officiated, leading students and campus staff on guided tours through the aircraft. Video later played as part of a local TV news report shows people cheering and generally enjoying the entire event in the pastoral site on the grass Quad in the middle of the college student union, dorms and athletic buildings.[103] The video shot by the local TV station does not show a small group of students who, despite the short advance notice, managed to create some posters to protest the event: 'A college campus is not the place for War-machines!' In fact, the college campus security took it upon themselves to remove protesting students to a place far from the cameras and the gathered spectators.

One political science professor sent a one-line mass email to the entire college community about four hours after the initial email communication: 'What is the purpose of this little stunt?' And with that, a veritable email firestorm was ignited for a few days on our

102. Michael Wilson, 'FYI-Chinook helicopter to land in Quad Thursday/ Transport LV ROTC Cadets to Training.' Email to All-College and Seminary. Moravian College, 23 April 2008.

103. See 'Military Helicopter Picks up Lehigh Valley ROTC Cadets,' WFMZ-TV Online, 24 April 2008. See www.wfmz.com/, accessed 28 August 2008.

campus.[104] Yet, if 'Chinook-gate' (as certain members of our community began to refer to it) illuminated the reality of the incursion of war-culture into higher education even in this seemingly unlikely place, a liberal arts college in a mid-sized town at least an hour away from any major city, it also highlighted the power and prevalence of sacrificial rhetoric as a masking and glorifying canopy that always accompanies, protects and energizes war-culture. In the midst of researching and writing this book, I was fascinated but unsurprised to see this rhetoric emerge almost immediately as the controversy about the helicopter landing began to swirl. In response to the first email by the political science professor, 'What is the purpose of this little stunt?' a second professor of economics weighed in,

> I can think of three worthy purposes, off hand: Those who *sacrific* salaries and stable home lives, if nothing else, to the service of their country deserve our support. Until the lion lies down peaceably with the lamb, we must encourage young people to consider similar *sacrifices* (italics mine).[105]

In this and further emails from this professor, sacrificial rhetoric dominated. He wrote about what he viewed as the need to 'support those whose sacrifices make our freedoms, including the freedom to wave a peace flag'... Moreover, it is just these 'sacrifices [that] make the freedom of speech.' Such 'sacrifice...makes freedom possible' and is 'required' if we, as a 'privileged minority' in the world, wish to continue to enjoy freedom of speech and other rights.

The economics professor thus smoothly aligned the presence of the military helicopter on our campus with a portrayal of war as necessary sacrifice. Moreover, his emails argued that the necessity of war as sacrifice is not something to be questioned; in fact, he claimed, its very necessity demands compliance – we are not to question or protest, for that is akin to diminishing the central players (soldiers) in this drama. No one challenged the sacrificial theme in this narrative to my knowledge, and even those who disagreed with the same professor relied upon it, such as one student who

104. Gary L. Olson, 'Re: FYI-Chinook helicopter to land in Quad Thursday/ Transport LV ROTC Cadets to Training.' Email to All-College and Seminary. Moravian College, 23 April 2008.

105. George D. Brower, 'Re: FYI-Chinook helicopter to land in Quad Thursday/Transport LV ROTC Cadets to Training.' Email to All-College and Seminary. Moravian College, 23 April 2008.

suggested in his email that making sacrifices (including, he noted, the 'ultimate sacrifice') only makes sense when one knows it's going to be 'worth it and make a lasting positive impact.'

The appearance of sacrifi ial rhetoric during 'Chinook-gate' was far from an aberration. In fact, it goes with the territory. Communication scholars have investigated why this is the case, and how such rhetoric operates. Sacrificial rhetoric in the purpose of war-culture has a way of inflating the measurement of real dangers and lifting the possibility of attack to a transcendent level. This same over-inflation disables critical thinking and pragmatic political critique. The rhetoric of sacrifice is ritualized speech, and channels and legitimates violence by covering the activities of killing with a sacred canopy made up of values such a loyalty and freedom. It 'rationalizes war as in the service of the greater glory of God,' Robert Ivies writes. '[The] secular quest for security [is converted] into a prayer for redemption and a sacrament of atonement through the sacrifice of a scapegoat in whom we have invested all the evil of the world.' Safety becomes a matter of salvation in the rhetorical universe of sacrificial U.S. War-culture. Moreover, as also is evident from the same economic professor's emails, this rhetoric transforms the idea of 'safety' into a feminized, risky and fragile undertaking. The demonic, even barbaric enemy will violate our safety, and we must do whatever is necessary to be protected. Sacrificial rhetoric in the purpose of war-culture enables dehumanization of those considered the enemy, and depersonalizes those other real flesh and-blood, complicated and multifaceted human beings who all too often are conflated into a one-dimensional portrait, 'the troops.' Ivies remarks, 'In war culture, disembodied abstractions and stone monuments supplant living memories of loved ones sacrificed for country and cause...our own soldiers are dehumanized by reducing them to depersonalized heroes.'[106]

The chapters of this book explore American acculturation to the rhetoric and logic of sacrificialism in war-culture. I also will show the complicity of Christian understandings, practices and doctrines of sacrifice in the service of war-culture, and the need to challenge Christianity and its practitioners to greater awareness and action. The predisposition toward sacrificial constructs deeply shapes

---

106. Robert L. Ivies, *Dissent from War* (Bloomfield, CT: Kumarian Press, 2007), pp. 56, 61, 79.

our perceptions and equally profoundly impacts our response to the realities of antagonism and conflict. If 'the military-industrial-academic [and on and on] complex is a huge systemic behemoth that must be engaged by numerous groups from multiple sites of intervention,' this book takes on the pedagogical, spiritual and political challenge to investigate the site of war-culture's intertwined relationship with the rhetoric and cognitive framework of sacrifice [107] The same relationship charges, masks and sacramentalizes war and war-culture, and works to hold at bay pragmatic critique, ethical discernment and the potential to imagine a different reality. War-culture affects everyone who lives in the United States, and many, many more who live in countries outside our borders. Once we become conscious of the deadly links between sacrifice and war-culture, there is no going back.

107. Giroux, *University in Chains*, p. 79.

Chapter Two

BUILDING AND MAINTAINING THE DRIVE TO WAR:
VICTIMAGE RHETORIC, FRAMING, AND THE LANGUAGE OF SACRIFICE

*Our nation is being tested in a way we have not been tested since the start
of the Cold War. We face an enemy determined to bring death and suffering into our homes. The War on Terror is not over and will not be over
until either we or the extremists emerge victorious. If we do not defeat
these enemies now, we will leave our children to face a Middle East over-
run by terrorist states and radical dictators armed with nuclear weapons.
We are in a war that will set the course for this century.*

President George W. Bush
Address to the Nation
11 September 2006[1]

Introduction

To illuminate the dynamic relationship between sacrificial rhetoric
and war-culture, this chapter analyzes a contemporary case study:
official government proclamations in the United States in the years
that followed the attacks on the World Trade Center's Twin Towers
in 2001. In countless public speeches to the nation and in addresses
to smaller groups, President George W. Bush and other prominent
leaders in U.S. government skillfully and unabashedly emphasized
'the necessity of sacrifice' to build and maintain the case for war in
Afghanistan and Iraq. Though other research and reporting about
this period investigate various alleged government deceptions used
to argue for regime overthrow in Iraq, the purpose behind this case
study is different. My aim is to examine closely the prevalence of

1. 'Fact Sheet: The Fifth Anniversary of September 11, 2001,' The White
House: President George W. Bush, Sept. 11, 2006, http://georgewbush-white-
house.archives.gov/news/releases/2006/09/20060911-2.html, accessed 3
January 2010.

exaggerated sacrificial language from this period, which, despite intense attention to other aspects of this same history, has been too little analyzed by journalists and scholars. It was precisely such rhetoric, based on sacrificial mandates and metaphors, that buttressed the case for war, silenced protest, and inhibited the asking of important questions both before and after the United States went to war in Afghanistan and Iraq. In fact, both the quantity and hyperbolic quality of official sacrificial rhetoric from 2001 – to the present, makes this a particularly salient case for our study.

At the same time, as we shall see, this is hardly the first time government leaders have resorted to the usefulness of sacrificial language and schemes in order to popularize agendas of various sorts. For instance, by the late 1980s, biblical theologian Elsa Tamez critiqued the devastating consequences of the discourse of sacrifice used by government officials to shore up neoliberal economic systems of Latin America. Tamez probed the public use of subconscious metaphors using religio-psychological themes from Christianity, noting their destructive impact on the lives of the most dispossessed in her society. This language's inhumane consequences cannot be overestimated, as she wrote, 'The traditional concept of death as necessary for the salvation of all translates [into] the economic claim that people need to accept sacrifices, in the hope that at some future time they will manage to obtain the goods and services necessary for life.'[2] Theological language about the necessity of Jesus' sacrificial death for salvation 'slipped,' or was manipulated to support neoliberal economic aims in Latin America. Sacrifice – meaning in this particular case the severe curtailing of social safety nets, including funds to support health care, food supply, education, etc. – was 'necessary' in order to meet international demands to repay national debts. As one Latin American theorist summarized,

> Human sacrifice is transformed exclusively into a moral obligation. This is occurring today with the payment of Third World debt, which has become a veritable genocide that costs always more in human sacrifices and that destroys even more of the natural world.[3]

2. Elsa Tamez, *The Amnesty of Grace: Justification by Faith from a Latin American Perspective* (Trans. Sharon H. Ringe; Nashville, TN: Abingdon, 1993), p. 157.

3. Franz J. Hinkelammert, *Sacrificios Humanos y Sociedad Occidental* (San Jose, Costa Rica: Editorial Departamento Ecumenico de Investigaciones, 1991), p. 36 (translation mine).

Global bodies such as the International Monetary Fund, not to mention Latin American political leaders, relied on sacrific al language to justify austerity measures required for the maintenance of an utterly unbalanced and unjust economic system. According to one proponent of such sacrificial discourse

> A free society demands a certain morality that as a last resort cuts life supports: we must say no to the maintenance of every life, because it will be necessary to sacrifice individual lives in order to preserve a greater number of other lives. As a result, the only moral laws are those that lead to a "calculus of lives" in ratio to private property and the contract.[4]

This sacrificial economic rhetoric resulted in a mystification and glorification of economic demands that were placed on the poorest of the poor. Moreover, as a result of these economic programs, ever-larger sectors of humanity in Latin America were increasingly excluded, to the extent that their most basic needs went unmet. Most perverse, sacrificial language assigned responsibility for the cost of the economic system to those with the least means for participation in the market economy and who were most injured by it: the poor – 'the majority are excluded, and their life hangs always in the balance.'[5]

This chapter's case study draws on the significance of Tamez' insight in order to analyze the resurgence of the discourse of sacrifice in the U.S. since 9/11, and the inauguration of the 'War on Terror.'

The Leitmotif of Sacrifice in U.S. Governmen

Following 9/11, sacrificial language was pushed to the forefront of political discourse in the United States, and operated as a leitmotif of the Bush Administration. For instance, in remarks addressing military families in Idaho, in August 2005, President Bush said, 'A time of war is a time of sacrifice, and a heavy burden falls on our military families…And America appreciates the service and the sacrifice of the military families.'[6] He continued a bit later in his

4. Free market economist Friedrich von Hayek, as quoted in Hinkelammert, *Sacrificios Humano* , pp. 32–33 (translation mine).

5. Tamez, *The Amnesty of Grace*, p. 38.

6. 'President Addresses Military Families, Discusses War on Terror,' 24 August 2005, The White House: President George W. Bush, http://georgew-bush-whitehouse.archives.gov/news/releases/2005/08/20050824.html, accessed 4 January 2010.

speech, 'In this time of call-ups and alerts and mobilizations and deployments, your employers are standing behind you, and so is your government. The country owes you something in return for your sacrifice.

President Bush's stump speech on the campaign trail before his re-election regularly featured sacrificial discourse

> The American spirit of sacrifice and service and compassion and love is alive and strong and therefore, I boldly predict that out of the evil done to America will not only come a more peaceful world, but out of the evil done to America will be a more compassionate America, where the great hope of this country, the great vibrancy of the American Dream, will be alive and well in every corner, in every neighborhood here in America.[7]

As the war in Iraq continued and an end or exit strategy retreated further and further into the distance, Bush said, 'the war on terrorism will take time and require sacrifice... yet we will do what is necessary.'[8] At the end of his presidency, as the number of deaths of soldiers fighting in Afghanistan and Iraq climbed to over 4,000, President Bush justified the number of deaths by insisting that the outcome of the war 'will merit the sacrifice. [9]

Of course, as communications scholar Robert Ivies has pointed out, sacrificial discourse is almost compulsory in times of war. 'Victimage rhetoric' is based on a series of binaries portraying the enemy as savage and uncivilized, aggressive and irrational, contrasted with the image of the U.S. as rational, tolerant of diversity and peace-and-freedom loving.[10] Thus, in the Revolutionary war, the British were described as 'monstrous savages breathing out thirstings for American blood'; in the late 1800s the Governor of

---

7. Quoted in Stuart Taylor Jr, 'How Bush Can Save International Law, Not Sacrifice It,' *National Journal* 35, Issue 16 (2003): 1207–1209.

8. George W. Bush, 'Address to the Nation Regarding Iraq,' 7 September 2003, The White House: President George W. Bush, http://georgewbush-whitehouse.archives.gov/news/releases/2003/09/20030907-1.html, accessed 4 January 2010.

9. Karen deYoung and Michael Abromowitz, 'Bush Says Wars "Will Merit the Sacrifice"', *Washington Post*, 25 March 2008, http://www.washingtonpost.com/wp-dyn/content/story/2008/03/24/ST2008032403176.html?sid=ST2008032403176, accessed 28 May 2009.

10. Robert Ivies, 'Images of Savagery in American Justifications for War', *Communications Monographs* 47 (1980): 281.

California, Peter H. Burnett, insisted that 'a war of extermination will continue to be waged between the two races until the Indian race becomes Extinct'; Polk's war-message of 1846 included such language as description of Mexico as 'a system of outrage and extortion…shedding the blood of our fellow-citizens on our own soil'; and Roosevelt described the war-effort against Germany as the 'victory of the forces of justice and of righteousness over the forces of savagery and barbarism.'[11] The emphasis in victimage rhetoric is Manichean division of the entire world into enemy and friend. Such division perhaps most aptly was summed up in the phrase frequently spoken by the president and members of his inner circle of advisors in the years following 9/11: 'whoever is not with us is against us.'[12]

The logic of victimage rhetoric works by depicting the enemy as irrational, savage, primitive and uncivilized, *in order* to evoke an emotional response that coercive and violent response is the one 'necessary' option. Ivies writes, 'While the savage has acted against order, the victim has been forced to respond in its defense.'[13] Not only does this rhetoric have strong historical continuity, appearing regularly at times of potential or actual war, but the words themselves are 'highly salient' in the culture, that is, 'noticeable, understandable, memorable and emotionally charged.'[14] The use of 'necessity' in victimage rhetoric is something I will return to later when I discuss the religious significance of sacrificial discourse

The key point of victimage rhetoric is that it releases the guilt people otherwise might feel as a result of causing the death or injury of the other. Any potential culpability is mitigated through laying all responsibility squarely at the feet of the enemy – it was *his* irrationality, savagery, etc., that provoked this, the only possible response. Ironically, this same rhetoric assigns to the U.S. the role of victim (or

11. Ivies, 'Images of Savagery', p. 287. See also Rosemary Radford Ruether, *America, Amerikkka: Elect Nation And Imperial Violence* (London: Equinox Publishing, 2007), p. 51.

12. 'Bush Says It's Time for Action,' *CNN.com*, 6 November 2001, http://archives.cnn.com/2001/US/11/06/ret.bush.coalition/index.html, accessed 20 April 2006.

13. Ivies, 'Images of Savagery', p. 290.

14. Robert M. Entman, 'Cascading Activation: Contesting the White House's Frame after 9/11', *Political Communication* 20 (2003): p. 417.

protector of other perceived victims in the world), in other words, as the put-upon, maligned and abused object of the enemy, or as the heroic guardian of order, despite the fact that in the Iraq war at least, the United States clearly was the aggressor. The perceived enemy must be sacrificed. As Ivies emphasizes, 'by sacrificing the savage, the representatives of civilization simultaneously cleanse their world of sins that have caused their fall from the Eden of peace and redeem themselves as defenders of freedom and reason.'[15] In this way the aggressiveness and 'preemptive' hostility of the U.S. was disguised by emphasizing the role of the nation as victim and as the agent of purification. Though Ivies wrote his analysis in 1980, it eerily foreshadows key words and phrases that became common-place in U.S. political discourse following 9/11.

Investigation of the use of 'framing' as a rhetorical strategy moves the analysis of victimage rhetoric one step further. Framing creates a simple, readily understandable and accessible narrative by draw-ing upon familiar cultural symbols, understandings and forms of discourse to assert control over understanding and interpretation. In other words, according to communication experts, framing is 'the central process by which government officials and journalists exercise political influence over each other and over the public.'[16] In the case of the wars against Afghanistan and Iraq, the dominant frame Americans easily recognize included four simple steps. First, the stage was set by Sept. 11 and the death of thousands of citizens. Second, terrorists were to blame. Third, a moral judgment ensued: the agents of assault are evil. Fourth, the remedy to this problem: war against the perpetrators. Framing takes place through the strategic selection and underscoring of particular events or issues, while in-tentionally leaving out or dismissing others, and then shoehorning those events so as to force a particular interpretation, evaluation or solution. Moreover, words and images are chosen for their 'cultural resonance' and achieve magnitude through regular and prominent repetition of the narrative.

Through such framing, 'the attacks of Sept. 11 gave the second President Bush an opportunity to propound a line designed to re-vive habits of patriotic deference, to dampen elite dissent, dominate

15. Ivies, 'Images of Savagery', p. 292.
16. Entman, 'Cascading Activation', p. 417.

media texts, and reduce the threat of negative public reaction, (in other words) to work just as the Cold War paradigm once did.'[17]

The sacrificial mandate in this language was aimed at multiple targets. First, as already emphasized, victimage rhetoric demands the sacrifice of the enemy to restore order. But this is not the end of sacrificial action. Second, this same language stresses the necessity of the sacrifice that those fighting will need to make in order to vanquish this same evil. However, as in the speeches of Bush quoted above, while there was no hesitation about sacrifice of the 'enemy,' and little hesitation in the framing of war regarding the necessity of self-sacrifice for those in the military (what exactly this sacrifice entails is defined below), an altogether new twist in this rhetoric occurred.[18] This twist is particularly significant in terms of understanding this case study.

According to communications scholar Timothy Cole, in order to be successful, the rhetor must 'align his or her intentions with audience expectations [so that] images presented to advance policy... resonate with public values, even as they attempt to shape them; conversely dissonance created by implausible dramatic accounts will fail to persuade.'[19] In the case of the wars in Afghanistan and Iraq, the rhetoric of sacrifice was shaped in a purposefully strategic fashion so as to coincide with perceived American cultural values and expectations. In particular, this rhetoric had to deal with the limits of American acceptance of the hardships and challenges that very well would accompany any such action initiating long-term war. The creation of the framing of victimage rhetoric, thus, emphasized that the sacrifice to restore the order disrupted by terrorists would *not* be paid by the American public. Cole writes, 'The president did not call for sacrific s from the civilian population, propose tax increases to cover costs, or bolster the Veterans Administration, but he did the opposite – urging Americans to consume more, asking Congress to cut taxes and VA services.'[20] When speaking to the American public, in response to a question regarding how the public should honor the memory of those who died in 9/11, the

17. Entman, 'Cascading Activation', p. 424.

18. Timothy Cole, 'The Rhetoric of Sacrifice and Heroism and U.S. Military Intervention', *Bring 'Em On: Media and Politics in the Iraq War*, Lee Artz and Yahya R. Kamalipour (eds) (New York: Rowman and Littlefield, 2005)

19. Cole, 'The Rhetoric of Sacrifice and Heroism', p. 141.

20. Cole, 'The Rhetoric of Sacrifice and Heroism', p. 143

president replied, 'Americans should return to their lives, be reso-
lute and live the values that exemplify American exceptionalism...
Live your lives and hug your children....be patient in what will be
a long struggle, keep praying for the victims of terror and for those
in uniform.'[21] On the other hand, in speeches to military audiences,
President Bush regularly emphasized their sacrificial action, as in
a speech to Westpoint graduates when he said, 'you will stand between your fellow citizens and grave danger.'

This is perhaps the most surprising, even cynical, aspect of the
frame for war in Afghanistan and Iraq. For, while one would expect
pro-war victimage rhetoric together with an equally strong call for
military readiness and sacrifice, should it not also call for the public
to share some part of the burden? Cole suggests that the decision *not*
to call for public sacrifice was strategic on the part of the administration, which focused instead on an appeal for public support and
quiescence. Why? And how does the very language of sacrifice itself
play into such an appeal?

To assert frame control, the government used rhetorically savvy
public relations skill. Of course, in this case the power asserted by
the Bush Administration expanded to the creation of an entirely
new Pentagon unit to produce intelligence findings more supportive of the Iraq-terrorism link than the CIA had offered.[22] Is it possible that the same attention to controlling the frame extended to a
realistic assessment of just how far the public would go to support
these efforts, and accordingly, an adjustment of the frame to match
that assessment? In this respect we must remember the reality of
public wariness regarding pro-war sentiment that is a legacy of the
'Vietnam syndrome,' and the considerable difficulties experienced
with nation building in previous recent administrations.

Emphasizing the sacrifice of the military (while reassuring other
Americans that they would not be required to make any substan-
tial changes or 'sacrifices') was congruent with current American
popular cultural values promising results 'without cost, effort or
sacrifice. [23] In this frame, the emphasis on military sacrifice discouraged questions regarding the inevitable cost to the American public
at large, from the much larger number of soldiers killed than was
initially anticipated, to the loss of funds to the war that could have

21. As quoted by Cole, 'The Rhetoric of Sacrifice and Heroism', p. 148
22. Entman, 'Cascading Activation', p. 428.
23. Cole, 'The Rhetoric of Sacrifice and Heroism', pp. 151, 140

served other national needs, and the costs associated with needs of wounded veterans, etc. Spotlighting the sacralized military sacrifice had the intended consequence of veiling, discouraging or mystifying hard questions about the true nature of these decisions and their impact on the nation as a whole.

Thus, it would seem that the most overt request made of the public was quietistic submission to the fatherly authority of a president who would 'protect us' as we were admonished as a 'traveling public' to 'get on board.''Do your business around the country. Fly and enjoy America's great destination spots. Get down to Disney World in Florida.'[24] Such overt paternalism in presidential admonition only serves to underscore the awareness among political scientists regarding the proclivity of state violence to result in a reproduction of masculinist subjectivities and values.[25]

Analyzing the Specifically Religious Content in this Discours

More pointedly, following 9/11 in the United States, this same rhetoric of sacrifice was employed by a 'born again' president well-versed in the art of using religious language to 'signal' and rally evangelical American Christians. Helpful and fascinating though a communications/rhetorical analysis is, there has been insufficient analysis of the religious content and connotations of the discourse of sacrifice in the political scene and American public. In the *Columbia Journalism Review,* Gal Beckerman notes that while we live in a country with a majority of people who acknowledge deep religious commitments, journalists and media scholars are too often ill-equipped to investigate or deeply understand the inner workings of religious doctrines, collective understandings and practices as they collide with politics and society.[26] Why? Part of the reason has to do with journalism's focus on the empirical, on 'objective reality,'

24. As quoted in Cole, 'The Rhetoric of Sacrifice and Heroism', p. 148

25. This was a recurring theme in many papers, presentations and general discussion at the UK Political Studies Association Women and Politics Annual Conference, 11 February 2006, University of Edinburgh that focused on the theme, 'Feminist Ethics, Feminist Politics and the States We're in: Critical Reflections in Uncertain Times.' See Chapter Three for further analysis of 'the logic of masculinist protection.'

26. Gal Beckerman, 'Why Don't Journalists Get Religion? A Tenuous Bridge to Believers', *Columbia Journalism Review*, Issue 3 (May/June 2004). See, www.cjr.org/issues/2004/3/beckerman-faith.asp, accessed 20 April 20 2006.

and on the practical need to get a story out immediately – both of which tend to be difficult to connect to the complex and intricate, and seemingly more 'static' inner workings of religious faith in the lives of individuals and communities.

Making matters more difficult, there are too few investigative reporters assigned to a 'religion desk', and those who are find themselves required to cover too much territory. Additionally, whereas much of the dynamism of religion in the U.S. can be located within the evangelical movement (encompassing over 26 percent of Americans according to recent polls), journalists frequently tend to lump all evangelicals together, failing to understand complex differences that lead to the self-affirmed membership of both Jimmy Carter *and* Pat Robertson in this movement. Finally, religious language itself can be a difficult code to decipher or translate. 'To grasp religion in a robust and full way, journalism would need to alter its basic notions of what news is, how religious people are interviewed, and the frame of politics as a way of understanding religion.'[27]

Given that reporting religion remains a challenge for journalism, religious studies scholars' investigation of the role of religion – and religious language – in politics provides a helpful antidote. For instance, Bruce Lincoln examined President Bush's own commentary about his religious conversion/practice in the president's campaign autobiography, *A Charge to Keep: My Journey to the White House*.[28] At an early moment in his own political development, when President George W. Bush was assigned by his father to serve as liaison with the Christian Right, he received critical religious/political coaching from Rev. Doug Wead that continued to influence his political activity throughout his entire presidency. According to Bush's own account, Wead not only introduced him to powerful people within the Christian Right, but counseled him regarding his own speech patterns, 'to win their support by showing he shared their values

27. Beckerman, www.cjr.org/issues/2004/3/beckerman-faith.asp. Also see 'Pew Forum on Religion & Public Life/U.S. Religious Landscape Survey,' 5 February, 2008, http://www.pewtrusts.org accessed 8 October 2010.

See David Domke and Kevin Coe, *The God Strategy: How Religion Became a Political Weapon in America* (Oxford: Oxford University Press, Updated 2010), for one helpful resource that explores the strategic use of religion for a wide variety of political purposes.

28. Bruce Lincoln, 'Bush's God Talk: Analyzing the President's Theology', *Christian Century* 121, no. 20 (2004): 22–29. George W. Bush and Karen Armstrong, *A Charge to Keep: My Journey to the Whitehouse* (New York: Morrow, 1999).

and spoke their language.' 'Signal early and signal often,' Wead encouraged. Lincoln writes, 'Although the elder Bush demurred from such practice, the younger took the lesson in earnest.' One could not miss the frequent biblical allusions and other symbolic religious language with which Bush peppered his speeches and public statements, his Texan drawl oftentimes thickening just at such moments. This was a key way Bush 'signaled his core constituency', and is an example of what Lincoln calls 'double coding.' The religious language, in other words, acted as 'the linguistic equivalent of winks and nudges.' Lincoln writes,

> If such things please you, he (Bush) wants you to know he is a faithful servant of Christ, acknowledges himself as same, and feels himself accountable to no Law save God's, no court save the Last Judgment. But if such things make you uneasy, he would prefer the question never arise.[29]

Such 'double-coding' conveyed a privileged relation to the base of the Christian Right while obscuring it from those who might be offended by such language because of Constitutional propriety.

Was the use of this religious language, then, merely cynical on the part of the Bush Administration? A result of *real politik* only focused on maximization of power and control over the citizenry? Such an analysis is too simplistic. According to Rosemary Radford Ruether, 'Most politicians are deeply self-deluded by their own rhetoric.' Belief in an exceptional (even 'elected' or 'chosen') role for American foreign policy as an outgrowth of American goodness and righteousness is not necessarily incompatible with the projection of American power and expansion of self-interest at any cost. 'Indeed, to combine being both practitioners of *real politik* and also self-deluded believers in the rhetoric of America's messianic role is the basic requirement of an effective American politician.'[30]

Theologian Mark Lewis Taylor places this into a larger perspective of a growing national 'religious romanticism' in the post-9/11 period. Describing the George W. Bush presidential administration, he writes, 'The Christian Right is better understood as a powerful romanticist movement in the revolutionary mode that has new powers in federal government and has created well-funded structures that affect federal policy.'[31] Taylor focuses less on George Bush's personal piety

29. Lincoln, 'Bush's God Talk', p. 23.
30. Ruether, *America, Amerikkka*, p. 2.

and more on the influence of the Christian Right as an organized and dynamic social force in this period. Religious romanticists, Taylor asserts, 'seek to bring back notions of the United States of America not just as an exceptional nation but also as what historian Martin Marty has analyzed as "righteous empire."' Thus, this administration was characterized by the following: the use of the Bible as a 'guidebook,' semi-compulsory weekly Bible studies in the White House, revival meetings held by senior officials such as John Ashcroft, the use of religious symbols in government documents, symbolic representation of religious leaders at key political moments, and regular meetings with religious leaders across the country. All in all, the Bush Administration crafted a 'Christian ritualized ethos in governance.'[32] The aspect of such governance most pertinent to this case study is the use of religious language. Taylor writes,

> It is important to see that when a Christian ritualized ethos is marked at as many points as it is in the Bush regime, it lets loose into government culture one of the most powerful traits of religious symbols: their active power, in anthropologist Clifford Geertz's language, to "establish powerful, pervasive and long lasting moods and motivations" in people.[33]

To summarize, then, we must analyze the use of sacrificial discourse not only in terms of the way it plays into a political frame dependent on victimage rhetoric, but by focusing on its specifically religious content. This means investigating the multivalent religious threads residing in the language of sacrifice that operate with 'active power' to establish moods and motivations in both religious and non-religious peoples' psyches, lives, understandings and practices. Political theorists have long been aware of the potency of religious images and discourse, as Taylor writes, 'Leo Strauss, one of the theorists informing several key neoconservative Bush appointees, in fact, encouraged wise rulers to deploy strong doses of state-oriented religion to unite the polis, even if the virtuous leaders of that polis do not themselves believe in that religion.'[34] The conclusion to be drawn is: consistent and repetitive use of sacrificial language within the larger

---

31. Mark Lewis Taylor, *Religion, Politics, and the Christian Right: Post-9/11 Powers and American Empire* (Minneapolis, MN: Fortress Press, 2005), p. 52.

32. Taylor, *Religion, Politics, and the Christian Right*, pp. 55–57.

33. Taylor, *Religion, Politics, and the Christian Right*, p. 57.

34. Taylor, *Religion, Politics, and the Christian Right*, p. 67.

discourse of 'the war on terror' let loose into the wider culture a kind of power to shape the mood, motivation and response of the general public. This public disposition acquiesced to a paternal authority that would act on its behalf and was mystified by a shield of religious sanctity. Moreover, this message disingenuously assured the public that the sacrifice only would execute righteous punishment 'far from home,' as opposed to any that would require hardships on the part of the American public at large.

Official presidential speeches and statements are a key place to see the dynamics of this communicative strategy in action. For instance, in President Bush's speech to the American people that alerted the public to the onset of war in Afghanistan, he remarked on the 'patience' that would be required of the American people, including 'patience in all the sacrifices that may come.'[35] But specific sacrifice from the American non-military citizenry was left undefined. Instead, in this speech Bush moved immediately to discussion of the military: 'Today those sacrifices are being made by members of our Armed Forces who now defend us *so far from home* (italics mine), and by their proud and worried families.' He closed his speech with the story of a fourth grade girl who told him that though she did not wish for her military father to fight, nevertheless, she was 'willing to give him' to the president for this battle. Bush concluded by saying, 'an entire generation of young Americans has gained new understanding of the value of freedom, and its cost in duty and in sacrifice.' If the story about the little girl was meant to pull at the nation's heartstrings, this also is language that was very carefully crafted to encourage trust that the president would keep the sacrifice far from the American homeland, execute righteous punishment to restore order, and limit any national sacrificial mandate to a military community trained to accept and prepare for such sacrifice as its reason for being

Military Sacrificial Identity Formatio

In fact, this same speech and its emphasis on sacrifice leads to questions about the dynamic of sacrificial identity formation in U.S.

---

35. The speech is reproduced in its entirety in Bruce Lincoln, *Holy Terrors: Thinking about Religion after September 11* (Chicago, IL: University of Chicago Press, 2003), pp. 99–101.

military culture. Political philosopher Jean Bethke Elshtain has argued that 'the will-to-sacrifice' may be constitutive not only of military identity, but of our very civic selfhood, male and female alike.[36] She writes,

> The Spartans, the model for later civic republicans and early modern state Builders, honored but two identities with inscriptions on tombstones – Men who had died in war and women who had succumbed in childbirth: Both embodied the sacrificial moment of civic identity.

Moreover, in Western Christianity at least, religion fed into this development of civic/military sacrificial self-identity: over time, the Christian virtue of *caritas* (Christian love for God, self and neighbor) was increasingly applied to sanctify and justify death for 'the fatherland.' Yet another 'slippage' occurred here, as understandings about giving oneself to God blended with notions about a sacred death incurred on behalf of the sovereign earthly leader, or sovereign nation.

That is, the young man who willingly sacrificed his life did so not only for the abstract male sovereign/deity, but also for 'the mother country bound by citizens speaking the mother tongue.' As Elshtain says, 'Mother and mother's milk serve as a foundation for civic-spiritedness and willingness to die.'[37] Such is the ambiguity of sacrificial dynamics. What began as the model of the Christian martyr who died for his faith, over time slid into the image of the soldier faithful even unto death, 'the model of civic self-sacrifice. [38] Elshtain claims (quoting Max Weber as her source) that up to the present day, without such sacrificial justification, the state rests only on the power of coercion. The development of identity as a citizen relies on sacrificial categories: 'only a preparedness to forfeit one's life rounds out, or instantiates in all its fullness, devotion to the political community.'[39]

But does it? We might immediately point out the significant discrepancy Elshtain fails to underscore between male and female

---

36. Jean Bethke Elshtain, 'Sovereignty, Identity and Sacrifice , *Gendered States: Feminist (re)Visions of International Relations Theory*, V. Spike Peterson (ed.), (London: Lynne Rienner Publishers, 1992), p. 144.
37. Elshtain, 'Sovereignty, Identity and Sacrifice', p. 142
38. Elshtain, 'Sovereignty, Identity and Sacrifice', p. 144
39. Elshtain, 'Sovereignty, Identity and Sacrifice', p. 147

experiences of sacrifice in her own examples, the male example of sacrifice occurring within the context of war, the taking of life and violent loss of one's own; contrasted with the female experience of self-giving through the bringing of new life into the world via child-birth. In contrast to forfeiting one's life as demonstrating devotion to a larger community, feminist theologian Daphne Hampson describes the experience of self-giving in childbirth as one of 'supreme connectedness.'[40] Though these ideas are explored in greater depth in later chapters, at this point some questions may be raised. Is such sacrifice unto death really 'necessary' for the development of a viable political identity? Are there other realities, practices and understandings that may be drawn upon to think about the meaning of civic identity, citizenship and belonging?

Notwithstanding such questions, Elshtain's highlighting of the slippage of sacrificial discourse from religious to civic interpretations, brings to mind my own visits in recent years to a military ethics course at the U.S. Naval Academy in Annapolis. Listening in to midshipmen's class discussion, I heard a word repeated over and over again: 'honor.' At one point I raised my hand to ask for a definition of the word which clearly, more than any other, defined both the method and goal for the ethical task that was being deliberated by the class, i.e., how to conduct and participate in warfare without losing one's soul. My question was met with laughter from class members and professor alike. The professor noted, 'Well, we have talked a lot about this word and struggled to define it for ourselves without much success. What we can say is, we know it when we see it!'

I understood the discursive world the professor was pointing to further when the students on the course made their own oral presentations investigating warrior ethics. Almost without exception, the theme of the free self-sacrifice of the warrior was paramount,

40. In her chapter, 'Feminist Ethics,' Hampson describes the emergence of the self as one 'centered in relation.' She writes, 'In using such a phrase I wish to capture the sense that the self is both "centered" and "relational."... it is not until we have a certain integration, a certain centeredness, as I have called it, that we can be sufficiently free of ourselves to be present to another.' The centered and relational self continues to give life in the act of childbirth; what a different conception of civic identity as compared with the destruction of the self and other through warfare! See *After Christianity* (Valley Forge, PA: Trinity Press, 1996), p. 106.

symbolized most powerfully for me by a powerpoint presentation offered by one group of students (all male, I might add), including a slide portraying one of their members kneeling, as if in prayer, head bowed and holding a samurai sword in his hands, in front of an Academy wall decorated in a way very much resembling an altar, inscribed with the names of all the Academy graduates who have been killed in wars since the Academy's beginning.[41] Whether the kneeling student was praying for himself, or for the country, or worshiping at the feet of those who had died, was a question I did not ask in that setting; nevertheless, the unconscious and unquestioned interplay of religious and nationalistic self-sacrificial expression illustrates exactly that slippage noted by Elshtain.

The centrality of notions of self-sacrifice for the formation of these midshipwomen and men, tellingly, also is highlighted in textbooks of military ethics such as *The Code of the Warrior*, in which the author writes about the importance of 'linking warriors' moral obligations to their function.' Leaders and citizens alike need to be clear and certain about the 'price its [the nation's] warriors pay for its defense.' What does this mean? Three necessary conditions must be met to justify the sacrifice of warriors' lives: first, both leaders and citizens must recognize the depth and seriousness of warriors' sacrifice; second, warriors themselves need to be clear about the purpose and need for their sacrifice; and third, the state must demonstrate concern and provide adequately for the needs of warriors after the time of battle is over. The author concludes,

> A mother and father may be willing to give their beloved son or daughter's *life* for their country or cause, but I doubt they would be as willing to sacrifice their child's soul [42]

Clearly, the quasi-religious language of sacrifice on the part of the U.S. Administration, redirected away from a wary American public out of fear of their resistance, easily meshed with sacrificia

41. This particular group of midshipmen had focused on Samurai warrior ethics in their presentation: thus the sword. While there were a small number of midshipwomen in the class each time I visited, I noted that albeit, not scheduled to make their oral presentations on the specific days I visited with my students, they were mostly silent. See Chapter Four for further discussion of tropes of masculinity in war-culture.

42. Shannon E. French, *The Code of the Warrior: Exploring Warrior Values Past and Present* (New York: Rowman and Littlefield, 2003), p. 10

self-understandings in military culture and practice in the post-9/11 period of the United States.

Additionally, delving more deeply into sacrificial elements of military identity and culture, we encounter a 'communal ecstasy' that explains a willingness to sacrifice, giving dying for others a mystical quality – here one sees the connection between the self-sacrifice of soldiers and the willingness of martyrs to die for their faith.[43] This dynamic, an 'anointing,' as it were, is all too vulnerable to abuse, such as the thousands of 'Hitler children' who died in martyrdom operations and last-ditch stands in Germany at the end of World War II. 'They had been fed on legends of heroism for as long as they could remember.'[44]

Finally, sacrificial self-identity in military culture is indelibly linked with the pragmatic value of unit cohesion, as stated in the *Soldier's Handbook* of the U.S. Department of the Army: 'The greatest means of accomplishing selfless service is to dedicate yourself to the teamwork that is the underlying strength of the Army.'[45] In his extensive study, *On Killing: The Psychological Cost of Learning to Kill in War and Society*, Lieutenant Colonel Dave Grossman emphasizes the significance of the presence or absence of fellow soldiers in terms of the individual soldier's decision regarding whether or not to kill. In the absence of group influence, many combatants chose *not* to kill the enemy. However, in the opposite setting, when soldiers *do* elect to kill, the motivation of group solidarity and communion is all-important. One example is Audie Murphy, the most decorated American soldier of World War II, who single-handedly took on a German infantry company, resulting in many German casualties. As Murphy simply said about his actions, 'They were killing my friends.'[46]

In our own time, the motives behind the actions of the terrorists who attacked the World Trade Center's Twin Towers have been analyzed as 'intensely and profoundly religious...as revealed by the instructions that guided their final days.'[47] And indeed, much

43. Elshtain, 'Sovereignty, Identity and Sacrifice', p. 146

44. Elshtain, 'Sovereignty, Identity and Sacrifice', p. 150

45. Department of the Army, *Soldier's Handbook* (Alexandria, VA: Byrrd Enterprises, 1998), pp. 3–3.

46. Lieutenant Colonel Dave Grossman, *On Killing: The Psychological Cost of Learning to Kill in War and Society* (New York: Little Brown and Company, 1995), p. 155.

47. Lincoln, *Holy Terrors*, p. 16.

attention has focused on an assumed 'irrational' or 'evil' mentality that induces suicide-bombers to sacrifice themselves. It likewise has been emphasized that this same mentality largely is influenced by religious fundamentalism. Yet far too little analysis has addressed the trajectory of a 'communal ecstasy' embedded in sacrificial self-understandings, and justified through the values of heroism, religious notions of sacrifice and military practices of unit cohesion. This same self-identification slips easily between roots in religion and roots in patriotism and nationalism, and may reveal the associated motivation of self-sacrifice at stake among *both* suicide bombers and soldiers fighting through more regularized, nationalized forms of warfare.

In sum, the frame for war in the post-9/11 period depended deeply upon notions of this equally unquestioned and sacralized self-sacrificial military identity. The frame for war wouldn't have worked without it – if Cole is right and Americans, generally speaking, wouldn't have stomached any kind of personal hardship in the face of war. In fact, American unconscious acceptance and expectation of just this military identity becomes all the more apparent when we consider how long it took for members of the military and American civilians to begin to question why such a heavy burden was placed so indiscriminately on such a small percentage of the American people.

What's Wrong with All This? Applying Feminist Theological Methods of Critique

To think through more deeply the troubling prevalence of sacrificial discourse in our case study, I turn to methods of investigation from feminist theology and ethics. Because feminist analyses of sacrifice address a wide variety of issues, and because feminists have theorized critiques of sacrifice for over thirty years, their body of work is especially useful. Methods to critique sacrificial frameworks include the following elements: first, feminists trace the inequalities that are imposed on various populations via sacrificial demands from religious doctrines and systems (including inequality related to gender, class, race/ethnicity, sexual orientation, disability and more). Second, feminist suspicion regarding self-sacrificial notions of self-identity leads to tracing the mechanics or functions of sacrificial language and practice in human self understanding and action.

Third, they question understandings of virtue linked to suffering. Finally, feminists work to unmask the mantles of quasi-religious sanctity, glorification or mystification that frequently shroud sacrificial mandates of varying kinds. To see an example of such investigation at work, we might turn to the work of Rebecca Parker, who analyzes the impact of Christian sacrificial language and belief on women's lives. Parker writes,

> Christian theology presents Jesus as the model of self-sacrificing love and persuades women to believe that sexism is divinely sanctioned. (Women) are tied to the virtue of self-sacrifice, often by hidden social threats of punishment. We keep silent about rape, we deny when we are being abused, and we allow our lives to be consumed by the trivial and by our preoccupation with others. We never claim our lives as our own. We live as though we were not present in our bodies.[48]

Whereas traditionally, theologians have tended to shape their work for audiences that share their religious heritage, feminist and other liberation theologians attend more fully to the multivalent social and cultural consequences of theological claims. In other words, feminist methods address the ever-changing cultural landscape that plays a role in the formation of religious doctrine, and attempt to describe the diverse impacts of religious ideas, language and practices on society at many different levels. As Linell Elizabeth Cady puts it, 'religious ideas are strategies with identifiable social effects. [49]

With these motives in mind, feminist interrogation of the reemphasis on sacrifice such as that in our post-9/11 case study, therefore, must lead to the following questions: what are we to say about the sheer costs of sacrifice laid so directly on one group of our citizens, i.e., the military, reservists and their families? A certain suspicion emerges having to do with the inequitable distribution of costs, and leads one to suspect the rationalization behind the 'necessity' for sacrifice in the first place – if the rationalization was more convincing, wouldn't there be less hesitation and cynicism regarding bracing the American citizenry as a whole to bear their fair share?

48. Rita Nakashima Brock and Rebecca Ann Parker, *Proverbs to Ashes: Violence, Redemptive Suffering and the Search for What Saves Us* (Boston, MA: Beacon Press, 2001), p. 36.

49. Linell Elizabeth Cady, 'Identity, Feminist Theory and Theology,' *Horizons in Feminist Theology: Identity, Tradition and Norms* (Minneapolis, MN: Fortress Press, 1997), p. 30.

Moreover, how are we to understand the 'communal ecstasy' of excited self-sacrifice that emerges as a psychological reaction when those whose sacrifice is demanded find themselves in a marginalized place of extremity and danger? Recall the example of the 'Hitler children' from above. The groundwork for 'communal ecstasy' is laid through a discourse that emphasizes self-sacrificial, heroic military identity. Furthermore, as we saw in President Bush's sacrificial rhetoric, the cover of quasi-religious glorification inhibits honest questioning of the motives behind sacrificial mandates and self-sacrificial acculturation. This rhetoric mystifies practical analysis of the issues at stake and the costs involved in such an endeavor. The moral and financial/material costs to the nation as a whole are pushed to the side at best, and completely repressed at worst (despite insistent repetition, such as that from President Bush, that the sacrifice would only take place 'far from home').

Finally, and far from least important, this same language justifies a supposedly righteous demand to sacrifice the enemy to execute punishment and restore order. In other words, any realistic and comprehensive investigation of complaints, resentments and even hatreds against the United States is circumvented by the binary portrait of 'us and them' encouraged by sacrificial victimage rhetoric

All in all, shining the light of suspicion on the sacrificial constructions in U.S. War-culture leads to the following insights: 'The necessary sacrifice' of war is a quasi-religious canopy that mystifies analysis of the true nature of war. Language of sacrifice slips from specifically Christian religious formulations into national 'secular' tropes, such as in military schools and State of the Union addresses. Such practices and cognitive frameworks result in an unquestioned presumption *for* war, and a sacralized, sacrificial national identity in American civil religion that is strongly connected to war and the 'need' for an invincible military. The incalculable worth of life is minimized through sacrifice's exchange system in which supposed goods are traded for other goods, such as in the calculus of Just War principles (including proportionality, just cause, discrimination, double effect and more).[50] As feminists have emphasized, sacrificial exchange systems regularly rely on the most vulnerable members of societies as sacrificial collateral. But this insight is shrouded through

50. Chapter Three analyzes the dangers of sacrificial exchange systems in Just War thinking that is linked with sacrificial rhetoric

the sanctified 'necessity of sacrifice' that neatly masks material economic and social power interests at stake. Thus, glorification of the soldier's sacrifice obfuscates more realistic analysis of his/her experience, even as the sacrifice of the 'enemy' plays easily into victimage rhetoric to dehumanize the other and promote a smooth slide away from the reality of the his/her suffering. Finally, this rhetoric and these practices have great resonance in the American public at large, so they go unquestioned, and the imagination of the American collective is sharply disciplined away from the perception of alternatives outside of sacrifice to meet the needs of a suffering and conflicted world

What response is called for in the face of abusive sacrificial dynamics? According to Elsa Tamez, because sacrificial discourse justifies unjust and destructive social structures, it must be resisted. Challenging the sacrificial norms in Latin American economic discourse, Tamez writes,

> If the inequitable economic system has used sacrificial language to accomplish its goals, there is something perverse or ambiguous in that language. It is therefore crucial to take up again the theme of sacrifice in order to reread it from another angle [51]

An important clue to this dangerous use of sacrifice emerges in connection with the ideology of 'necessity.' Tamez writes, '...the death of Jesus is not necessary in order to accomplish a particular purpose but rather is the inevitable result of a specific cause.'[52] In Tamez' setting, the problem lies in the way the language of sacrifice was colonized by elite power brokers of economic systems in Latin America. They drew upon specific understandings of Christian atonement to emphasize the ideology of a 'necessary sacrifice' in order to demand the self-sacrifice of the least powerful people.

In Christian theology one finds the wording of 'necessity' most often connected to Christian salvation images of *satisfaction, penal substitution, sacrific* and *christus victor*. All these salvation images have roots in early Christianity, though they have come into prominence in varying Christian communities during different historical epochs. In *satisfaction* theories of Christian redemption (coming into full development in the eleventh century), Jesus' suffering and

---

51. Tamez, *The Amnesty of Grace*, p. 157.
52. Tamez, *The Amnesty of Grace*, p. 158.

death satisfies the offense to God's honor, or mends the rupture in the moral wholeness of the universe created by the reality of human sin. *Penal substitutionary* theories, which became prominent during the time of the European Reformation and which dominate the American Christian landscape today, emphasize Jesus as the surrogate or substitute for the rightful punishment a wrathful God assigns to sinful humanity. *Sacrific*, the most ancient of these images, comes out of cultic practice in which the offering up of an unblemished animal, or the pouring out of grain or cereal, purifies, cleanses and/or unifies the faithful before God. Finally, the image of *christus victor*, based on experiences of the battlefield, portrays Jesus as a warrior who fights by way of his suffering and death to liberate humanity from the clutches of Satan, evil and the consequences of sin. In each of these images, Jesus' suffering and dying action is 'necessary.' It recompenses the offense to God, repairs the rupture in the universe, pays the price, and wins the battle. However, it is just this element of 'necessity' that we should question, according to Tamez. 'The *necessary* sacrifices fall under the reign of the law, of sin and of death. All…who would speak of the necessity of human sacrifices negate the resurrection of Jesus and thereby also justific - tion by grace.'[53]

Penal substitutionary interpretations of Christian salvation in particular emphasize retributive notions of justice. Jesus, the innocent one, freely takes on sin and punishment in the place of sinful humanity, thus becoming the scapegoat. Punishment is unavoidable; the price must be paid. In this way, *penal substitutionary* understandings utilize logic identical to that in victimage rhetoric, demanding sacrifice (which may be the sacrifice of the adversary, the surrogate, or both) to restore order. This same mechanism may be linked to military identity development; just as Jesus freely offers himself in place of sinful humanity, so the soldier offers himself, 'without thought of recognition or gain,' as the Soldier's Handbook states.[54] Moreover, one frequently finds such patterns embellished with *christus victor* imagery, so that the portrait of Jesus 'paying the price' occurs on the battlefield as Jesus wages war against sin and the devil.

This connection between salvation imagery and the operations and portrayal of war is troubling indeed. However, the ideology of

53. Tamez, *The Amnesty of Grace*, p. 158.
54. Department of the Army, *Soldier's Handbook*, pp. 3–3.

'necessity' has linked together Christian atonement theory with Just War ideology at least since the time of Augustine, Bishop of Hippo, who lived in the fifth century. Scholar R.A. Markus writes,

> Augustine evokes the great evils, the horror and savagery of war, only to reaffirm his view...that a wise man will wage just wars and lament the *necessity* which lays this duty upon him. The language of "necessity" is the language in which Augustine appealed to Roman officials and generals in Africa, just as it is the language in which he speaks of public duty.[55]

While, in the United States, we have heard our government officials making just this same link between sacrifice and necessity (recall President Bush's words in this vein, 'The war on terrorism will take time and require sacrifice...Yet we will do what is necessary'), an important part of the framing of sacrificial discourse in the post 9/11 period was to discourage citizens from questioning this same necessity too deeply. One wonders, for instance, about the refusal of the president over many months during his first term to meet with Cindy Sheehan, mother of deceased soldier Casey Sheehan, killed in Iraq. In an email to her supporters from the summer of 2005, Sheehan outlined the topics she wished to raise in a private meeting with President Bush, topics that clearly disrupted the streamlined, unquestioned link in the ideology of sacrifice and necessity

> 1) What is the noble cause that everyone is dying for?
> 2) If it is so noble, do you encourage your daughters to enlist?
> 3) Stop using the name of my son to continue the killing.
>
> — God bless
> Cindy Sheehan

However, according to various editorialists in the United States, even this act on the part of one citizen did not escape the powerful force of framing to prevent any possible disruption of an uninterrupted ideology. Frank Rich of *The New York Times* wrote,

> The hope (of the administration) this time was that we'd change the subject to Cindy Sheehan's 'wacko' rhetoric and the opportunistic left-wing groups that have attached themselves to her like

55. R.A. Markus, 'Saint Augustine's Views on the "Just War"'. W.J. Shiels (ed.), *The Church and War: Papers Read at the Twenty-first Summer Meeting and Twenty-second Winter Meeting of the Ecclesiastical History Society* (Oxford: Blackwell, 1983), pp. 10–11.

barnacles…(in order to silence) her message of unequal sacrifice and fruitless carnage.[56]

Mothers of soldiers who have died, daughters of the deployed and widows all represent 'an especially salient political category' during times of war because of their usefulness to political and intellectual elites as symbols of national sacrifice. Citizens are encouraged to grieve with them and thus underscore the meaningfulness of the war. In contrast, the ridiculing and sidelining of Sheehan makes sense when we take into account the potentially deeply disruptive nature of her questions to the national sacrificial trope in the Iraq war. In fact, while the same sacrificial narrative suggests that the sacrifice of widows, children and mothers should be met with support, encouragement and the thanks of a grateful nation, all too often the actual circumstances faced by these women and girls reveal an altogether different and much harsher reality.[57]

The abusive potential inherent in sacrificial identity formation and mandates is sufficient to make one wonder if sacrifice may ever be justified ethically. To be sure, various feminist theologians reject any positive or normative portrayal of sacrifice within Christianity on the grounds of just such potentially dangerous application to any marginalized collective. However, Bruce Chilton's anthropological and textual studies of sacrifice reveal surprising insights. It is doubtful that we may ever arrive at a definitive theory of sacrifice because it operates in such varying ways in different cultures and epochs, and because it is impossible to recreate the internal mechanics in particular of ancient sacrificial practices. Nevertheless, at the very least, anthropologically speaking, we can describe various factors involved in sacrifice as they emerge in different contexts. In his study of sacrifice in the ancient world Chilton identifies three such descriptive elements; sacrifi e is 1) pragmatic, 2) affective, and 3) involves some sort of ideological transaction (that is, an affirmation of belief and community).[58] The virtue of generosity may both compel and emerge out of sacrificial practices, as he writes

56. Frank Rich, 'The Swift-Boating of Cindy Sheehan', *The New York Times*, 21 August 2005 , Op Ed., p. 11.

57. Cynthia Enloe, *Nimo's War, Emma's War: Making Feminist Sense of the Iraq War* (Berkeley, CA: University of California Press, 2010), pp. 62–63.

58. Bruce Chilton, *The Temple of Jesus: His Sacrificial Program Within a Cultural History of Sacrifice* (University Park, PA: Pennsylvania University Press, 1992), pp. 39–41.

> Communities that practice sacrifice understand themselves to exist within a sacrificial compact, such that their generosity within rituals is met by the generosity they desire…the generosity that sacrifice demands is worthwhile… [59]

One example of such sacrifi ial activity described by Chilton takes place in the chapel at the college where he teaches, when a group of Guatemalan women gather together to eat tortillas and drink wine in a room that has been adorned with photographs of dead relatives who were victims of state terror. As they eat, they sing together in the mood of a family reunion. Chilton writes,

> What is done provides a paradigm of the value of certain elements and gestures, the *pragmata* of sacrifice: the foods, their preparations, things done at the time and in the space of the meal. Emotions are engaged, often in an ambivalent manner…the Guatemalan dead join the living only in song. Presence and absence are balanced through a ritual exchange which is as affective as it is pragmatic… ideology and affect and pragmatics are united in any sacrificial moment.[60]

What is so surprising in Chilton's description is the mutuality, the give and take, the sense of communion and generosity that may emerge in the sacrificial action taking place, a sensibility altogether unlike the connotations surrounding contemporary discourse of sacrifice in the post-9/11 U.S

In contrast to Chilton's example, post-9/11 sacrificia political discourse had very little to do with 'generosity within rituals met by the generosity one desires.' In fact, post-9/11 sacrificial language derived not a small amount of its resonance from having collided with certain widespread atonement images that dominate the popular American religious scene, not only the image of sacrifice, but sacrifice conflated with *christus victor* (righteous revenge)and *penal substitutionary* (righteous surrogacy) understandings of Christian salvation.

It has long been recognized that despite the enormous variety of images, metaphors and theories of redemption in the history of Christianity, Christian salvation in the U.S. tends to be popularly understood and expressed through the metaphor of *penal*

---

59. Chilton, *The Temple of Jesus*, p. 31.
60. Chilton, 'Sacrificial Mimesis', *Religion* 27 (1997): 225–30, 227.

substitution.[61] The theory of *penal substitution*, of course, emphasizes the *necessity* of an innocent substitute (Jesus) who self-sacrifices (by receiving God's rightful punishment) in place of sinful humanity in order to achieve salvation. Moreover, the image also draws upon *christus victor* imagery, so that the transaction taking place is multiplied to the level of a cosmic battle between the forces of good and evil. Scholars have noted that a vast amount of Christian practice in the U.S., including preaching, liturgy, hymnody and catechesis, illustrates the meaning of Christian salvation through images such as these.[62]

Yet in addition to specifically Christian practice, these images are a part of popular culture; one only has to think back to the widespread popularity of Mel Gibson's film, *The Passion*, to see such resonance at work in the American public. The film's images of punishment beyond one's wildest imaginings, conflated with sacrificial and cosmic battleground imagery, all combined to create an effect that deeply resonated with a significantly large swath of the American public, if movie box-office totals are to be believed. The punitive, grotesquely violent, Manichean, sexist and anti-semitic tones in Gibson's film have been thoroughly analyzed by a host of religion and film scholars.[63] Yet we dare not compartmentalize these specifically religious images of sacrifice in popular culture from the political discourse of sacrifice that likewise became a formative element of the post-9/11 culture of the United States.

In fact, a 2005 study that surveyed Americans regarding their religious and political commitments demonstrated that 'religious traditionalists' were much more inclined to believe the Iraq war was justified than centrist or modernist mainline Protestants, Jews,

61. This is especially true in popular culture, but also remains the case in the many ecclesial cultures.

62. See, for example, the work of New Testament scholar Joel B. Green: *Recovering the Scandal of the Cross: Atonement in New Testament and Contemporary Contexts* (Downers Grove, IL: Intervarsity Press, 2000); and Joel B. Green and Jon Carroll, *The Death of Jesus in Early Christianity* (Peabody, MA: Hendrickson, 1995).

63. See J. Shawn Landres and Michael Berenbaum (eds), *After the Passion Is Gone: American Religious Consequences* (New York: Altamira, 2004). Also, Kelly Denton-Borhaug, 'A Bloodthirsty Salvation: Behind the Popular Polarized Reaction to Gibson's *The Passion*,' *Journal of Religion and Film* 9, no. 1 (April 2005).

Catholics, other faith groups or non-religiously-affiliated people in the U.S. 'Religious Traditionalists' also demonstrated higher levels of support for the doctrine of pre-emptive military action. At the same time, 'evangelical centrists' fell far below the mean with regard to the question of protecting human rights.[64] Along just these same political/religious divisions, evangelical Christians and conservative or 'traditionalist' Catholics were the most ardent supporters of the Gibson film, though it also found a highly receptive audience far beyond these specific groups.[65] We dare not miss the important connections between the political proclivities of these groups and the dominant religious images that are deeply resonant in their lives. *Penal substitutionary* imagery and understanding, so dominant in American religious consciousness (and subconsciousness), meshed with the ideology of the necessity of warring sacrifice. This meshing led to 'powerful, pervasive and long-lasting moods and motivations' that all too easily became available and malleable for alignment with the idea of war as the best, indeed, the only option.

Thus, when President Bush called on sacrificial language to describe the meaning of the war in Iraq, not only did he 'signal his base,' he additionally dipped into an enormous, partly conscious and perhaps even more largely subconscious pool of resonance in the American public at large. 'Cultural Congruence' describes 'the ease with which –all else equal – a news frame can cascade through the different levels of the framing process and stimulate similar reactions at each step.'[66] Cascading here refers to the transfer, the movement of any given political message through a variety of groups, including the administration, other elites, the media and the public. The most powerful frames are those that move most easily across groups; moreover what makes such movement possible is that 'the most inherently powerful frames are fully congruent with schemas *habitually* used by most members of society.' September 11 is an example of such congruence; in the American public consciousness, the 9/11 terrorists quickly 'assimilated to the common schema of

64. James L. Guth, John C. Green, Lyman K. Kellstedt, and Corwin E. Emidt, 'Faith and Foreign Policy: A View from the Pews', *Faith and International Affairs* 3, no. 2, (Fall 2005): 5–6.

65. See Julie Ingersoll, 'Is It Finished? *The Passion of the Christ* and the Fault Lines in American Christianity' in Landres and Berenbaum (eds), *After the Passion is Gone*, pp. 75–87.

66. Entman, 'Cascading Activation', p. 422.

Islamic terrorism.' In contrast to the ease of assimilation on Sept. 11, an example of a lack of congruence may be seen in the 1988 downing of an Iranian civilian airliner by a U.S. naval vessel, killing 290 people. 'Research shows the media frame discouraged any dissonant interpretation – one holding the U.S. as morally culpable.'[67]

To conclude this case study, the post-9/11 period demonstrates a dynamic in which a number of compelling forms of sacrificial discourse coalesced, each in its own way a familiar, resonant part of American culture. These same discourses collided and blended with one another, creating a deeply congruent field ripe for the abuse of notions of sacrifice, seen in the following

- The ideology of victimage rhetoric overtly demanded the sacrifice of the enemy and the self-sacrifice of the military to restore order, and justified the violence/killing that ensued. Political/ military sacrificial discourse collided with highly resonant and habitual images in religion and culture at large, based on *penal substitution*, *sacrificia* and *christus victor* atonement metaphors, stressing punitive, hyper-violent, polarizing and binaried heuristic methods for understanding and interpreting events.
- Such rhetoric depended on the affect of anger toward and fear of the enemy, combined with a righteous justification for retributive action; perhaps the complete opposite of the affect of generosity Chilton notes in his study of ancient and contemporary sacrificial practices. In terms of sheer efficacy, one must recognize that anger, fear and retribution have the potential to unify a population over against the enemy just as much as (or even more than) the practice of generosity. This is the challenge for religion in general, and Christianity in particular.
- The *pragmata* of this sacrifice did not depend upon the practical, everyday elements of food and drink and implements to prepare and share them, as we see with the example of the Guatemalan women, but highly evolved, technological weapons of war capable of wreaking almost unimaginable damage on people, their property and the environment at large.
- Purposefully veiled communication regarding the operations and costs of such sacrifice laid the heaviest part of the burden on the American military and their families, and took advantage of sacrificially-oriented identity formation within that military

67. Entman, 'Cascading Activation', p. 423.

population. Thus the administration cynically was protected from a potential public outcry, loss of votes and money through the careful message that the American public at large would not bear any of these costs. In addition, as in the case of Elsa Tamez' context, here too the sacrificial population included a significant, if not majority, portion of members of the military forces coming from the lower-middle and working-classes of the United States.

• The religious under- and overtones in the discourse of sacrifice shrouded the presidential administration initiative with a mantle of glorification, creating a frame with theological connotations that made it powerful, emotionally compelling and understandable; and simultaneously a frame powerful enough to subvert, divert, and dilute important questions that needed to be asked and considered, a frame that encouraged quietistic response to a paternal authority.

Signs of the Frame Interrupted

And yet...in the second term of Bush's presidency signs emerged indicating that the cultural congruence of the current frame could be on the wane. Cole recognized that such might be the case when he concluded his argument with the following words:

> The use of a rhetorical frame that assumed public wariness and found congruence with elements of the popular culture that promise results without effort, cost or sacrifice has perhaps now found the limits of its persuasiveness in the turbulence of postwar Iraq.[68]

One might point to the indictment of Scooter Libby, and the actions of the congress to insist on hearing a report regarding possible manipulation of pre-war intelligence, not to mention the sharply decreasing measure of public approval of the Iraq war, as signs of a weakening frame. In addition to these developments, however, we can point to a growing collection of smaller, yet significant signs that emerged in the culture. The persistence of Cindy Sheehan and her supporters might be cited as one example of such burgeoning signs. In conclusion to her email outlining the topics she wished to

---

68. Cole, 'The Rhetoric of Sacrifice and Heroism', p. 151

discuss with the president, she included the unequivocal statement: 'Stop using the name of my son to continue the killing.' In this vein Lewis Taylor notes that military families and veterans are among others who formed groups during this same period in order to engender what he calls, 'prophetic spirit,' defined as 'a way of being that is always at work broadening and deepening the horizons of our lives and, in the process, giving rise to ever new awareness of breadth and depth in our understandings of being.'[69] An important part of such awareness has to do with asking those hard questions discouraged and dissimulated by the current frame.

Interestingly, at the opposite end of the spectrum from Sheehan and other similar families, Taylor also makes note of a group of 'just war against terror scholars,' in other words, scholars who advocated for warring response after 9/11, including Elshtain, whose insistence on the irremediable evil of terrorists and necessity of a violent response contributed not only to public fear but to a hesitancy to ask probing questions that might give us more and better information for our deliberation about the best way forward. In Taylor's estimation, Elshtain's 'resistance to dissenting understanding' with respect to the war on terror 'is consistent with the rhetoric of evil.'[70] 'Necessity' played into this dynamic as well, insisting that something must be sacrificed/p nished, instead of focusing on how and why things went so wrong in the first place.

An additional insistent challenge to the preferred frame of the Bush Administration were growing signs that the military might be at the breaking point, as the self-sacrificing warrior culture moved to a level of crisis. In November, 2005, the top general in the Army Reserve described his troops as 'degenerating into a broken force' as a result of the 'demands placed on the Reserve by the Iraq and Afghanistan wars.' A former army lieutenant outlined the situation with the following words: '[Soldiers] feel like they're the only ones sacrificing...they're starting to look around and say, "You know it's me and my buddies over and over again, and everybody else is living life uninterrupted."' Increasingly it became a greater part of public awareness that the military was paying the cost not only through loss of life and horrific injuries, but

69. Taylor, *Religion, Politics, and the Christian Right*, p. 97.
70. Taylor, *Religion, Politics, and the Christian Right*, p. 25.

in rising divorce rates, financial problems, post-traumatic stress disorder, and a host of other ills.[71]

Finally, even in the popular culture of Doonesbury, questions regarding the discourse of sacrifice arose with greater force. In a cartoon in which a news commentator questions the president regarding the expected duration of the war, cartoonist Gary Trudeau spotlighted the familiar rationale from President Bush: 'We must remain in Iraq to ensure that those who've given their lives didn't die in vain.' But the fictional newsperson keeps the question going: 'What if our troops are still dying at the current rate a year from now? What about two years? Five years?' The presidential voice from the TV remains constant: 'Again, we'll stay the course. We cannot dishonor the upcoming sacrifice of those who have yet to die...'[72]

At the same time, the powerful political machinery of framing largely continued to hold sway. For instance, in late November 2005, his approval ratings severely declining, President Bush gave a major speech to announce a new document, available on the official White House website, called 'National Strategy for Victory in Iraq.'[73] In the title and 16 subtitles of the document alone, the word 'victory' appeared no fewer than eight times. *The New York Times* noted in its 4 December 2005 report that the word 'victory' was repeated like a mantra by the president no fewer than 15 times and also appeared in a visual backdrop with the words 'Plan for Victory.'[74] It soon became apparent that while the administration had touted the new document as a policy statement from the Pentagon to outline its strategy for fighting the Iraq insurgency, the obvious goal of both document and speech was to sway American public opinion, to create a new frame that might have the chance of disrupting growing disapproval (up to 65 percent, according to a *Newsweek* Poll) in the

71. Bob Herbert, 'An Army Ready to Snap,' *The New York Times*, 10 November 2005, A29. By April, 2006, no fewer than six generals publicly had called for the resignation of Donald Rumsfeld.

72. Gary Trudeau, *Doonesbury, The New York Times*, 9 October 2005.

73. 'National Strategy for Victory in Iraq', The White House: President George W. Bush, 30 November 2005, http://georgewbush-whitehouse.archives.gov/news/releases/2005/11/20051130-2.html, accessed 4 January 2010.

74. Scott Shane, 'Bush's Speech on Iraq War Echoes Voice of an Analyst', *The New York Times*, 4 December 2005.

American public regarding the war and the president's leadership as Commander in Chief.

With a bit of investigative digging, the true author of the report, Peter D. Feaver, a Duke University political scientist, was discovered. The Times reporter wrote,

> Feaver was recruited after he and Duke colleagues presented to administration officials their analysis of polls about the Iraq war in 2003 and 2004. They concluded that Americans would support a war with mounting causalities on one condition: that they believe it would ultimately succeed.

Dr. Feaver's research on public opinion regarding the Iraq war is readily available. In one article, 'Casualties are the First Truth of War,' he strongly opposes what he describes as the common post-Desert Storm political/military philosophy that 'higher casualities will translate into a precipitous decline in public support.'[75] On the contrary, according to Feaver's own research of polls from the first two years of the war 'if political leaders remain calm and convey confidence that the mission will be successful, then the price [i.e., high causalities] can be paid.' Thus the new and almost overwhelming focus on 'victory' (the State of the Union Address in January 2006 likewise parroted the word incessantly). To add to the impression of an attempted public opinion coup, it might be noted that Dr. Feaver joined the National Security Council staff as a special adviser in June 2005; while Lt. Gen. Martin Dempsey, the top American military official in charge of training Iraqi troops, told a surprised group of reporters that he had never seen or heard of the document before its public release. Such blatant attempts at framing to infl - ence public opinion are enough to encourage one to transpose a few of the words in Dr. Feaver's *Weekly Standard* article to create an alternate title, 'Truth is the First Casualty of War.'[76]

At the same time, and most unfortunate, the move from an emphasis on 'sacrifice' to 'victory' still made it possible for this language to operate under the same mantle of religious sanctific - tion/glorification, given the popular American interpretation of

75. Peter Feaver, 'Casualties are the First Truth of War,' *Weekly Standard* 008, Issue 29, (April 7, 2003).

76. The phrase, 'truth is the first casualty of war' has been attributed to various political figures and poets, going back to Aeschylus. See, http://www.guardian.co.uk/notesandqueries/query/0,5753,-21510,00.html for examples.

Christian salvation. Religion scholars long have urged that *christus victor* salvation metaphors, with their cosmic battleground imagery and dualistic division of the world into evil and good, as well as their unrelenting focus on 'victory' as the ultimately assured and unassailable single goal and definition of salvation, are portrayals that Christians and citizens in general must critique with greater self-awareness. Especially in the lives of privileged Christians living in 'first-world' nations, these images contain great capacity to bless war-making, alienate and demonize groups perceived as 'different' and encourage abandonment of any methods that promise less than absolute certainty.

The same frame emerged yet again in connection with 'the surge' of 20,000 additional forces sent to Iraq in 2007. Once again, President Bush declared that the result of this latest action would be nothing less than 'victory.' But now the definition of victory shifted. 'Victory in Iraq will bring something new in the Arab World...a functioning democracy...[However,] a democratic Iraq will not be perfect.' At the same time, even this more modest frame of victory continued to be tied to the same sacrific al mandate addressed to the American military and their families:

> In these dangerous times, the United States is blessed to have extraordinary and selfless men and women willing to step forward and defend us. These young Americans understand that our cause in Iraq is noble and necessary – and that the advance of freedom is the calling of our time. They serve far from their families, who make the quiet sacrifices of lonely holidays and empty chairs at the dinner table. They have watched their comrades give their lives to ensure our liberty. We mourn the loss of every fallen American – and we owe it to them to build a future worthy of their sacrifice [77]

The loss of over 4,400 members of the military by 2010, not to mention the devastating injuries sustained by tens of thousands more, makes it difficult for Americans to hear such language as this without experiencing a deep emotional reaction.[78] However, without deeper awareness and analysis regarding the operations of the rhetoric of necessity, sacrifi e and victory, citizens are vulnerable to

77. 'President's Address to the Nation,' The White House: President George W. Bush, 10 January 2007, http://georgewbush-whitehouse.archives.gov/news/releases/2007/01/20070110-7.html, accessed 4 January 2010.

78. 'U.S. Military Deaths in Iraq War at 4,424,' *The Associated Press*, 6 October, 2010, http://www.washingtonpost.com, accessed 08 October 2010.

manipulation, simplistic thinking, and the tendency not to question, just as this latest frame of 'victory' encouraged.

Reframing the Question

Christian ethicist Larry Rasmussen suggests that we adopt different language to shift the terms of the conversation about war and non-violence in our society. Searching for the 'civic counterpart' of rendering equality through baptism; defining the possibility of 'eucharistic economics'; developing methods for 'binding and loosing through forgiveness' to move past retribution – Rasmussen would have us bring these religious images, metaphors and practices imaginatively into the civic realm to seek out parallels appropriate for a pluralistic and troubled world. He writes, 'following Jesus as "premeditated reconciliation" would be more accurate than "non-violence."'[79] He continues,

> Pacifist practices are not just a firewall for containing conflict. They are the evangelical practices these traditions see as a whole way of life. Just peacemaking is the hard task of developing these as civic practices and not only ecclesial ones.

This is the 'hard task' facing people of religious faith and other advocates of non-violence who resist the kind of conflation of religious language and images with the practices and tools of war that are so very much a part of our cultural moment.

Perhaps Rasmussen's proposal is not unlike theologian Denny Weaver's exercise in imagination, when he responds to the 'ultimate question' consistently thrust in the face of advocates of non-violence, i.e., 'What would you do about Hitler? Or – What would you do if a crazed person came after your mother/father/wife/child with a gun?' Weaver's response is to highlight the patent unfairness of such questions. He writes,

> The temptation is to believe that violence, or structures and movements of violence, are the ultimate moral agents in God's world, and that by serving those agents one advances the purposes of the reign of God.[80]

79. Larry Rasmussen, 'In the Face of War,' *Sojourners Magazine* 34 no. 1 (2005): pp. 12–17.

80. J. Denny Weaver, 'Responding to September 11 – and October 7 and January 20: Which Religion Shall We Follow?' *Conrad Grebel Review* 20, no. 2 (Spring 2002): pp. 79–100, 90.

The 'ultimate' question itself is unfair on at least two grounds; first, it places pacifists in the position of being responsible for the long build-up of frustrations that produce 'people who do terrible things'; and second, it assumes that there are insufficient numbers of pacifists in the world to make any measurable difference anyway. In response, Weaver writes,

> For the "What-about" question to be fair, pacifists need equal time to prepare and equal numbers of people involved – say three peace academies (parallel to the Naval Academy, West Point, and the Air Force Academy) graduating several hundred men and women each year highly trained in nonviolent techniques, plus standing reserve companies of thousands of men and women trained in nonviolent tactics, all of whom have access to billions of dollars to spend on transportation and the latest communications equipment...[81]

I find much to appreciate in the imaginative thrusts of both Rasmussen's and Weaver's proposals. However, the gist of the argument in this chapter moves in a different direction, to throw into greater relief the ambiguity residing in the communicative dynamic of primary religious symbols and metaphors themselves. This very ambiguity creates the capacity for misuse and even abuse of these images in the service of political and commercial/economic goals. Because images and practices of 'sacrifice' communicate so profoundly both at communal and individual levels, they embody transformative *and* manipulative capacity. In addition to the proposals of Rasmussen and Weaver, an equally hard task involves encouraging greater public analysis and awareness regarding the multivalent operations of the ambiguous symbol, 'sacrifice.' How can such a task be accomplished? An indispensable step lies in something very simple: that is, demonstrating that 'the emperor has no clothes.' In other words, we must:

- pull back the veil of religious mystification and glorification that so neatly has swathed administration admonitions, justifications and explanations regarding 'the necessity of sacrifice' (think back to President Obama's justification for war in his acceptance of the Nobel Peace Prize, discussed in the introduction to this book);

81. Weaver, 'Responding to September 11', p. 92.

- shine a harsh light on the crude and even cynical practice of borrowing religious language for the purpose of framing to manipulate public interpretation and approval;
- encourage greater public and ecclesial debate regarding the construction of an ethically justifiable role for religion in the political public square;
- demonstrate the importance of deeper theological interpretations of primary religious symbols beyond popular cultural understandings;
- deepen the analysis of these symbols in military acculturation and identity formation;
- promote increased awareness of the ways the discourse of sacrifice or victory may be manipulated in the public realm.

All of these emphases constitute for U.S. citizens indispensable steps we must encourage if we are to adequately understand, much less respond to our current political and cultural moment in history, and our relationship with the rest of the world.

Also ahead is the task of more substantive investigation into the links between 'necessity' in Just War ideology and in the atonement metaphors of *penal substitution, christus victor* and *sacrific* in Christian history and theology. Chapter Three takes up this examination, and reveals another kind of 'slippage,' one similar to the one we discover between the self-sacrificial identity of the martyr and that of the soldier, so that the 'necessity' of war becomes a buttress supporting the 'necessity' of Christ's suffering and death and vice versa.

Is it possible to imagine discourse and practices of sacrifice that compel and produce generosity? Is it possible to 'rehabilitate' sacrifice for Christian doctrine and practice? Chapter Four explores these important questions. But this chapter concludes with Chilton's description of the Guatemalan women's practice of sacrifice, singing – albeit ambivalently – with the memories and spirits of those killed by the state, sharing food, drink and grief, and searching for hope. Here is one image of generosity juxtaposed with our heightened awareness about our political, cultural and religious post-9/11 reality. In a world of fragile human institutions, with great capacity to manipulate even as we hope that they will promote human flou - ishing, in a world that feels all too often not safer, but more polarized and dangerous, (re)discovering and (re)imagining generosity is more urgent than ever.

Chapter Three

A DEADLY NEXUS: 'NECESSITY' – CHRISTIAN SALVATION AND WAR-CULTURE

To learn to tell the truth… requires the never-ending work to discover the connections between the contingencies that constitute existence. Such connections are displayed in narratives that at once constitute who we are but also hide from us who we are. For we desire to deny our contingency by living as if the way things are is the way things have to be. Violence lies in our attempt to show the "necessity" that the way we live is the way we must live… If we are to live truthful lives we must recognize that any truth to be had in this life requires the ongoing, never-ending discoveries of the connections made possible by a truthful story.

– Stanley Hauerwas[1]

Introduction

In the spring of 2007, when a small group of white middle-aged women from the 'Fairmont, Minnesota Peace Club' persuaded the local town council to endorse a resolution in favor of a Department of Peace in the federal government of the U.S., all hell broke loose. The morning after the council unanimously passed their resolution, the irate telephone calls and messages began. A hearing convened to listen to responses from the townspeople on the topic revealed that most critics' fears had little to do with what a Peace Department actually would do in the federal government. Individual speakers warned that this was 'a humongous push to get the United Nations' foot in the door,' to 'take away our sovereignty,' and would send a message to enemies of the U.S. that we are 'weak and afraid to fight,' not much more than 'a bunch of wussies,' according to a former

1. Stanley Hauerwas, *Performing the Faith: Bonhoeffer and the Practice of Nonviolence* (Grand Rapids, MI: Brazos Press, 2004), p. 17.

Navy bomber pilot in Vietnam. Needless to say, the resolution was rescinded before the ink was dry on the paper.[2]

The actual proposal for a Department of Peace in the federal government dates back to the Founding Fathers of the United States and in its most current iteration has been supported by at least 60 Democrats in Congress. This latest incarnation is in the shape of a bill that advocates sophisticated approaches to conflict resolution, including a 'Peace Academy' to train armies of mediators who might spread out to the U.S. and around the world, and proposes the creation of a position as Peace Secretary in the president's cabinet. What then, one wonders, is such immediate, uninformed and passionate resistance all about? What does it tell us? How should we 'read' it culturally? 'I didn't think it was controversial,' said one club member, referring to the effort to have the resolution passed. 'I thought everybody wanted peace.'

The purpose of this chapter is to investigate the cultural, discursive and especially the religious preconditions that give rise to such reactions in the United States. Specifically, I argue that the naturalization of war-culture in the United States is buttressed by an ideology of 'the *necessity* of war-as-sacrifice.' We see this ideology at work in the narrative from the Minnesota Peace Club. Examination of the public outcry reveals two dominant assumptions that are at work in the townspeople's responses: first, not killing, or other-than-violent methods of addressing conflict, are assumed to be unreliable, ineffective and effeminate. Second, violent response is masterful, determinative and in a word, 'necessary.' What feeds into and energizes such assumptions in the post-9/11 culture of the United States? As one scholar writes, '... the basic political consciousness ... has continued to be shaped by the belief that only violence can either keep the peace or produce change. The willingness to wage war and engage in the preparation for war is still overwhelmingly thought to provide the only practical, if admittedly precarious, approach to world peace.'[3] Yet, as I will show, this secular formulation regarding

---

2. 'Peace Department Proposal Rattles Small Town', Daniel Zwerdling, *Weekend Edition, National Public Radio*, 24 March 2007. http://www.npr.org/templates/story/story.php?storyId=9083208, accessed 22 January 2010.

3. Richard Falk, 'Renouncing Wars of Choice: Toward a Geopolitics of Nonviolence', *The American Empire and the Commonwealth of God* (Louisville, KY: Westminster John Knox Press, 2006), pp. 79-80.

the 'necessity of war' gains traction and energy from religious impulses, especially religious notions of sacrifice [4]

If the introductory story represents a popular example of the operation of the ideology of the necessity of war in the U.S. context, a second example comes from the level of policy makers and public intellectuals. Within six months of 9/11, in a document titled 'A Letter from America,' over 60 prominent writers, members of think tanks and academics unequivocally called for a U.S. declaration of war. Drawing upon the rhetoric and logic of Just War theory in their argument, the letter's authors emphasized that war was the required and 'necessary' response to the attack on the Trade Towers. Their recommendation to go to war stands out all the more, given that the signatories simultaneously acknowledged that the target to be attacked, Al Qaeda, resided in no fewer than 40 different countries.[5] We will return to exploration of this letter later in this chapter.

Rhetorically, the discourse of 'the necessity of war-as-sacrifice' reinforces and privileges a certain logic; *ideologically* it operates so as to discipline the imagination that might otherwise develop alternative views of thinking, being and acting in the world. I intend to bring this link of necessity to the surface for analysis, though it primarily rests beneath the surface of conscious awareness. This examination helps us to understand more deeply both the roots and the operations of U.S. War-culture that increased in scope in the post-9/11 era.

4. Legal scholar Mary Ellen O'Connell defines the legal principle of 'military necessity' as '... the obligation that force is used only if necessary to accomplish a reasonable military objective.' In contrast to the rhetoric of 'necessity' that encourages the lurch toward war as the only sensible and effective means for addressing conflict, proper deliberation regarding the legal principle of 'necessity' requires specific training in the law of war. O'Connell argues that the use of drones in Pakistan from 2004 forward demonstrates precisely a lack of such training and regard, in that CIA operatives and contractors (who receive no such training) largely were responsible for the decisions to strike targets. By 2009, these strikes resulted in the deaths of approximately 750–1,000 unintended victims in comparison with the deaths of 20 al-Qaeda or Taliban leaders. See Mary Ellen O'Connell, 'Unlawful Killing with Combat Drones: A Case Study of Pakistan, 2004–2009,' in Simon Bronitt (ed.), *Shooting to Kill: The Law Governing Lethal Force in Context*, Forthcoming, Notre Dame Legal Studies Paper No. 09-43.

5. The letter is reprinted in full in a longer justification for the response of war to the World Trade Center Twin Tower Attacks written by Jean Bethke Elshtain, *Just War Against Terror* (New York: Basic Books, 2003), pp. 182–207.

Chapter One explored the analysis of U.S. War-culture from the perspective of political scientists, economists, sociologists and communication scholars. U.S. War-culture reveals a history of U.S. economic and military dominance in the world and determination to prevent any meaningful challenge to it, and may be defined as the interpenetration of the culture, ethos and practices of war with ever-increasing facets of U.S. culture, institutions, and imagination. Scholars have characterized the United States as an 'empire,' due to its: '1) triumphalist unilateralism, 2) war, 3) nationalism, 4) political and economic inequality, and 5) torture.'[6] For instance, to focus on just one aspect of empire, scholars analyze militarization as a pillar of the U.S. economy, such as was investigated so compellingly in Eugene Jarecki's documentary, *Why We Fight.*[7] The film highlights the danger of an unrestrained military complex wielding power in the U.S. through four key constituencies in our society: 1) the military, 2) the defense industry, 3) Congress, and 4) think tanks. Moreover, the economics of militarization are tied to the growing wealth gap in the U.S., as more and more wealth was concentrated in the hands of fewer individuals, especially in the period beginning with the 1980s. By the time of the economic crisis in the United States in 2007, one political scientist described the wealth-gap in the United States in the following terms: 'The top 1 percent of Americans is now receiving the largest share of national income since the pre-Great Depression year 1928. The top 10 percent get 48.5 percent of total income, an obscene rate of inequality.'[8] A symbiotic relationship between corporations and legislative government in the military industrial complex relies on enormous defense budgets and results in huge profits made by private industry from military production and activity; as one scholar describes it, this is a 'well-oiled machine greased by opportunistic relationships between political leaders, military personnel and defense contractors.'[9]

6. As enumerated by Mark Lewis Taylor in 'American Torture and the Body of Christ: Making and Remaking Worlds', in Marit Trelstad (ed.), *Cross Examinations: Readings on the Meaning of the Cross Today* (Minneapolis, MN: Fortress Press, 2006), p. 264.

7. Director Eugene Jarecki, Sony Pictures, 2006.

8. Gary Olson, 'The Rich Are Very Different from You and Me,' *Z Magazine*, 5 January 2007, see, http://www.zmag.org/zmag, accessed 5 March 2007 Chapters One and Five explore the economic facet of U.S. War-culture in greater detail.

9. Marc Pilisuk with Jennifer Achord Rountree, *Who Benefits from Global Violence and War: Uncovering a Destructive System* (Westport, CT: Praeger Security International, 2008), p. 101.

Yet the net culmination, never mind the consequences, of increasing militarization and empire remain outside the consciousness and awareness of many Americans, perhaps even the majority of citizens. How can this be?

In order to answer this question we must explore what lies beneath the assumptions that support war-culture and the ideology of 'the necessity of war' in the United States. What energizes support for war-culture? How may assumptions and narrow forms of discourse be unmasked? If we agree that violence as stems at least in part from various discursive practices, and that analysis of the roots of violence involves making visible the symbols and rituals giving rise to violent acts, then one important key to unlocking this puzzle has to do with returning to language itself. Systems of language buttress our interpretations and values regarding both the 'justifiability' of violence at the level of the state, and revulsion or ridicule regarding alternative considerations. This is far from a new method of analysis; in the 1960s this very process was described by Herbert Marcuse as 'linguistic therapy,' an excavation of language with the purpose of freeing words, concepts and discursive systems from enslavement by the powers.[10] Similarly, Thomas Merton's 'War and the Crisis of Language,' is a beautiful essay from the same period that investigates the tautological language used to create a concrete barrier around the ideology promoting the Vietnam War.[11] It is the discursive classifications and frameworks embedded in any society that shape its members' thinking and determinations regarding what is 'real.' At the same time, investigating and shining light on 'what is real' is also a profoundly theological exercise, as we have learned from Ignacio Ellacuria and Jon Sobrino in El Salvador. As Sobrino says, 'the first step in any humanization... (is) simply to be honest about the world.'[12] In this investigation, I propose an excavation of those discourses and processes that shape our sense of what is 'real'

10. Herbert Marcuse, *An Essay on Liberation* (Boston, MA: Beacon Press, 1969), p. 10. Moravian College Professor of Philosophy Carol Moeller referred this resource to me.

11. Thomas Merton, 'War and the Crisis of Language', in Thomas Merton, edited and with Introduction by Gordon C. Zahn, *The Nonviolent Alternative* (New York: Farrar, Straus and Giroux, 1971, rev. ed. 1980). Moravian College Professor of Religion Don St. John made this work known to me.

12. Jon Sobrino, *Jesus the Liberator: A Historical-Theological View* (trans. Paul Burns and Francis McDonagh; Maryknoll, NY: Orbis Books, 1993), p. 234.

with respect to the foundation of U.S. War-culture and U.S. cultural assumptions regarding 'the necessity of war-as-sacrifice.' This is an exercise in honesty about the context of the United States.

The urgency of the post-9/11 historical moment demands a return to and refinement of just this kind of examination and exploration. In this period, the rhetoric of necessity, war and sacrifice reemerged linguistically as a tautology that encircled not only justification for the Iraq war but the discourse of the security state generally speaking. Through tracing this rhetoric to its roots in two ancient forms of discourse, Just War tradition and the language of Christian salvation, some clarity about the incongruity in our own society may surface. I close this section with a powerful quote from Merton's essay that describes his own excruciating awareness of the danger of war-buttressing tautologies, and his frustration and anger in response:

> The language of the war-maker is self-enclosed in finality. It does not invite reasonable dialogue, it uses language to silence dialogue, to block communication, so that instead of words the two sides may trade divisions, positions, villages, air bases, cities – and of course the lives of the people in them… Our side is always ahead. He who is winning must be the one who is right. But we are right, therefore we must be winning. Once again we have the beautiful, narcissistic tautology of war – or of advertising… there is no communicating with anyone else, because anyone who does not agree, who is outside the charmed circle, is wrong, is evil, is already in hell.[13]

The Logic of Masculinist Protection

The normalization of war-culture certainly is not new, but its dominance and pervasiveness grew significantly in the post-9/11 period in the United States. Political philosopher Iris Marion Young analyzes the dynamics of the U.S. government in the post-9/11 period as the ascent of a security regime based in the logic of masculinist protection.[14] She writes, 'One of the things I have learned since Sept. 11, 2001, is how easily the state actions and political culture of a democracy like that of the United States can shift in authoritarian

13. Merton, 'War and the Crisis of Language,' p. 244.
14. Iris Marion Young, 'Feminist Reactions to the Contemporary Security Regime,' *Hypatia* 18, no. 1 (Winter 2003).

directions.'[15] According to Young, the security regime is characterized by the prominence of the state's militaristic identity, its cen-
tralization of power and punishment of forms of dissent, and its
elevation of security as the highest value, far surpassing freedom
or autonomy.

Such a setting discourages us from asking questions and favors
explicit obedience. For the duty of the state to protect its citizens is
framed so as to outweigh other aspects of democratic practice, such
as honoring individual freedom, due process and public accountability. As a result, the primary focus of state energy and initiative
is directed to military and security concerns. At the same time, however, all of this is couched in language emphasizing dangerous outside forces ready to perpetrate aggression against us. In this way the
state maintains the posture of victim/defendant, while in reality it
pursues an active militaristic agenda.

In particular, what characterizes the post-9/11 state is, as Young
states, 'the patriarchal right (which) emerges from male specializa-
tion in security.'[16] The right of the patriarchal leader is founded
on his promise to protect. In return, citizens are to trust that our
leaders are making the right and necessary decisions to protect us.
Young writes, 'Because he bears this responsibility of leadership
… and because he takes risks and is ready to sacrifice, those under
his protection owe him deference and indulgence.'[17] According to
Young's account, female subordination is linked to the position of
being the protected one, and state hierarchical power sometimes
wears the mask of militarized aggression and, at other times, the
mask of virtuous love for those under the umbrella of protection.
The overarching message is this: 'You subordinate your actions
to our judgment of what is necessary, and we promise to keep
you safe.'[18] The willingness of the patriarchal leader to 'sacrifice,
moreover, increases citizens' quiescence and compliance. It would
be ungenerous to question, much less protest such self-giving.

That the vast majority of citizens failed for so long to recognize
the post-9/11 masculinist protection governmental scheme, only
serves to show just how naturalized such arrangements became for
us in this period. Among many examples of this dynamic, we might

15. Marion Young, 'Feminist Reactions', p. 225.
16. Marion Young, 'Feminist Reactions', p. 224.
17. Marion Young, 'Feminist Reactions'.
18. Marion Young, 'Feminist Reactions', p. 226.

remember Larry King's televised interview of former Head of the CIA, George Tenent, who in May 2007, spent a number of weeks circulating among television and other media outlets in the U.S. to promote his book, *At the Center of the Storm: My Years at the CIA.*[19] In this interview, Tenent repeatedly insisted that the 'enhanced interrogation' methods he authorized as Head of the CIA could not be described as torture and did produce important intelligence that aided the nation's security interests.

As in other interviews, in this televised encounter with Larry King, Tenent refused to discuss any particular events or details regarding either specific methods used in interrogations of terrorist suspects, or potential attacks that were prevented. With emphatic words and tone, he asserted his right as former Head of the CIA to insist that listeners take his word at face value without any proffered evidence to back up his claims. His supposed 'expertise' in security was enough to demand compliance and trust. Frustrated, at one point Larry King asked, 'But did it [the interrogations of supposed terrorists] produce useful information? Were you able to provide enhanced protection against attacks?' Tenent's response, firmly and unhesitatingly affirmative, while once again refusing to supply any specific details that would provide any evidence for his claims, revealed the very dynamic outlined by Young. Here was a blatant display of unquestioned privilege Tenent assumed in his role as intelligence expert/protector of the nation, a sense of patriarchal right that asked for and relied upon the citizenry's compliant faith in his intelligence/security expertise. U.S. citizens were to believe Tenent when he insisted that our government did not participate in or authorize acts of torture – because he said so. Further, we were to believe that 'enhanced interrogation methods,' whatever that phrase means, provided us greater security. We were not permitted to question further, but told that such questions would jeopardize the very security the protector labored to provide us. In fact, Tenent is only the tip of the iceberg in 'Top Secret America'; since 9/11 the industry of security expertise and secrecy has exploded within the United States. According to one investigation, 'The top-secret world

19. George Tenent, *At the Center of the Storm: My Years at the CIA* (New York: HarperCollins, 2007), *Larry King Live* featured the interview with Tenent on 30 April 2007. See *CNN Homepage: Larry King Live,* http://www.cnn.com/CNN/Programs/larry.king.live/, accessed 20 December 2009.

the government created in response to the terrorist attacks of Sept. 11, 2001, has become so large, so unwieldy and so secretive that no one knows how much money it costs, how many people it employs, how many programs exist within it or exactly how many agencies do the same work.'[20]

The fear, anxiety, anger and sense of helplessness felt by so many in the U.S. in the months and years following 9/11 no doubt proved fertile ground for the reification of this framework. But was it a 'good deal'? Having submitted to such a scheme, according to Young, there is much for U.S. citizens to be worried about. In the post-9/11 period, public decision-making autonomy seriously eroded, with dissent characterized as not only 'unpatriotic' but even 'ungrateful.' Legislative and judicial branches were weakened. In addition, the rights and dignity of many individuals, especially immigrants, certain ethnic minorities and foreigners, came under not only severe scrutiny but harassment, and in not a few cases, outright abuse as people were subjected to bodily harm, loss of livelihood, imprisonment and worse, without due process of law. By the time of the release of the torture memos by the Obama Administration in 2009, remembering Tenent's earlier insistence and U.S. citizens' compliance seems like a bad dream. Among other stories, we might remember Maher Arar, a Canadian citizen who was detained in 2002 by U.S. officials, when he changed planes at Kennedy International Airport on the way home from a vacation in Tunisia. Through the process of 'extraordinary rendition,' he was sent to Syria, where he spent a year imprisoned, and where he claims, he was tortured. Released in 2003, he later was exonerated by Canadian officials who asserted that he had no connections with terrorism. To date, all Arar's attempts to hold the United States accountable through its legal system have resulted in failure.[21]

All in all, Young summarizes, the system of masculinist chivalry expresses genuine concern and desire for its citizens' wellbeing, but within a clear hierarchy, separating those who have the right to decide from those placed in the feminine position, whose responsibility it is to demonstrate subordination.

20. Dana Priest and William M. Arkin, 'Top Secret America: A Hidden World, Growing Out of Control,' *The Washington Post*, 19 July 2010.

21. Benjamen Weiser, 'Appeals Court Hears Case of Canadian Citizen Sent by U.S. to Syria', *The New York Times*, 9 December 2008.

What feeds into this mindset? Why was it not more seriously questioned and held up for examination? What makes it plausible, in other words, what 'energizes' it? To answer to these questions we must dig beneath the foundation of the masculinist security regime to two supports undergirding it, first, the discourse of the Just War, and second, the language, symbology and practice of Christian atonement, especially sacrificial atonement.

In the United States, Just War discourse was the most all-encompassing framework that impacted discussion and analysis of 9/11 and 'the War on Terror.' The contours of the debate largely focused on how to *apply* the theoretical categories of Just War correctly, assuming that Just War theory provided the most compelling framework for analyzing most ethical quandaries associated with terrorism and war.[22] The 'Letter from America' is a case in point. Just War principles of just cause, legitimate authority, right intention, last resort, proportionality, probability of success, and noncombatant discrimination all may be found in this manifesto.

Yet reading this public letter from February 2002, with the benefit of years of hindsight, reveals how fraught with ambiguity the moral principles of Just War are in any application, and how easily they bend in diverse ethical directions. For instance, the writers of the 'Letter to America' asserted that 'the principles of just war teach us that wars of aggression and aggrandizement are never acceptable. Wars may not legitimately be fought for national glory, to avenge past wrongs, for territorial gain, or for any other nondefensive purpose.'[23] However, this principle of right intent, powerfully underscored in the letter, seems less and less certain as we look back with the perspective of hindsight. It appears more doubtful with every passing year that the wars in Afghanistan and Iraq have been free from the taint of revenge, empire building, or the imposition of democracy.[24]

22. See, for example, Michael Walzer, *Arguing about War*, Chapter entitled 'The Triumph of Just War Theory (and the Dangers of Success)' (New Haven, CT: Yale University Press, 2004, in which he argues for the ascendancy of Just War theory over any other method.

23. 'Letter to America,' p. 189. In Jean Bethke Elshtain, *Just War Against Terror* (New York: Basic Books, 2003).

24. In fact, as early as September 2002, a forum to debate the ethics of the looming Iraq war was organized through the Pew Forum on Religion and Public Life, and demonstrated the complex and uncertain nature of determining

In Just War thinking, an additional understanding of right intent that justifies going to war involves protection of those whose lives are endangered. Accordingly, the writers of the 'Letter from America' further justify their call to war on the basis that 'innocent people who are in no position to protect themselves will be grievously harmed unless coercive force is used to stop an aggressor...'[25] Yet one wonders, were there no other ways to address the needs of security outside of the wars that followed 9/11? Was some other response outside of the lurch toward war ever considered as a viable possibility?

In this same letter, the authors assert that the members of Al Qaeda had 'possible access to, and willingness to use, chemical, biological and nuclear weapons.'[26] Perhaps more than anything else, this perceived danger leads the authors of the letter to claim, 'In the name of universal human morality, and fully conscious of the restrictions and requirements of a Just War, we support our government's and our society's decision to use force of arms against them.'[27] However, as we have seen in the intervening years, adequately determining the intelligence behind the claims of weapons of mass destruction proved to be all too subject to error and failure, according to the 9/11 Commission.[28]

These 60 leaders who signed the 'Letter from America' had every good intention to 'seek to apply objective moral reasoning to war' in order to 'defend the possibility of civil society and a world community based in justice.'[29] But their very application of Just

the ethics of war in Iraq through reliance on Just War theory. Gerard Bradley, William A. Galston, John Kelsay and Michael Walzer debated questions of preventive/preemptive war, regime change as an acceptable end of Just War, and evidentiary claims regarding weapons of mass destruction in Iraq. See 'Iraq and Just War: A Symposium', *Pew Forum on Religion and Public Life*, 30 September 2002, http://pewforum.org/events/?EventID=36, accessed 27 October 2009. Among other resources, see Larry May (ed.), *War: Essays in Political Philosophy* (Cambridge: Cambridge University Press, 2008), for an anthology of essays that explore these and other compelling problems of Just War theory.

25. 'Letter to America', p. 189. In Elshtain, *Just War Against Terror*.

26. 'Letter to America', p. 192. In Elshtain, *Just War Against Terror*.

27. 'Letter to America' , p. 192. In Elshtain, *Just War Against Terror*.

28. See the *9/11 Commission Report*, National Commission on Terrorist Attacks upon the United States, http://govinfo.library.unt.edu/911/report/index.htm, accessed 11 October 2008.

29. 'Letter to America', p. 189. In Elshtain, *Just War Against Terror*.

War principles to the events of 9/11 and its aftermath, and their unswerving conclusion regarding 'the necessity of war-as-sacrifice' raise many more questions than answers. In this respect it is well worth thinking about Young's analysis in connection with the letter's use of Just War principles and thinking. As the authors of the 'Letter from America' make their case about the justice of this recommended war, they reference the fifth century writing of Augustine of Hippo: Augustine is a 'seminal contributor to just war thinking.' And indeed, the roots as well as the development of Just War thinking are in need of further investigation.

Augustine, the Just Judge and the Paterfamilias

In the post-9/11 period, Just War discourse was the dominant lens through which both U.S. leaders and most citizens interpreted terrorist events and the U.S. response. But is it possible that these same Just War theoretical frameworks played into the masculinist security regime outlined by Marion Young? In this section I explore one of Augustine's key writings related to the development of Just War theory, Book XIX from *The City of God*. I suggest that a feminist analysis of Augustine's ethic demonstrates that Just War theoretical perspectives emphasizing 'the necessity of war-as-sacrifice,' may in fact be linked to masculinist power structures and operations, and that at a minimum, a much more critical reading of Just War frameworks is in order.

Evaluating the 'Letter to America' with the benefit of hindsight throws into relief the palpable sense of threat felt in the United States in the months and early years following 9/11. In fact, massaging this very sense of threat regarding the possibility of continuing terror and violence 'against the homeland' proved to be a useful mechanism for shoring up the masculinist security regime. Here I will not enter into debate (though there indeed has been lively discussion) regarding the degree to which this threat was based in actual data, and the degree to which it was a useful political tool for the power structures in the U.S. My point is to underscore that measures of security and military response (or aggression) that in other situations might be thought of as extreme, in the post-9/11 climate were portrayed unrelentingly as 'necessary,' given the articulation of the dangers faced by the United States.

In other words, the populace was hammered with political discourse highlighting the potential of civil disintegration as a result of the specter of continuing terrorism on an increasing scale of violence. Understandable enough. In fact, it is possible to trace fear regarding civil destruction as a foundational element at a very early stage in the development of Just War theory, in the writing of St. Augustine. My particular concern here is Augustine's writing on war near the end of his life, as the threat of invasion from outsiders to the Roman Empire drew ever closer, bringing with it the likelihood of society's unraveling.

Augustine scholars emphasize the importance of exploring his thinking only in the immediate context of his own intellectual biography. His ideas changed, sometimes quite radically, over the span of his career.[30] Accordingly, *The City of God* reflects the precarious political situation that faced Augustine near the end of his life; already his society had witnessed the scandal of the sack of Rome in 410, and Africa was anticipating imminent invasion by the Vandals, with only the Roman legion as a buttress before what appeared to be coming civil chaos.[31] By the time of this writing, what had become preeminent in Augustine's thinking about politics was the question regarding use of power to secure some protection against social and civil disintegration, and the importance of 'securing a breathing space' as a barrier to keep conflict in check [32]

Given such an historical context, it is not difficult to understand Augustine's concern for protecting and maintaining civil order, even as he endeavored to call Rome to task for its corruption, and lust for

30. See R.A. Markus, 'Saint Augustine's Views on the "Just War"'. W.J. Shiels (ed.), *The Church and War: Papers Read at the Twenty-first Summer Meeting and Twenty-second Winter Meeting of the Ecclesiastical History Society* (Oxford: Blackwell, 1983). The third and longest stage in Augustine's thinking with respect to war has been described as 'a "hell on earth" era' in *The City of God*. See Alan J. Watt, 'Which Approach? Late Twentieth-Century Interpretations of Augustine's Views on War,' *Journal of Church and State* 46.1 (Winter 2004): 106.

31. See Lisa Sowle Cahill, 'In Readiness of Mind,' *Love Your Enemies: Discipleship, Pacifism, and Just War Theory* (Minneapolis, MN: Fortress Press, 1994), p. 66; Eugene TeSelle, 'Toward an Augustinian Politics,' in William S. Babcock (ed.), *The Ethics of St. Augustine* (Atlanta, GA: Scholars Press, 1991); Judith Chelius Stark (ed.), *Feminist Interpretations of Augustine* (University Park, PA: Pennsylvania State University Press, 2007).

32. Markus, 'Saint Augustine's Views on the "Just War"', p. 10. Also see, Judith Chelius Stark, 'Introduction,' *Feminist Interpretations of Augustine*, p. 7.

power. While the peace of the earthly city is in no way a substitute for the ultimate of heavenly peace, it is an extremely important social good that the ruler is obligated to preserve, and even analogically, an instrumental contribution to the wellbeing and progress of Christians called to heavenly peace.[33]

Yet in addition to the looming uncertainty of invasion and societal unrest, Augustine's writing about war also was influenced by his belief about the way the evils of war should be assessed. War has a positive function in Augustine's thinking, even an ethical purpose; war can be the means for restoration of the moral order in which various goods are appropriately distributed, and desires rightly grounded and arranged in their proper place. John Langan writes, 'The restoration of the right internal order of dispositions and desires constitutes a sufficient justification for resort to violence.'[34] Preservation of one's own life as a justification for violence, as in a Hobbesian conception of natural right, is not found in Augustine. On the contrary, even the evil a ruler may incur is not seen by Augustine as a justification for revolution, but as an opportunity for the faithful to be tested in virtue and reproved by God. However, for Augustine, the use of violence as a tool to restore individuals and society that have fallen into misplaced dispositions and desires, is not only permitted, but is a lamentable 'necessity' that rests on the shoulders of those occupying various leadership roles, be they within families, courts or states.

In Book XIX of *The City of God*, one key source for scholars focusing on Augustine's contribution to Just War theory, Augustine poses a fascinating juxtaposition of two figures: the tragic but wise judge, and the *paterfamilias*. His reflections on the vagaries of peace and violence all revolve around these two figures in Book XIX, and both finally are important analogues for Augustine's ethical analysis of the civil ruler waging war.[35]

33. John Langan, S.J., 'The Elements of St. Augustine's Just War Theory,' in William S. Babcock (ed.), *The Ethics of St. Augustine* (Atlanta, GA: Scholars Press, 1991), p. 179.

34. Langan, 'The Elements of St. Augustine's Just War Theory,' p. 175.

35. *Augustine, Bishop of Hippo, City of God* (trans. Henry Bettenson; Baltimore, MD: Penguin Books, 1972). *Against Faustus, Letters* 138 and 139, and *On Free Will* also are identified by scholars as key texts for investigation of Augustinian ethics on war and peace. Watt, 'Which Approach?', p. 112.

Augustine's pessimism in this period is clear from his description of the fragile nature of earthly happiness and its susceptibility to decay. The human body, mind and virtue itself, all are too easily overcome and dismantled. He summarizes, 'We are beset by evils, and we have to endure them steadfastly until we reach those goods where there will be everything to supply us with delight beyond the telling, and there will be nothing any longer that we are bound to endure.'[36] Indeed, peace (on earth) itself is 'a doubtful good,' since not even the household is free from traitors. If even the household may be described as a place of potential hostility and division, Augustine writes, then what of the earthly city or the world at large? Is there any hope at all for stability and peace?

At this juncture Augustine introduces the first member of the critical pair in this section, the tragic but wise judge. As Augustine emphasizes the impossible but necessary social role the judge finds himself occupying, a truly fascinating discussion of torture ensues. In the fifth century Roman context, the judge seeks the truth in a given case by torturing witnesses.[37] Though the accused may in fact be innocent, the judge orders such torture in order to retrieve intelligence. This is the first potential injustice the judge must confront, and in Augustine's mind, the judge's actions arise out of his intention to avoid a worse injustice, that is, sentencing a supposed 'criminal' to execution for a crime he did not commit. In words that sound astonishingly contemporary, Augustine acknowledges the conundrum the judge faces. The accused may very well confess to a crime he has not committed in order to avoid torture. After the prisoner's execution the judge still does not know for sure whether the right person justifiably has been punished. Augustine's writing is full of emotion as he laments this impossible situation, '… will our wise man take his seat on the judge's bench, or will he not have the heart to do so? Obviously, he will sit; for the claims of human society constrain him and draw him to this duty; and it is unthinkable to him that he should shirk it.'[38] This is the supposed 'necessity' of brute and unjust violent action, unavoidable because of human

36. Augustine, Bishop of Hippo, City of God, 19.4.
37. Of course, much contemporary scholarly literature on torture refutes the notion that reliable information may be secured through torture's application. Among many resources, see Darius Rejali, Torture and Democracy (Princeton, NJ: Princeton University Press, 2007).
38. Augustine, Bishop of Hippo, City of God, 19.6.

ignorance, yet 'necessary' because '… the exigencies of human society make judgment also unavoidable.' The best the judge can do, in Augustine's estimation, is to acknowledge the necessity of his role even while he hates it, and cry out, as the psalmist does to God, 'Deliver me from my necessities!'[39]

For Augustine, the tragic but wise judge is the analog to the ruler who also faces the 'necessity of waging just wars.'[40] Like the wise and tragic judge, the ruler laments the tragic 'necessity' of his situation: '… a man who experiences such evils, or even thinks about them, without heartfelt grief, is assuredly in a more pitiable condition…'[41] In both cases, 'necessity' is the factor that compels the one in charge to violence, including violence that might prove to be unjustifiable. In the end, 'necessity' comes to mean that there is no other recourse than violence.[42]

Nevertheless, the purpose behind the ruler's waging of war is to bring about peace. As Augustine says, '… it is an established fact that peace is the desired end of war.'[43] And there is no one who does not wish for peace; animals seek out their own kinds of peace; even robbers live in a type of peaceful association with other robbers. But how shall we understand the nature of this 'peace'? Augustine launches into a typology of peace that lays the groundwork for the second major figure in his juxtaposition, the *paterfamilias*. There is peace of the body in ordered proportion, peace of the soul in ordered appetites, and peace among men in agreement between minds (I intentionally reiterate Augustine's exclusive language here, for this

39. Augustine, Bishop of Hippo, *City of God*, 19.6.
40. Augustine, Bishop of Hippo, *City of God*, 19.7.
41. Augustine, Bishop of Hippo, *City of God*, 19.7.
42. For a history of the legal principle of 'military necessity' in the U.S., see Burrus M. Carnahan, 'Lincoln, Lieber and the Laws of War: The Origins and Limits of the Principle of Military Necessity,' *The American Journal of International Law*, Vol. 92 (April, 1992): 213–31. Carnahan writes, 'That military necessity was originally a limit on state action, and should still function as a limit, seems to have been forgotten… military necessity is widely regarded today as an insidious doctrine invoked to justify almost any outrage.' See page 230. 'Necessity,' in this understanding, is meant to act primarily as a restraint on violent action, though, as Carnahan acknowledges ruefully, popular reference to 'necessity' today tends to serve exactly the opposite purpose, to support and rationalize violent action.
43. Augustine, Bishop of Hippo, *City of God*, 19.12.

peace between men turns out to be very different if women are introduced into the equation).

Next Augustine moves to describing the peace of the household and this is where we must begin reading his text more slowly, for this peace is described as 'the ordered agreement among those who live together about giving and obeying orders.'[44] The peace of the fifth century household in Augustine's Roman context depends on knowing who gives the orders, and who is responsible for subordinating oneself to those orders. In contrast, the peace of the Heavenly City is '… a perfectly ordered and perfectly harmonious fellowship in the enjoyment of God, and a mutual fellowship in God.'[45] In other words, the peace of the Heavenly City appears to result in a less coercive and hierarchical set of relationships than those required for the peace of the earthly household.[46]

For Augustine, such ordering of the household is nothing less than expressive of God's intended creation. In the divinely inspired 'order of nature,' and as the given framework of human society, the man has responsibility for his household. He is the *paterfamilias* who 'takes care of his own people.' Not out of 'lustful domination' but from a 'dutiful concern for the interests of others,' the male head of household has the unquestioned right to give orders to wives, children, servants/slaves. In matters of worship there is 'equal affection' for all the members of the household, but in other aspects of life, the sharp distinction between different genders, children and slaves is to be maintained '… in respect of the temporal goods of this life.'[47]

44. Augustine, Bishop of Hippo, *City of God*, 19.13.

45. Augustine, Bishop of Hippo, *City of God*, 19.13.

46. Yet even this heavenly communion is predicated, for Augustine, on a transformation of women's reproductive body parts involved in sex and childbirth. Rosemary Radford Ruether, 'Sexuality, Gender and Women, *Feminist Interpretations of Augustine*,' p. 63.

47. Augustine, Bishop of Hippo, *City of God*, 19.16. Feminist interpreters of Augustine largely agree that he accorded women the status of being created in God's image. Yet immediately this status begins to shrink, for women's *imago dei* is meant only in a spiritual sense, not nearly as fully as men, and is expressed at all with great hesitation. According to Stark, 'We are left to imagine… what might have happened had Augustine drawn out the implications of his own paradigm of interrelationship, based on equality, mutuality and reciprocity, that he discovered as the inner life of God. He brought these insights to bear on the inner life of human beings, but not to human beings themselves

As the *pater*, the male head of household is entrusted with the right and responsibility to reprove those who threaten domestic peace. This may take place through word or physical blows, '… or any other kind of punishment that is just and legitimate.' The point is that Augustine understands such reprisal to be '… intended to morally readjust (the offender) to the domestic peace from which he had broken away.'[48] It is an act of kindness and love. Almost immediately after this passage Augustine draws the reader back to the larger circle of the city, for which the household is the microcosm: 'now a man's house ought to be the beginning, or rather a small component part of the city…'[49] From an overarching perspective, Augustine's understanding of the ethical role of the *pater*, as well as the judge, may be traced back to his emphasis on the two great commandments: Love God, and love your neighbor as yourself. Thus, these patriarchal figures are to do no harm, but to enact 'kindness' through restraining those socially located beneath them, by punishing their sin and returning them to the 'natural order' of social relations. In the end, Augustine tautly pulls the line of continuity through the judge, the *pater*, and the ruler who wages war with a summary statement: the peace of the earthly city is fundamentally *based* on relations '… concerning the giving and obeying of orders to the establishment.'[50] From start to finish, this is a hierarchical system with a given power structure justified through divine intention [51]

and their relationships.' Judith Chelius Stark, 'Augustine on Women,' *Feminist Interpretations of Augustine*, p. 238.

48. See Rosemary Radford Ruether, 'Sexuality, Gender and Women,' regarding Augustine's comparison of the marital relationship to master and slave. 'The good Christian wife distinguished herself by her total abnegation of her will to that of her husband, even if he be violent and ill tempered,' p. 57.

49. Augustine, Bishop of Hippo, *City of God*, 19.16. As Eric Gregory has noted, an ethic of care that fails seriously to analyze structural realities of patriarchy and parochialism all too easily infantilizes and otherwise diminishes and harms the objects of care. See, Eric Gregory, *Politics and the Order of Love: An Augustinian Ethic of Democratic Citizenship* (Chicago, IL: University of Chicago Press, 2008), pp. 171–75.

50. Augustine, Bishop of Hippo, *City of God*, 19.17.

51. Ruether writes that in this later stage of his life, Augustine's writing about God imagery is 'purged' of any mothering traits, instead focusing on God as the strict *paterfamilias*, whose punishing love is retributive, though 'meant for the son's own good.' See 'Sexuality, Gender and Women,' p. 63.

My interest is in the connection between chivalrous patriarchal rule and the development of Just War theory. We can sum
up Augustine's argument by underscoring that the wise but tragic
judge, the *paterfamilias*, and the civic ruler all foreshadow Young's
contemporary analysis of chivalrous patriarchal rule based in protection. Just as in the current masculinist scheme, what is at stake
for Augustine is the drive to preserve civil stability and order that is
perceived to be at risk because of outside threat. Augustine assumes
the patriarchal right, indeed, the 'necessity' of all three figures to exercise control and execute various forms of control – even violence
– and likewise assumes the unquestioning subordination of those
beneath these authorities in the social hierarchy. The protection
of the patriarchs provides ongoing societal stability. But not only
is stability at stake, moral order is involved here as well. All three
patriarchs provide moral oversight through punishment and violence. Thus, the right or necessity to torture and execute, to wage
war, and to give orders and punish within the household result
in an architectonic whose levels cohere. These actions correspond
not only to the patriarchs' responsibility for social stability, but are
an essential part of their duty to maintain the moral order itself,
albeit an earthly moral order that can never rise to the moral perfec-
tion of the Heavenly City. This is the 'love-as-killing paradox' in
Augustinian ethics, made 'necessary' by the depth of evil and sin in
the world. As one scholar writes,

> The famous dictum: "Love and do as you will," – is a way of justi-
> fying the use of harsh measures for the correction of those in error;
> as long as one is motivated by love, one can follow one's instincts
> and go about chastising... There is solicitude, but of a patriarchal
> sort; the subordinates are given no rights of participation, let alone
> resistance.[52]

Clearly, this description of Augustinian ethics calls to mind Young's
insight regarding the various masks worn by the patriarchal ruler,
the mask of aggression intermixed with the mask of protection for
those he loves. But Young protests that the right to security ought

---

52. TeSelle, 'Toward an Augustinian Politics,' p. 151. Lisa Sowle Cahill
writes, '... love can come to mean, not nonviolence, but a particular attitude
motivating violent acts. Augustine unites love to violence by speaking of them
together as punishment, which has in view the good of the offender.' See Lisa
Sowle Cahill, 'In Readiness of Mind,' *Love Your Enemies*, p. 79.

not to be brokered through the requirement of unquestioning sub-mission. In contrast to Young's critique, for Augustine,

> "Peace" then is the object of this hierarchical society: peace in the Empire as a whole and peace in the "families", both large and small, of which it was made up. According to both official pro-nouncements and no doubt much popular practice, such peace could best be secured by a "loving" relationship between the various inferiors and superiors: such would be case in the "ideal" society. But where the "love" of an inferior failed, it could be re-inforced by blows and whippings, a discipline by inconveniences, or, in the case of states, by war.[53]

Thus, Augustine's writing near the end of his life combines an ancient version of a patriarchal protective scheme with the intellec-tual roots of Just War tradition. Moreover, as Young suggests, not only in ancient times but today as well, the promise of protection, especially in a time of fear of civil disintegration, all too easily may lead, even in democracies such as the United States, to a reemer-gence of these paternalistic and hierarchical regimes that require subordination. Indeed, additional characteristics from the ancient masculinist security regime find a parallel in our contemporary U.S. political context. For instance, language commonly was used in the post-9/11 period to justify the 'War on Terror' as a moral im-perative designed to rightly punish wrongdoers, or to 'advance the cause of democracy' in places characterized as primitive and under-developed morally and socially. Here the contemporary patriarchal right exceeded even the demand for unquestioned obedience and subordination from those protected, to include an additional right, the moral superiority to know what was best for one's 'enemy,' and the right and responsibility to punish the enemy 'for his own good,' 'in order that democracy may advance.'[54] In this way we see how in

53. John M. Rist, *Augustine: Ancient Thought Baptized* (Cambridge: Cambridge University Press, 1994), p. 212.
54. In his State of the Union speech in January 2007, announcing his inten-tion to escalate the number of troops in the Iraq war, President Bush offered the following rationale: 'These young Americans (U.S. troops) understand that our cause in Iraq is noble and necessary – and that the advance of freedom is the calling of our time' (see, The Whitehouse, http://www.whitehouse.gov/news/releases/2007/01/20070123-2.html, accessed 4 January 2010. In con-trast to President Bush's rationale, Just War tradition considers such 'civilizing wars' as a kind of 'secularized holy war/crusade.' In other words, this rationale

both the ancient and contemporary cases, the role of male protector carries with it the sense of moral guardianship, entailing not only entitlement to make decisions, enforce one's will, and assume or enforce the compliance of the subordinate, but in addition, the right to foist one's own sense of moral good on the other, whose responsibility it is to receive it gratefully.

The 'love-as-killing paradox,' embedded in masculinist protective schemes and found in the roots of Just War thinking, is alive and well up to and including our own historical moment. Scholars trace the way this discourse threads its way through the further development of Just War thinking beyond Augustine in the Reformers and, in the twentieth century, in theologians such as Paul Ramsey and Reinhold Niebuhr.[55] This discourse continues the portrayal of war as 'necessary'; moreover, the 'sacrifice' incurred through war is also 'necessary' and, if tragic, nevertheless a moral good.[56]

If, as Young asserts, the post-9/11 period in the U.S. thoroughly was characterized by the rise of a masculinist security regime that proffered protection in exchange for subordination, this dynamic was linked rhetorically to the discourse of Just War with the leitmotif of necessity and sacrifice as its driving force. The dominance of this rhetoric in the West since the time of Augustine surely is part of the energizing electricity that gives the 'necessity of war-as-sacrifice' its current power and sway, but there is still more to be said. Remember the strong outcry from the conclusion of the 'Letter from America': 'In the name of universal human morality, and fully conscious of the restrictions and requirements of a Just War, we support our government's, and our society's, decision to use force

is little more than a thin veneer that provides a pretext to cover empire's true colonizing intent. See Gary Simpson, *War, Peace and God: Rethinking the Just War Tradition* (Minneapolis, MN: Augsburg Fortress, 2007), p. 65.

55. See Cahill, *Love Your Enemies*, for a thorough investigation of this history.

56. In fact, Niebuhr's analysis of conflict is modulated with his sense of irony and suspicion of human tendencies to justify violence in order to protect power. Though Elshtain acknowledges Niebuhr's distrust and hesitation along these lines, and while she in fact finds the same doubt and hesitancy in her study of Augustine's writing on war, she does not focus on masculinist elements of patriarchal power embedded in Just War theory from its roots in Augustine onwards. See Niebuhr, *Moral Man and Immoral Society* (New York: Scribner's Sons, 1960); Elshtain, *Augustine and the Limits of Politics* (Notre Dame, IN: University of Notre Dame Press, 1995).

of arms against them.'[57] How shall we understand and interpret this unequivocal call for war?

Scholars propose various answers to this question. For instance, Mark Lewis Taylor focuses on the adamant Manichean assumptions regarding Al Qaeda that drove the framework of *this* fight as representative of a larger cosmological battle between good and evil. In his mind, the broad brushstrokes of a cognitive framework emphasizing irredeemably evil and irrational terrorists stoked the flames and worked against other dynamics. He would have wished to see more Americans inquiring about the relationship between a long history of U.S. interventionism abroad, all too often to serve corporate economic interests, and reactive resentment on the part of Bin Laden (and others) regarding U.S. military presence on Saudi soil. Instead of the turn to victimage rhetoric, we should push for a more comprehensive theological exposition of evil, as well as a deeper historical analysis of U.S. interventionism, as a more productive way forward.

But the lurch toward war was influenced not only by cognitive frameworks that regard evil as a cosmic generative force to be battled within a historical context; Jeffrey Stout in addition considers the significance of the ideology of necessity that in any historical time of exigency may be called upon and manipulated by political leaders. 'Beware of leaders pleading necessity,' he warns us. Especially when leaders' immoral acts become public, such as the condoning of torture or bombing of civilians, all too commonly they may declare that the exigency of the moment required such extreme and 'necessary' measures in order to preserve the social good of security. He writes, 'The necessity excuse belongs to a vicious cycle that has been detrimental to democracy in contexts as different as the final phase of the war against Japan, nuclear deterrence during the Cold War, the Balkans in the 1990s, the Israeli-Palestinian conflict, and the global struggle against terrorism.'[58]

Strict Father Morality and Politics

In addition to the analyses above outlined by Taylor and Stout, a deeper investigation into discursive elements that provide a

57. 'Letter to America,' p. 192. In Elshtain, *Just War Against Terror.*
58. Jeffrey Stout, *Democracy and Tradition* (Princeton, NJ: Princeton University Press, 2004), p. 186.

foundation for the rise of the masculinist security regime is in order. Along with exploring the links between the masculinist security regime and Just War discourse, in this section I turn to the work of cognitive linguist George Lakoff, who analyzes common patterns of thinking to show how they are shaped by cognitive metaphors that are widely shared in the public discursive realm. Our accepted ways of thinking, writing and speaking, make possible social worlds and specific dynamics of power.[59] But these accepted ways of thinking are mostly unconsciously used to perceive, think, analyze and judge. Humans draw upon conceptual metaphors, through which they use one domain of experience to help interpret another. Lakoff writes, 'We use an elaborate system of concepts (in our thinking), but we are not usually aware of just what those concepts are like and how they fit together into a system.'[60] According to this analytical framework, human minds make sense of puzzling phenomena by drawing on available and dominant cognitive metaphors for the purpose of interpretation, understanding and action. Lakoff's analysis of cognitive metaphors is a helpful methodological tool for understanding the discursive elements that energized the masculinist security regime, and that cemented connections between this regime, 'necessity' and 'sacrifice' in the post-9/11 period.

In particular, we can draw on Lakoff's exploration of subconscious cognitive metaphors to better grasp the way that people in the U.S. make political judgments. Family-based metaphors explain what seem to be political paradoxes. For instance, conservatives see no contradiction in their position as right-to-life advocates who *also* are in favor of capital punishment; and liberals support welfare and education political initiatives, *and also* the right to abortion. Not only do the family paradigms explain *why* certain seemingly inexplicable stands on unrelated issues go together (i.e. gun control goes with social programs); the conceptual models of two different family types represent world views that shape and enforce choice of key topics, words, and forms of reasoning in both liberal and conservative discourse.[61]

59. See Judith Perkins, *The Suffering Self: Pain and Narrative Representation in the Early Christian Era* (London: Routledge, 1995), p. 6.

60. George Lakoff, *Moral Politics: How Liberals and Conservatives Think* (Chicago, IL: University of Chicago Press, 2002, 2nd edn), p. 4.

61. Lakoff, *Moral Politics*, pp. 32–33.

The place to begin is with the familial models outlined by Lakoff, the 'Nurturant Parent and the Strict Father,' both of which are connected to the equally unconscious cognitive metaphor of 'the Nation as Family.' As Lakoff writes, 'It is the common, unconscious, and automatic metaphor of the Nation-as-Family that produces contemporary conservatism from the Strict Father morality and contemporary liberalism from Nurturant Parent morality.'[62] Specific beliefs and values underlie each of these metaphors. The Strict Father family model begins with the conviction that the world is inherently dangerous and subject to evil, and underscores the Father's responsibility to support and protect the family, and to set family policy:

> He [the Strict Father] teaches children right from wrong by setting strict rules for their behavior and enforcing them through punishment... He also gains their cooperation by showing love and appreciation when they do follow the rules. But children must never be coddled, lest they become spoiled; a spoiled child will be dependent for life and will not learn proper morals.[63]

Strength and authority are strongly emphasized in Strict Father morality. In fact, morality is conceptualized *as* strength, as in having moral backbone. One builds this strength through self-discipline and hard work, and through asceticism and self-denial (otherwise one is morally flabby and self-indulgent). The Strict Father has the responsibility for modeling and building this same kind of strength in his family. At the same time, Strict Father morality is accompanied by a certain understanding of evil as a force that strength is needed to counter. Evil has no truth on its own, and can never be empathized with or understood; the only way to deal with evil is to combat it.[64]

It's not difficult to see how Strict Father morality grows from a hierarchical understanding of leadership with a clearly defined

62. Lakoff, *Moral Politics*, p. 13.

63. Lakoff, *Moral Politics*, pp. 65–66. Lakoff explores the views of James Dobson and his Center, 'Focus on the Family,' as one clear proponent of the Strict Father model. At the same time, Strict Father cognitive frameworks may be utilized by individuals in their own family life but not at the level of politics, or vice versa; some individuals may employ more of a nurturant family dynamic within their individual family but look to a Strict Father model at the level of their political thinking and decision-making.

64. Lakoff, *Moral Politics*, pp. 74–76.

authority figure, the male parent, whose oversight provides guidance for those subject to him. This moral order legitimates certain power relations as the natural order, and is undergirded by a 'folk theory,' with God at the top, adults over children, men over women, people over animals and plants, etc.[65] This means that dominance is tightly linked to moral authority, and morality becomes equivalent to staying within the hierarchical boundaries set forth by the paradigm.

The 'Strict Father' cognitive framework, Lakoff asserts, undergirds conservative political thought and morality. Conservatives tend to promote Strict Father morality in general, highlight the importance of self-discipline and sacrifi e, and work with a moral system of reward and punishment. They support the pursuit of self-interest on the part of those who are self-disciplined, and punishment for those who are lazy, insufficiently self-reliant, and/or those who stray from the moral hierarchies in the Strict Father paradigm.[66]

It should be obvious that the Strict Father cognitive metaphor shares many of the same characteristics I have already explored in Young's investigation of the masculinist security regime. Along with Augustine's *pater*, just judge and civil ruler, this model evinces the assumption of a supposedly benign patriarchal hierarchy based on an understanding of natural order or divine intention. All three models, moreover, share very similar understandings of the nature of evil as inexplicable and irredeemable, something only to be fought against. Finally, all three assert the right to violence as a form of justified punishment or moral pedagogy, in other words, violence as the tragically 'necessary' and moral response to evil.

Having outlined Lakoff's analysis, we can return to the questions posed at the beginning of this chapter regarding the vehement reaction of the Fairmount townspeople in response to the women's peace group. What motivated their thinking and emotion; why did a proposal for a governmental department for peace cause such a ruckus? Lakoff would point to the 'plausibility structure' that subconsciously informed the reaction of the townspeople. In fact, the post-9/11 elevation of a masculinist security regime response in the U.S., and the emotional response of Fairmount, MN, to the Peace Department Proposal, were not accidents; similar conceptual

65. Lakoff, *Moral Politics*, p. 81.
66. Lakoff, *Moral Politics*, p. 163.

metaphors came together that encouraged specific ways of thinking, interpreting and valuing, not only in the Minnesota small town, but also in a group of more than 60 top leaders and academics, and indeed, a majority within a nation. As Lakoff summarizes,

> Many people think that words are "mere words" – just labels for aspects of an objective reality. Cognitive linguists know better. The way we use language both reflects how we think about something, and can impose on other people a way of seeing the world. Language matters, and the ideas (often metaphorical ideas) expressed by language matter.[67]

Lakoff's work helps us to better understand the plausibility structure at work that promotes the idea of war as the only and necessary response to conflict. However, his analysis can be pushed even further. Thus far we have been exploring the links between Just War thinking and masculinist protective orders, but Just War theory is also deeply embedded in a broader Christian discourse about necessity, suffering and salvation. In the next section of this chapter we will see that the plausibility structure of 'the necessity of war' gains further voltage from Christian convictions, practices and language regarding sacrifice and salvation. This is the additional element of the cognitive framework we need to understand in order adequately to analyze the U.S. post-9/11 context.

Increased Voltage: Christian Sacrifice Electrifying the Nexus of Necessit

In the section above I noted how the 'Strict Father' family metaphor emphasizes a system in which one builds up moral strength through obeying moral authority, and by staying within prescribed moral boundaries. Here I further explore Lakoff's investigation of the metaphors involved in the concept of sacrificial exchange.

According to Lakoff, the dominant cognitive metaphor for morality is that of wealth, or 'keeping the moral books.' In this framework, wellbeing is equivalent to financial riches, and loss of wellbeing is a 'cost.'[68] He writes,

> The metaphor by which we conceptualize well-being as wealth is a metaphor that is ubiquitous and important in our conceptual systems. Whenever we are not talking literally about money, and

---

67. Lakoff, *Moral Politics*, p. 399.
68. Lakoff, *Moral Politics*, p. 44.

we ask whether a course of action is "worth it," we are using this financial metaphor to treat the resulting well-being or harm as if they were money and to see if the course of action is sufficiently "profitable. [69]

According to Lakoff, various moral schemes are related to the concept of moral accounting, including reciprocation, retribution, restitution, revenge, altruism and more. Within these schemes, the words, 'owe, debt, and pay' all are financially-based terms that are commonly used. However, this is not only a secular moral metaphor, but has strong ties to Christian understanding as well.

Both the Strict Father and the Nurturant Parent cognitive metaphors interpret suffering as a way of either acquiring moral credit, or paying off moral debt.[70] More to the point, this cognitive framework is tied to both liberal and conservative Christian frameworks. Lakoff describes the way in which Christian atonement is most popularly understood in just these terms. Jesus, through his suffering, pays off 'mankind's Original Sin debit'; he 'makes the ultimate sacrifice' in order to 'balance the sins of the entire human race.'[71] Thus, suffering is calibrated in a kind of moral arithmetic through which one is imputed moral credit at both historical and metaphysical levels. While various theological accounts might dispute this as a crude exposition of the inner workings of salvation, Lakoff's point is that cognitively, this is the popular understanding that tends to be at work in American Christianity.

Whether this calculus measures Jesus as sacrificed by God the Father to suffer more than the total possible suffering of humankind forever (as in a Strict Father/*penal substitutionary* morality scheme), or equates Jesus as the perfect nurturer who sacrifices himself by suffering to balance the sins of the entire human race out of solidarity and empathy with the plight of humans (as in a Nurturant Parent/*moral exemplar* dynamic), the point remains the same. Suffering becomes a necessary mechanism for human well-being, or, to put it in religious terms, suffering is necessary for human salvation. Moreover, this cognitive framework, the 'necessity' of suffering and sacrifice for salvation, collides with and melds together with the 'necessity' of the Just War, so much so that both

69. Lakoff, *Moral Politics*, p. 45.
70. Lakoff, *Moral Politics*, p. 249.
71. Lakoff, *Moral Politics*, pp. 249, 259.

the soldier's and Jesus' death are referred to with identical terminology: both are regularly described as 'the ultimate sacrifice.'

The mutual, even electric attraction between the 'necessity' of sacrifice in war and the 'necessity' of sacrifice in popular Christian understanding and practice has not been lost on theologians. What is at stake here are the 'deep-seated issues of power and authority, and the mythologies, theologies and underlying assumptions' in the subconscious subterranean field that lies beneath. As theologian Mary Condren has written,

> The work of sacrifice is the work of power: it is the work of excluding, rejecting and vilifying those uncomfortable parts of ourselves and projecting them on to a victim... The work of sacrifice is the work of war: the instant solutions of the politics of aggression, and the spurious power gained by demonizing the Other.[72]

'The necessity of war-as-sacrifice' not only masks power relations, but promises quick, powerful and effective solutions, as we have seen in one too many Hollywood war-films. In addition to Condren's reflections, one might turn to Jürgen Moltmann's analysis of the links between Christian pastoral care and the battlefield during World War I:

> Glorification of the war and sanctifications of the soldier's sacrifice on the front by bishops of the Protestant national churches were even worse, because they conveyed the message that Christ is present in the soldier who gives his life for his friends, and anyone who is killed in the noble cause of his Fatherland will be forever engraved in the memory of his people. One can still find monuments of Christlike dying soldiers in the memorials of World War I.[73]

All this leads to the conclusion that what we have before us is a deadly nexus. Just war discourse, influenced by the assumptions of the masculinist security regime, gains further traction from moral/religious notions of sacrifici l exchange. Put differently, Just War discourse undergirds the masculinist security regime, even as religious

72. Mary Condren, 'The Theology of Sacrifice and the Non-Ordination of Women,' in Elisabeth Schüssler-Fiorenza and Hermann Haring (eds), *The Non-Ordination of Women and the Politics of Power* (Maryknoll, NY: Orbis Books, 1999), p. 56.

73. Jürgen Moltmann, 'The Cross as a Military Symbol for Sacrifice,' in Marit Trelstad (ed.), *Cross Examinations: Readings on the Meaning of the Cross Today* (Minneapolis, MN: Augsburg Fortress, 2006), p. 262.

language permeated by sacrificial images and understandings also enlivens the same nexus. When we examine Just War thinking more carefully, we see that it operates precisely *through* the mechanism of sacrifice; it is the sacrality of the sacrificial exchange through which the losses and damages associated with war are justified and made meaningful. Moreover, the power and ubiquity of sacrificial images and mechanisms in Just War bleed into and are empowered by sacrificial understandings and images that emerge from Christian understandings of salvation. Just as the sacrifice of Jesus is declared theologically necessary for Christian salvation, so the mechanism of sacrifice explains, rationalizes and transcendentalizes the necessity of the Just War.

Current and all-too-painful examples of just this plausibility structure may be found among liberals and conservatives alike in the United States in the quest to interpret the significance of the wars in Iraq and Afghanistan, and most specifically, the deaths of those fighting these wars. On the political right, in a May 2007 issue of *The American Legion*, an article narrated the story of soldier Adam Galvez, killed by an Improvised Explosive Device (IED) in Iraq. When interviewed for the article, his father said, 'He died a hero, and that's all I need to know as a father.' Adam's mother remained insistent regarding the need to support the mission of the war, saying,

> People may not agree with the reason we went to war, but while our troops are over there, we can't be telling the world that what they are doing is wrong. If we say that we support them, we have to support what they're doing.[74]

In this way Mrs. Galvez linked a positive interpretation of her son's death with emphasis on the necessity of the mission behind warring action. The writer of the article concluded, '… for those who have made the supreme *sacrific* in this war, the United States must prevail in Iraq.' Mrs. Galvez continued,

> I told President Bush last summer that the biggest insult anyone could hand me would be to pull the troops out before the job is complete. If we're going to quit, at that point I'll have to ask, "Why did my son die?"[75]

74. Matt Grills, 'Death, Not in Vain,' *American Legion* (May 2007), p. 30.
75. Grills, 'Death, Not in Vain,' p. 34.

Thus, in Mrs. Galvez' mind, what was at stake was the worthiness of this exchange, the life of a young man in exchange for the success of what is declared to be a necessary war. A positive valence to this sacrificial exchange depends upon success in the overall mission. According to this understanding, the just nature of the Iraq war necessitates and makes meaningful the sacrifice of young men such as Adam Galvez, even as it implies that backing away from war would be an injustice.

On the other hand, on the political left, the question was framed in much the same terms by the woman who has been called the 'face' for the anti-war movement in the United States, Cindy Sheehan. On 28 May 2007, writing in her online diary, she publicly resigned her role as spokesperson, telling her supporters and the world that she was doing so because she came to the conclusion that her son's death as a U.S. soldier fighting the Iraq war was meaningless. Not only is it impossible to justify the Iraq war, however (and it is here that we need to pay attention to the cognitive metaphor operative in this logic), if the American people could be made to see the injustice of the war and could be motivated to act against it, then Casey's death would not be in vain, but a meaningful sacrifice. What is so fascinating in this context is the similarity of Sheehan's sacrificial plausibility structure to that of the Galvez family. Sheehan wrote,

> … it is so painful to me to know that I bought into this system for so many years and Casey paid the price for that allegiance… Goodbye America … you are not the country that I love and I finally realized that no matter how much I sacrifice, I can't make you be that country unless you want it.[76]

Most painfully, to Mrs. Sheehan, Casey 'paid the price' through his suffering and sacrifice. Mrs. Sheehan's analysis is striking regarding the nature of the cost that was paid by way of Casey's death; in her mind, Casey's death was in part due to her own allegiance, her 'buy in' to the system of 'empire of the good old U.S. of A' with which she aligned herself for so many years. Mrs. Sheehan's conviction is built upon the notion that her son's death might become meaningful if her work as an anti-war activist has an effect in changing U.S. policy; still most telling is that while Mrs. Sheehan's conclusion about the

76. Cindy Sheehan, 'Good Riddance, Attention Whore,' (28 May 2007), *The Daily Kos*, http://www.dailykos.com/storyonly/2007/5/28/12530/1525, accessed 4 June 2001.

just nature of the Iraq war is the mirror opposite of that espoused by Mrs. Galvez, both interpretations rely on exactly the same logic. In both cases, the plausibility structure remains the same: sacrifice is an exchange between the state and the subject, a form of currency through which moral credit is bartered and accounted. Moreover, moral credit accumulates through suffering, and finally, it is justified by way of 'necessity,' a term that is left basically undefine

From 9/11 onward, President George Bush repeatedly framed the rationale of both the wars in Afghanistan and Iraq in terms of the sacred and necessary sacrifice of members in the military (and their families).[77] President Barack Obama continued use of the same language as his Administration began. Theologians have not missed this important and problematic connection. One only need look so far as the terminology used to describe both the military and the religious settings. In the trope of 'the ultimate sacrifice,' Jesus' sacrifice 'bleeds' into and informs the meaning of the sacrifi e of soldiers in death. At times of potential or actual war, the resurgence of the masculinist security regime is electrified by the discourse of sacrifice so as to undergird the assumption of the 'necessary' Just War. Chapter Four explores this electrical interplay further and raises questions about the continuing viability of sacrificial frameworks in Christian self-understanding and practice.

Conclusion

The ideology of 'the necessity of war-as-sacrifice,' energized by the twin discourses of the Just War and sacrificial religious understandings, resurged in the U.S. masculinist security regime in the post-9/11 period and is in need of further investigation and critique. I here wish to offer four ways forward in this important process.

First, deeper investigation of the relationship between sacrifice, necessity and masculinist security regimes is in order. Especially in times of fear or crisis, when possible disruption to political and social orders appears all too likely, sacrificial rhetoric lubricates the machinations of unequal power relations, social, political and economic. While Chapter Two's analysis of the rhetoric from the Bush Administration is a case in point, we should not relax our alertness to the ongoing danger of this dynamic. When President Obama accepted the Nobel Peace Prize, and spoke very frankly in his speech

77. Chapter Two explores this rhetoric and its significance.

about the 'necessity of the sacrifice of war,' though many other aspects of his speech were criticized, this foundational logic went unchallenged. Does 'peace entail sacrifice,' as he claimed? Is it an unquestionable given that the only way to 'purchase' global security for the United States is through '… the blood of our citizens and the strength of our arms'?[78] As we have seen, the religious underpinning of the 'ultimate sacrifice' discourages critical analysis of the methods, mechanisms and operations of U.S. War-culture; and use and abuse of familiar religious symbology mystifies and disciplines the imagination and discourages non-militarized avenues of response to conflict

Second, we must raise greater consciousness regarding the nefarious interplay between 'the ultimate sacrifice' and Just War discourse. The conflation of religious symbol and Just War terminology imbues the violence of war with a sacred canopy that also renders it impermissible to challenge. Nevertheless, what we see more often than not in our contemporary political moment is the distancing and dissimulation of such critical analysis. Too frequently Just War discourse blesses war through sacrificial language such as in the 'Letter to America.' This explains what seems an automatic reaction on the part of so many to warring response, framed as the only possible and 'necessary' reaction, and dismissing other non-killing methods as useless and untrustworthy, dangerous and even cowardly. Not only are non-warring responses seen as weak and ineffectual, killing methods assume a connection to divine intention.[79]

78. 'Remarks by the President at the Acceptance of the Nobel Peace Prize,' 10 December 2009, The Whitehouse.gov, http://www.whitehouse.gov/the-press-office/remarks-president-acceptance-nobel-peace-p ize, accessed 14 January 2010.

79. At times the Iraq war was linked to divine intention quite explicitly, falling into the category of 'holy war.' For instance, in May 2009, *The New York Times* reported on daily cover sheets, approved by Secretary of Defense Donald Rumsfeld for the Secretary of Defense Worldwide Intelligence Update. Only declassified in May 2009, these sheets originally were hand-delivered to the White House and initially were only seen by an audience including the president and inner circle. The cover sheets were comprised of 'triumphal color photos of the [Iraq] war headlined by biblical quotations.' For instance, following the first indications of trouble with 'Shock and Awe,' the daily sheet included Josh. 1.9 on the headline: 'Have I not commanded you? Be strong and courageous. Do not be terrified; do not be discouraged; for the LORD your God will be with you wherever you go.' Frank Rich, 'Obama Can't Turn the Page on Bush,' *The New York Times*, 17 May 2009.

Once again, an important aspect of what is shielded through this sacrificial language has to do with the economic stakes involved, and who serves to benefit through the mechanics of war. Thus the power dynamics behind warring response neatly become bracketed, hidden from view, through Just War's calculations of sacrificial exchange. Separating sacrificial mechanisms and discourse from Just War theoretical categories is a way to begin, so that we may better evaluate Just War theory's usefulness as a critical analytical tool to help us navigate a world filled with conflict. At the same time, one wonders whether Just War theory makes much sense outside of the largely invisible sacrificial relations upon which it appears to be based. All this points to the importance of a much more critical and thorough-going analysis of the history, culture and theory of Just War discourse. The contemporary analytical trend, focusing on how to correctly apply Just War principles, stops far too short.

We may hope that greater honesty about patriarchal dynamics embedded in Just War theory and thinking will help us distinguish valid principals from political expediency used to buttress inequitable power dynamics. However, while peace churches stand out as an exception, other Christian denominations frequently embrace enthusiastically and wholeheartedly Just War theoretical thinking, and are too uninvolved in critically analyzing the ways that specifically Christian forms of discourse and understanding may enliven (even if unintentionally) war-culture.

Third, a deeper investigation of the actual dynamics of sacrifice is in order. In the case of Just War as well as the Christian understanding conflated with it, sacrifice operates as a patriarchal operation of exchange. The loss of life, property and wellbeing in war is a kind of currency that is given up in exchange for that which is (supposedly) of greater worth. Theological critiques of this type of sacrifice emphasize, however, that it is those on the periphery of influence and privilege who most frequently are ground up in such systems of sacrificial exchange, even while, once again, the sacred religious canopy shields from view a more thoroughgoing analysis of power dynamics. We also need to think more critically about models of sacrifice themselves in order to analyze what is going on in various sacrificial methods and mechanisms, how they work, and why they hang together cognitively in the imagination. Cognitive linguists such as George Lakoff probe beneath what appears to be 'common sense,' in order to better understand the cognitive connections and operations behind the systems of logic people utilize. Chapter Four mounts a theological investigation of sacrificial models

Finally, it further must be acknowledged that religious institutions perpetrating uncritical portrayals of the work of Christ as the ultimate sacrifice for human salvation, unwittingly feed into war-culture. If the secular war-culture may be described as a 'male protection racket,' then Christian institutions that uncritically proclaim the necessary sacrifice of Jesus for human salvation feed into and electrify this secular frame of discourse.[80] Yet where in the landscape of Christianity in the U.S. does one find critique of such faith-oriented proclamation going on? Christians face a serious ethical mandate with respect to the issues this chapter has raised. Is it indeed possible to distinguish speech, values and practice regarding Christian forms of sacrifice, from those that magnify the necessity of war in a post-9/11 U.S. War-culture? Facing this question directly must lead, for Christians, to self-interrogation regarding their own proclamation, system of values and theological frameworks centered on sacrificial dynamics. Moreover, not only those of Christian orientation, but indeed, all U.S. citizens face additional questions: If we tried not to think about the losses of war as a form of sacrificial exchange, how else might we conceive of them imaginatively? What difference would it make? Chapters Four and Five take up these concerns.

American citizens remain unconscious of the dangerous and potentially destructive connections between the rhetoric of necessity, Just War thinking and sacrificial symbols. This lack of awareness contributes to justification of the war-culture in which we live, and sets the stage for our all-too-ready acquiescence to subservience in the masculinist security regime in the post-9/11 era. Worse yet, lack of consciousness only will increase our vulnerability in the future with respect to ever new calls and cries for war as the necessary, heroic, sacrifi ial action in the face of continuing threats. Thus, this chapter closes with a series of snapshot quotes, and invites the reader to pay close attention to the way this language operates. Listen for the language of necessity, war and sacrifice

> At times it becomes *necessary* for a nation to defend itself through force of arms. Because war is a grave matter, involving the *sacrific*

80. See the conclusion of Marion Young's article for this definition of the masculinist security regime.

and taking of precious human life, conscience demands that those who would wage the war clearly state the moral reasoning behind their actions…

     — 'A Letter to America'

For those who have made *the supreme sacrific* in this war, the United States must prevail in Iraq.

     — The American Legion

I have tried every day since he died to make his *sacrifice* meaningful. Casey died for a country that cares more about who will be the next American Idol than how many people will be killed in the next few months.

     — Cindy Sheehan

Jesus, through his suffering, pays off "mankind's Original Sin debit"; he "makes *the ultimate sacrific* " in order to "balance the sins of the entire human race."

     — George Lakoff[81]

81. Lakoff, *Moral Politics*, p. 249.

Chapter Four

Rehabilitating Sacrifice?

Anyone who has tried to debate the virtues of war with an eager cadet or loyal Marine knows what it must feel like to dispute the Resurrection with a priest. Warriors are intransigent on the advisability of war, and their resistance springs not from bullheadedness but from a kind of religiosity. Theirs is the hymn of the true believer.

— Susan Faludi[1]

Introduction

Thus far the project of this book has been to investigate the problem of the pervasive and mutually supportive relationship between the practices of war and war-culture, and the discourse of sacrifice, especially sacrifice as understood and practiced in popular Christianity in the U.S. After the first chapter, which introduced the reader to the penetration of war-culture in the United States, the second chapter explored the language of sacrifice used so successfully by U.S. government leaders following 9/11 (in a way below the conscious 'radar screen' of most Americans) to build support for and squelch protest against the Iraq war. Chapter Three investigated unquestioned assumptions in society and church about 'necessity': the 'necessity' of the 'just war' requiring sacrifice and its abiding link to the 'necessity' of Jesus' sacrifice for a sinful humanity. The purpose of this chapter is to face the theological conundrum that rises in our minds once we begin to see and understand the troubling nature of this relationship between sacrifice and war-culture: are there theological articulations of sacrifice in Christianity that can resist the dynamic of war-culture and sacrifice? Thus far it seems as though root understandings of sacrifice in Christianity

1. Susan Faludi, 'Let Us Prey,' *The Nation*, 12 May 1997, p. 24.

are bound to become ammunition in any doctrine of the necessity of war and war-culture. Are there ways of speaking about sacrifice in Christianity that can be mobilized to criticize such abuse? Do recent theological reconstructions of sacrifice help us in this respect? Do they go far enough? Or is the only truly ethical alternative – for those who wish to resist war-culture – to jettison religious sacrificial constructions altogether?

Sacrifice, War and the Nation-Stat

Before turning to Christian theological discourse on sacrifice, I take a brief pause to further reflect on the connection between 'religiosity' and war. Notwithstanding the ironic tone in the opening quote from Susan Faludi, the point she makes is worth thinking about further. It comes from her review of an important book very little considered by theologians, *Blood Rites*, by Barbara Ehrenreich.[2] Struck by the sacred canopy over war and war-culture, Ehrenreich wants to understand it. What is this 'religiosity' that accompanies the warrior and war-making milieu? What may we understand sociologically and anthropologically about human development and the feelings and passions that give rise to war? For Ehrenreich, understanding the religiosity that accompanies war-culture means getting to war-culture's roots in rituals of blood sacrifice.

Of course, ancient understandings and practices of sacrifice are notoriously difficult to unearth with any certainty. While scholars agree that cognitive frameworks and practices of sacrifice go back to extremely early human experiences and self definitions, pinning down exactly how sacrifice worked and how it was understood by early human communities is very difficult to do. In large part this has to do with the wide multivalent understandings and practices (still in evidence today) of sacrifice across context and chronological time. Another complexity has to do with the reality that practices and understandings of sacrifice, even ritual sacrifice, not only are specifically religious, but have strong ties to communal, social and political frameworks. Theological thinkers may find rich resources from a long history of anthropological analysis assessing the significance of sacrificial blood rites, values and representations that have

2. Barbara Ehrenreich, *Blood Rites: Origin and History of the Passions of War* (New York: Henry Holt and Co., 1997).

cemented and promoted all kinds of religious, political and social arrangements.[3] It would seem that from very early times, humans have been tempted by the notion that 'violence will save,' not only religiously, but socially and politically as well. As Walter Wink put it so well,

> Violence is so successful as a myth precisely because it does not seem to be mythic in the least. Violence simply appears to be the nature of things. It is what works.[4]

'Dulce et decorum est pro patria mori,' or in English, 'It is sweet and fitting to die for one's country,' is a poetic line that reverberates across the ages, from Roman poet Horace to its ironic usage by World War I era poet Wilfred Owen, not to mention even more contemporary musicians, poets and writers. Some psychoanalysts have explored the deep-seated assumption that the sacrifices war brings 'are good for people.' Witness the echo many centuries later in the reflections of a woman who lived through the London bombings of World War II:

> Oh, it was a marvelous time. You forgot about yourself and you did what you could and we were all in it together. It was frightening, of course, and you worried about getting killed, but in some ways it was better than now. Now we're all just ourselves again.[5]

The emotional and energetic communal ties forged through facing the rigors and dangers of war meet a deep psychological human need to be part of a community, by investing meaning and purpose into one's own group. This points to 'functionalist' definitions of religion, which emphasize not core doctrines or dogmas, or belief in various deities, but the functions of religion that serve various needs of individuals and society. Functionalist definitions of religion emphasize the following: 1) religion serves social functions that provide experiences of community; 2) religion provides existential functions that help people claim identity, meaning and purpose; and 3) religion makes possible transcendent functions

3. See Jeffrey Carter (ed.), *Understanding Religious Sacrifice: A Reader* (New York: Continuum, 2003), for a very helpful and expansive anthology of scholars on sacrifice, from the early nineteenth century through the twentieth

4. Walter Wink, *Engaging the Powers: Discernment and Resistance in a World of Domination* (Minneapolis, MN: Fortress Press, 1992), p. 13.

5. Quotations from Lawrence Leshan, *The Psychology of War* (Chicago, IL: Noble Press, Inc., 1992), pp. 16, 29.

through which people experience the numinous.[6] Such a defin-
tion of religion connects with the thinking not only of ancient poets
and statesmen (Juvenal wrote, 'Now we suffer the evils of a long
peace. Luxury hatches terrors worse than wars.'), but also modern
philosophers and social scientists who have proposed that war is a
positive way to maintain national health and communal purpose.
Thus, Hegel: 'War has the higher meaning that through it …the
ethical health of nations is maintained.' Likewise, Max Weber proposed that *caritas* and true loyalty for the nation-state requires the
shedding of blood as a seal of the sanctity of this relationship. The
death of the warrior achieves a 'consecrated meaning,' and confers
dignity upon the coercive power of the state.[7] The murky, yet deep-
seated ties between war and religion are strong, enduring and as a
result, largely invisible and outside the awareness of many, perhaps
even most people.

In modern times, the ineradicable link between sacrifice and war-
culture solidified in the rise of the nation state. 'The modern nation
at its birth was a nation in arms.'[8] Through dominant national symbols, such as the flag, anthems, festivals, memorials, etc., we see that
waging war and the rise of the nation-state in modern times are intimately intertwined, so much so that it becomes extremely difficult
to envision the modern state without war-culture as an essential ingredient of national self-identity and representation. Most important,
sacrifice functions as the hinge between religion, war-culture and
national self-identity. The wars leading to the birth of the modern
state are explained and justified by making sacred the death of the
soldier for the nation, such as is exemplified in national anthems like
The 'Marseillaise,' which proudly proclaims that when its young heroes fall, the sacred soil of France will reproduce them all.[9] Likewise,

6. Gordon Lynch, *Understanding Theology and Popular Culture* (Oxford:
Blackwell, 2005), p. 28. As one way to measure the appearance and degree of
functional religiosity, William T. Cavanaugh suggests the following: 'An em-
pirically testable definition of absolute, then, might be "that for which one is
willing to kill."' *The Myth of Religious Violence: Secular Ideology and the Roots of
Modern Conflic* (Oxford: Oxford University Press, 2009), p. 56.

7. Jean Bethke Elshtain, 'Sovereignty, Identity and Sacrifice', *Gendered States:
Feminist (re)Visions of International Relations Theory*, V. Spike Peterson (ed.),
(London: Lynne Rienner Publishers, 1992), p. 146.

8. See George L. Mosse, *Confronting the Nation: Jewish and Western Nationalism*
(Hanover, NY: Brandeis University Press, 1993), p. 16.

9. Mosse, *Confronting the Nation*, p. 16.

'My country, 'tis of thee/Sweet land of liberty/Of Thee I sing./ Land where my fathers died,' are the words of the American anthem learned by every generation of school children. The words of the anthem are paralleled by the famous dictum of Thomas Jefferson, 'The tree of liberty must be refreshed from time to time with the blood of patriots and tyrants.'[10]

Not only a religious artifact, then, sacrificial self-identity shares an intimate relationship with national identity and representation. Scholar Sarah J. Purcell describes just this close tie with respect to the beginnings of the United States:

> Military memory, especially memory of the Revolutionary War, is really at the heart of the American national identity…As has been true in many other countries, the shared memory of sacrific and the hardship of war has helped to define American values for over two hundred years.[11]

At the beginning of American history and even before the Revolutionary War's end, evolving American conceptions of nationalism were deeply influenced by military commemorations of martyrs and heroes. The development of nationalist self-identity in the United States was rooted in language that stressed the need for sacrifice for the common good of the nation, 'transforming the bloodshed, division, and violence of war into beautiful symbols of unity and national cohesion.'[12] For instance, the date of the battles of Lexington and Concord, 19 April 1775, became the occasion for a yearly commemoration in the new nation, celebrated with parades, feasts and toasts, art and fireworks, and always a public sermon.

Revd. Jonas Clarke, the Congregational minister who had witnessed the battle of Lexington, gave the first annual sermon, which was published a year later alongside a detailed narration of the battle itself. In his sermon, after calling people to remembrance of their sins and underscoring the providence of God's action in the workings of the war, Revd. Clarke proclaimed that the revolutionary soldiers 'bleed, they die, not in their own cause only; but in the cause of this whole people – in the cause of God, their country and

10. From Thomas Jefferson's letter to William Smith, Paris, 13 November 1787, *The Atlantic Monthly Online* (Oct.) p. 96, http://www.theatlantic.com/issues/96oct/obrien/blood.htm, accessed 11 November 2009.

11. Sarah J. Purcell, *Sealed with Blood: War, Sacrifice, and Memory in Revolutionary America* (Philadelphia, PA: University of Pennsylvannia Press, 2007), p. 1.

12. Purcell, *Sealed with Blood*, p. 3.

posterity.'[13] This hinge of sacrifice between war-culture, American self-identity and religion, taking root in the very beginnings of U.S. history, continued to grow and draw even more explicitly from Christian religious formulations later in American history.[14]

In fact, the intensity of the relationship between sacrifice and the nation-state reached its apotheosis in the development of what scholars term 'total war.'[15] The difference between this kind of war and its earlier forms largely had to do with the entry of new and more extensively deadly forms of technology, and increased combatants and victims in war. Total war's targets expanded far beyond the enemy soldier. Technological development widened the target focus to include centers of the production of weaponry and civilian support; as a result the dead included larger and larger ratios of civilians to each soldier killed (one might also mention in this regard the increasing destruction of the natural world and resulting environmental degradation, accelerating especially in twentieth century war).

The first total war that scholars identify in modern times is the American Civil War, which relied on mass armies (first constructed by Napoleon) with the added destructive power of new rifled muskets that multiplied target range by five times that of earlier wars.[16] The number of U.S. soldiers killed in the Civil War amounted to more than in both World Wars, plus the Korean and Vietnam wars combined, in all approximately 622,000 dead. Moreover, historians of religion note that it is *precisely* at the point of America's first total war that we discover language entering into political American discourse that compared the sacrifice of the soldier for his country to the sacrifice of Christ [17] Perhaps, scholars muse, it was the search

13. Purcell, *Sealed with Blood*, pp. 39–42.

14. See Jon Pahl's discussion regarding the nature of 'shifting sacrifices' in U.S. history, including the Pequot War of 1637, the Civil War, World Wars I and II, and the 'War on Terror' in the twenty-first century. Jon Pahl, 'Shifting Sacrifices,' *American Christianities*, Catherine Brekus and W. Clark Gilpin (eds), (Chapel Hill, NC: University of North Carolina Press, 2011).

15. See Chapter 4, 'Reductio Ad Absurdum: Total War', in Gwynne Dyer, *War* (New York: Crown Publishers, 1985).

16. Dyer, *War*, p. 77.

17. Historians of religion summarized this point during the discussion period from the History of Christianity Section and North American Religions Section, Theme: *War and Religion in North America*, American Academy of Religion, San Diego, CA, November 2007.

to find some cognitive framework large enough to encompass such devastating loss that led to this specific link. President Lincoln's famous letter to a grieving mother, said to have lost five sons during the Civil War, relies upon the sacrificial theme

> I pray that our Heavenly Father may assuage the anguish of your bereavement, and leave you only the cherished memory of the loved and lost, and the solemn pride that must be yours, to have laid so costly a sacrifice upon the altar of Freedom [18]

During the period of the First World War, with the experience of literally hundreds of thousands sacrificing themselves for the nation, this same cognitive connection grew even stronger. As one scholar writes,

> Christian symbols, indeed, the very figure of Christ, were present in the cult of the fallen soldier – and in Germany, Italy, and France, familiar Christian symbols represented national sacrifice. The First World War was a climax in the evolution of modern nationalism, and in its quest for totality the nation sought to co-opt Christianity.[19]

The reification of sacrifice as a cognitive framework within which to find meaning and purpose in the losses of war was cemented through the outpouring of energy and resources to memorialize this same sacrificial reflex in the European interwar period; in the U.S. context a very similar dynamic occurred even earlier with respect to the setting aside of public space for memorialization of Civil War battles such as Gettysburg and Antietam. Across Europe today one finds memorials in villages and towns such as the *Terre de France* (Earth of France), by sculptor Maxime Real Del Sarte. These memorials sprang up by the hundreds, if not thousands, in the interwar period. *Terre de France* features a young woman, sheaves of wheat,

---

18. 'So Costly a Sacrifice: A Letter to Lydia Bixby', *Abraham Lincoln: A Documentary Portrait through His Speeches and Writings*, Don E. Fehrenbacher (ed.) (New York: Signet, 1964), p. 269. While this letter was published in newspapers at the time, the original has never been found. In addition, the information inspiring the letter regarding the death of five sons turned out to be not exactly correct. Mrs. Bixby did have five sons and all served in the military; two of the five were killed and at least one was a deserter. The letter was understood at the time as the president's words of condolence not just to this particular mother, but to all grieving mothers.

19. Mosse, *Confronting the Nation*, p. 124.

and a cross at the foot of a grave decorated with a soldier's helmet. Del Sarte, the sculptor, described the symbolic meaning of this statuary memorialization in the following terms:

> Alone, dressed with simplicity that Millet would have liked, a peasant woman, primitive and healthy in her youthfulness, gathers the sheaves that have sprouted in the Earth around the tomb of the soldier who died for her.[20]

Nationalism has frequently been described and analyzed as a kind of religion, yet with insufficient attention to the dominant theme of sacrifice that binds the experiences of nationalism and Christian religion, forming a sacred canopy encompassing both religious *and* national self-identity and representation. The extensiveness of human resort to sacrifice makes it so ubiquitous as to reside largely 'off the radar screen,' of alert awareness and consciousness. As a result, analysis of sacrifice is simultaneously all the more difficult *and* all the more important. But the infusion of the sacred tone that justifies such sacrifice makes this construction all too   pervious to moral analysis and criticism.

Blood Sacrifice, Prey and Predato

Social sciences provide helpful methods to explore the troubling relationship between sacrifice, war, Christianity and nationalism. According to Barbara Ehrenreich, deep-seated connections between sacrificial understandings and war can be traced to early human experiences, not as warriors, but as the prey of large animals, especially cats, that roamed and dominated a significant part of the earth's landscape. In fact, the roots of scapegoating may be tied to just this same experience. Early humans directly experienced the threat of inevitable violence from animal predators. Moreover, this violence only dissipated once a member from the group was attacked and carried off, the 'sacrifice' of the one leaving the rest of the group safe, at least for the time being.

Ehrenreich explores the emotional trajectory of this experience, and suggests a link between the early human experiences of being preyed upon, and the beginnings of religion humanly understood.

20. Daniel J. Sherman, *The Construction of Memory in Interwar France* (Chicago, IL: University of Chicago Press, 1999), pp. 151–52.

The 'holy shiver' in the face of the awesome sacred is tied to the experience of terror in the face of the not-to-be-denied predator. At the same time feelings of group solidarity and community grow in part out of human experiences of banding together to ward off and prevent the animal's attack. Then, further emotions of altruism and self-sacrifice arise from the primal experiences of seeing that one must and will die in order for the rest to reside in safety (if only until the next attack).

Thus, early human experience as prey of large carnivorous animals helps to explain the hinge of sacrifice between religious and warring sensibilities. We can plot the course of human development by tracing the human trajectory from prey to predator. Human status as prey once figured largely in human self understanding, and rituals of blood sacrifice reenact the crisis of a predator's attack, increasingly drawing together both sides of this human developmental shift, the human as prey and as predator. This experience mirrors the duality of warriors' sacrifice – they both kill and die. Moreover, these schemes involve understandings of salvation as sacrificial exchange: one must fall prey so that the rest may be safe, at least temporarily.

Over time, Ehrenreich asserts, especially as humans began to develop more complex tools and weapons, they accomplished an astonishing feat, once their weapons and strategies enabled them to lessen their vulnerability as prey to become predators themselves. In fact, humans became such successful hunters, about 10,000 years ago, that most human cultures reached the point where there were insufficient numbers of large animals left to hunt. Competing theories attempt to explain the eventual disappearance of these large prey. However one explains it, the eventuality of insufficient animals as prey corresponds with the rise of pre-civilized warfare, largely a male-only rough sport for 'under-employed hunters.'[21]

Anthropologists have proposed various materialist theories behind the rise of war in human culture (involving disputes over land and access to water, etc.). Nevertheless, these theories can be eliminated much more easily than the rationale that 'war persists because it is a prestigious thing for men to do, that it is an exciting and even "religious" undertaking.'[22] The warrior experience reenacts

21. Ehrenreich, *Blood Rites*, p. 124.
22. Ehrenreich, *Blood Rites*, p. 124.

the triumph of the shift from prey to predator. Unlike other theorists, who place the rise of war in human civilization at men's feet through a biological connection having to do with testosterone and aggression, Ehrenreich's conclusion is more nuanced. War became an important mechanism through which masculinity itself was defined; in other words, it is the thing that 'makes men "men," and gives the adult male something uniquely "manly" to do.'[23] This is not because women are biologically situated to resist war (in fact they frequently have no less inhibition against fighting than do men), but because it is through war that men define the male role 'satisfactorily enough,' to quote Margaret Mead.[24]

What then of women's participation in war? In fact, there has been an enormous rise of female participation in warring violence across many contexts over the last 30 years, such that girls and women now comprise up to 40% of combatants in various ethno-separatist/guerilla conflicts. The same increase in numbers has been noted with respect to women suicide bombers. Scholar Cindy Ness ascribes this growth to three predominant causes: 1) blurring of the private/public spheres; 2) increasing recognition of the political utility of women; and 3) decreasing separation between combatant and noncombatant status in contexts of war.[25]

However, according to many researchers, the rise of women combatants has not led in many cases to greater empowerment over their own lives, or to a decrease in the structural forms of violence they face. For instance, feminist theologian, Mary Condren, traces the 'double jeopardy' women face with respect to war. On the one hand, in Western cultures, women bear the societal expectation to 'save the peace of the world.' On the other hand, when women attempt to expand their consciousness and activism in the public square of politics, they lose credibility. The stereotype of women as 'more peaceful' than men runs headlong into the social expectation that women should remain ensconced in the private sphere. Such contradicting roles place women in an impossible social situation. Condren summarizes, 'warfare, more than any other institution, plays a powerful role in the generation of symbolic capital for

23. Ehrenreich, *Blood Rites*, p. 127.
24. As quoted by Ehrenreich, *Blood Rites*, p. 129.
25. Cindy Ness, 'The Rise in Female Violence,' *Daedalus* (Winter 2007): 86–97.

patriarchal culture in which women's self interest is constantly and radically undermined.'[26]

Other feminists expand on the idea of women's double and even triple jeopardy as participants, advocates, protesters and victims in war. For instance, the Bush Administration's 'repackaging' of the Afghanistan war as a struggle for the emancipation of women may be traced to late-nineteenth-century colonial practices for 'introducing progress to underdeveloped societies, whose ill treatment of their womenfolk evidenced their backwardness.' This 'saving women trope,' or as other feminists have described it, the 'saving brown women from brown men' trope, has served as a rationalization for war since the 1970s at least in Afghanistan, and also was used by the Taliban as a rationale to gain local support in Kandahar. Meanwhile, the largest women's organization in Afghanistan, Revolutionary Association of the Women of Afghanistan (RAWA), consistently refused to support armed violence as an effective method for improving women's security and bettering their lives. As Jennifer L. Fluri writes, 'the "saving women trope" extends a legitimate reason for waging violent conflict, while marginalizing women as political and social agents. This solidifies men's roles as both perpetrator and protector in the shaping or implementing of military violence.'[27]

War also brings increased threat of sexual and other forms of violence to women both in and outside the military ranks. Widespread rape of women was systematically practiced in the 1994 Rwandan genocide, as well as in wars in Bosnia, Sierra Leone, and East Timor. At the same time, sexual assaults and rape of women soldiers in the Gulf wars have skyrocketed, according to the reports of servicewomen; domestic violence in military families is three to five times higher than in civilian ones; as Zillah Eisenstein writes, 'femininity has been militarized while the military has not been demasculinized.'[28]

26. Mary Condren, 'To Bear Children for the Fatherland: Mothers and Militarism,' *The Power of Naming: A Concilium Reader in Feminist Liberation Theology*, in Elisabeth Schüssler Fiorenza (ed.), (New York: Orbis Books, 1996), p. 117.

27. See Jennifer L. Fluri, '"Rallying Public Opinion" and Other Misuses of Feminism' pp. 143–49; and Alyson M. Cole, 'The Other V-word: the Politics of Victimhood Fueling George W. Bush's War Machine,' p. 119, *Feminism and War: Confronting U.S. Imperialism*, Robin L. Riley, Chandra Talpade Mohanty, Minnie Bruce Pratt (eds), (London: Zed Books, 2008).

28. Zillah Eisenstein, 'Resexing Militarism for the Globe,' *Feminism and War: Confronting U.S. Imperialism*, Robin L. Riley, Chandra Talpade Mohanty, Minnie Bruce Pratt (eds), (London: Zed Books, 2008).

Thus, though women participate in war, even as warriors, in greater numbers, their participation to date seems to have little impacted the practice of war as a powerful mechanism by which masculinity is defined, performed and enforced. In this way, through the phenomenon of war, men are initiated 'as men,' and create a male-only lineage for inheritance of various sorts of power, material and social.[29] Moreover, participating in the *sacrifice* of war delineates the true boundaries of power relations and exchanges. The initiation of the warrior in his first real battle may be compared to entry into the priesthood. Both of these rituals entail a kind of male-only rebirth and reproduction and simultaneously, a way of passing down power in patriarchal lineages. 'Through his first kill, a young man "earns his spurs," "bloods his spear," or even, as was said by Americans in Vietnam, "loses his virginity," thus marking his rebirth into the world of grown-up men.'[30]

We cannot sufficiently underscore the important role sacrifice plays in these power exchanges: in fact, the ritual of blood sacrifice is what unites religious sensibilities and war. Practices of blood sacrifice were widespread and multivalent in early cultures for a diverse set of purposes, including ensuring fertility of the land and consecration of various human constructions, be they buildings or tribal hierarchies, or to 'feed the gods.' Notwithstanding the plethora of sacrifice's purposes, the main point to emphasize here is the undeniable link between practices of blood sacrifice and practices of war. Ehrenreich summarizes the point:

> It was war that allowed human sacrifice to achieve a truly spectacular scale. Certainly, the sacrifice of a well-loved child within a tribal group would be a compelling spectacle in itself, but with war the process could be magnified to hundreds or thousands of deaths at a time.[31]

29. Ehrenreich, *Blood Rites*, p. 157. Ehrenreich draws on the theoretical work of anthropologist Nancy Jay and the role of sacrifice in the inheritance of power. See Nancy Jay, *Throughout Your Generations Forever: Sacrifice, Religion and Paternity* (Chicago, IL: University of Chicago Press, 1992). Jay also analyzes other sacrificially maintained transfers of power, including those that operate through sacrificial religious rituals such as the Eucharist in Christianity. See the *excursis* on Jay's analysis later in this chapter.

30. Ehrenreich, *Blood Rites*, p. 156.

31. Ehrenreich, *Blood Rites*, p. 66.

Thus, even while sacrificial practices lubricate patriarchal exchanges of power, at the same time this dynamic is mystified through its connection to religious understandings and practices. Blood sacrifice is at the heart of war-culture's and the warrior's 'religiosity.' Because of this, to question the cognitive framework of sacrifice, residing as a deep and largely unexamined anchor for warriors' identity, is tantamount to a kind of heresy. Interrogative protest about the nature and operations of sacrifice in war-culture is subject to the same charge. More troubling still, Christian proclamation that portrays the work of Christ as a sacrifice cements the architecture of this social structure in Western cultures such as the United States. To cast doubt on the soldier's mission as sacrifice is as unsettling, challenging and frankly, jarring to common sensibility, as to question the sacrality of Christ's sacrificial death on the cross.

Evaluating Theological Reconstructions of Sacrific

Here is a caution for Christian theology. We must beware that in our reception and interpretation of the Gospel we do not end up entering the passion story on the side of Jesus' murderers.

Mark Heim

Only a fool would try to remove an ink spot with more ink, or an oil spot with oil; how can anyone believe that blood stains can be removed by shedding more blood?

Bertha von Suttner[32]

At this juncture we may return to the question raised in the last part of this chapter's introduction: are there theological articulations of sacrifice in Christianity that can resist the dynamic of war-culture and sacrifice? To take up this question, this chapter surveys recent theological explorations of the role of sacrifice in Christianity, in order to evaluate the degree to which they disrupt the dangerous blurring of the boundaries described above between Christianity and sacrifice, nation, soldier and war. We have seen that frameworks emphasizing the sacred sacrifice of Jesus support, justify and provide a model for the sacrifice of the soldier – both deaths are

32. S. Mark Heim, *Saved From Sacrifice: A Theology of the Cross* (Grand Rapids, MI: William B. Eerdmans Publishing Co., 2006), pp. 125–26; von Suttner's quote taken from Jack Nelson-Pallmeyer, *Is Religion Killing Us? Violence in the Bible and the Quran* (New York: Continuum, 2003), p. 148.

'necessary' sacrifices in some way, serve a larger social/political or cosmic purpose, and provide an ethical blueprint for followers' imitation.

In addition, sacrificial cognitive frameworks are returned to again and again by individuals and communities in the face of losses of many different types. In the case of devastation incurred as a result of war, however, sacrificial constructions that are created to explain or justify violence impede deeper questioning and analysis about the true nature and causes of the conflict and losses experienced. In light of all this, we have to ask, is there a way to continue to maintain the framework of the sacrifice of Jesus without contributing to the problem of war and war-culture, without the sacrifice of Jesus adding to a sacred canopy that glorifies and mystifies the realities of war? Additionally, once we become more deeply aware of this sacred sacrificial framework in war and war-culture, what must this same awareness mean for Christian theology and practice?

A growing number of theologians who are aware of the dangers in sacrifi ial ideologies and theologies are responding in significant ways to this problem. I explore three different but related trajectories of response in this chapter, and along the way evaluate strengths, limitations and ongoing questions related to each. A first group of theologians acknowledges and criticizes the social dangers of sacrificialism (and scapegoating), and attempts to redefine Jesus' sacrifice as somehow different. Comparison and contrast within a second group of theologians reveals a tension in Christian theology between portrayals of the death of Jesus as surrogacy or as sacrament. Lastly, a third group of thinkers focuses on sacrificialism in neoliberal economic systems (in addition to war culture), and advocates leaving sacrificial frameworks behind altogether in theology, economics and national representation. While this is far from an exhaustive survey, it does illuminate some of the diversity of response and highlight ongoing theological issues and tensions that remain unresolved.

Reinscribing Sacrific

A first group of theologians sets out to differentiate the meaning of Jesus' ministry, life, death and resurrection from a long human history of social scapegoating and ensuing sacrifice. Representative of this group is theologian Mark Heim, who draws on Rene Girard's work to come to terms with a central conflict at the heart of the passion story in Christianity: the paradox at the center of the narrative of the crucifixion of Jesus, 'God's plan and an evil act, a good bad thing.'[33] The difficulty with understanding and faithfully embracing the narratives of Jesus' death has to do with multiple story lines (the 'stereophonic' quality, according to Heim) included in the Gospel accounts. On the one hand, these stories are emphatic about Jesus' sacrificial death as unjust and wrong. He is a victim of social scapegoating.

On the other hand, however, Jesus is supposed to die and sets his face to go to Jerusalem, the place of his coming torture and death. His death is part of a divine plan for salvation. How can such seemingly contradictory story lines be adjudicated? Heim claims that the Gospels are unreserved in their critique of social violence backed by religious rationale. As he argues this case, Heim draws on texts such as the woman accused of adultery and sentenced to die by stoning in John 7 and 8. A crowd energetically comes together to carry out her punishment. Here the Girardian scapegoating mechanism is in full swing, with the community bonded together in eagerness and animosity to wreak violence against a vulnerable victim. According to Heim, Jesus 'runs the tape backward,' when he targets the collective force of violence by insisting that one person step forward, 'Let anyone among you who is without sin be the first to throw a stone at her.' The destructive energy of the mob mentality is punctured like a balloon, and instead of stoning, the crowd melts away one by one.[34]

Heim's Girardian analysis requires some explanation in order that we understand both his critique of and embrace of sacrificial categories. Returning to the narrative in John, Heim describes the

33. Heim, *Saved From Sacrific*, p. 108. See also Brad Jersak and Michael Hardin (eds), *Stricken by God? Nonviolent Identification and the Victory of Christ* (Grand Rapids, MI: Eerdmans, 2007), for an anthology of essays written by thinkers working on questions related to nonviolent soteriological constructions. I acknowledge but here do not intend to analyze the theological enterprise of yet additional thinkers who continue to mount defenses of sacrifice as a central category in soteriology, such as Erin Lothes Biviano, *The Paradox of Christian Sacrifice: The Loss of Self, the Gift of Self* (New York: Herder and Herder, Crossroads, 2007), and Robert J. Daly, *Sacrifice Unveiled: The True Meaning of Sacrific* (London: T & T Clark, 2009).

34. Heim, *Saved From Sacrific*, p. 134.

dynamic of the crowd in the Gospel story as 'mimetic rivalry,' an archetypal unfolding of the escalation of social unrest that must and will result in violence against the scapegoat, in this case the sacrifice of the woman accused of adultery. Mimetic rivalry works in the following way: humans desire what others desire, and respond not only to others' actions, but to what we believe their intentions are. It is just this desire that leads to suspicion, unrest and ultimately, conflict. Mimetic desire appears to be intrinsic in human experience, and scapegoating mechanisms are both ubiquitous and ancient in human societies (while I rehearse Girard's theory here in order that we understand Heim's use of it in his theology, later in this chapter I will present various critiques of Girard).

According to Girard, 'the contagious escalation of violence is the archetypal social disease.' Moreover, because violence is a threat to the unity and stability of the community, it must be dissipated in some way. Release occurs when the tension is broken through the eruption of 'spontaneous and irrational collective violence' upon some distinctive or minority individual in the group (the sacrificial act). The violent act 'clears the air,' suspends reciprocal violence, and reestablishes peace. Moreover, without adequate legal systems or other institutions to mitigate such conflicts, 'the human community cannot get off the ground.' At the same time, a central feature of scapegoating violence is its invisibility with respect to the actual causes of the violence and the guilt or innocence of the victim. In fact, scapegoating violence works most effectively when it is most unquestioned, when it operates below the level of conscious thought. Here's where religion comes into the picture, providing a 'canopy of sacred awe' that suspends suspicions about the victim, the nature of the violence, and the innocence or guilt of the perpetrators. Religious sacrificial frameworks provide cover for closer examination of the sacrifice of communal scapegoating violence. As Heim sums it up, 'If it were obvious to all that sacrifice was a ploy in the ordinary round of rivalry and violence, a bone thrown to satisfy everyone's lust for revenge, it would be much less effective.'[35]

The 'sacrificial crisis' described by Girard continues well into our own time, according to Heim, though in our own age, dominated by the rise of technology and (supposedly) advanced society, many if not most individuals mistakenly believe that sacrifice is a

---

35. Heim, *Saved From Sacrific* , p. 51.

long-passed, 'primitive' stage we moderns and post-moderns have abandoned. Such thinking actually works well with Girard's insight that scapegoating sacrifice is most effective when it is most invisible and unrecognized. Humans have developed institutions to try to deal with mimetic rivalry, social conflict, and the escalation of violence, such as our legal and police systems, (and one might say, though Heim does not, the branches of the military as the coercive/ defensive arm of the legislative and executive branches of U.S. government). But Heim notes that all too often, our legal and political systems are consumed by the very sacrificial crisis they were designed to otherwise control or curb. Examples such as the Stalinist terror, the National Socialist terror in Germany, the U.S. red scare after World War I, the practice of racial segregation and more, all illustrate contemporary scapegoating violence. If anything, scapegoating sacrifice is more prevalent than ever, given advanced and sophisticated technological developments (such as media and advertising), that increase 'mimetic contagion.' Scapegoating sacrifice, moreover, continues to be very effective, because of its 'shape-shifting' capacity. As Heim says, 'there is always a special premium on a process that can unite a community precisely ...in the face of external threat of internal disintegration.'[36]

Nevertheless, even as Jesus' ministry unmasks the violence against innocent victims, Jesus' role is to be *sine qua non* of scapegoats, *in order*, Heim claims, to repeal scapegoating. This is where Heim attempts to clarify distinctions between the 'stereophonic' multiple narrative lines of the New Testament. His intention is to differentiate Jesus' work as sacrifice from the long history of scapegoating sacrificial violence that so defines the ways of the world. However, as I will argue below, it is precisely this place in Heim's argument where questions must be raised.

Heim points to a key scriptural passage that sheds light on these issues from the three Synoptic Gospels – the dialogue between Peter and Jesus immediately following Peter's confession that Jesus is the Christ, the Messiah. In this narrative, Peter's confession of Jesus as the Messiah leads to Jesus' passion prediction; he must go to Jerusalem and undergo great suffering, be killed and raised on the third day (Mt. 16. 21-23; Mk 8.31-33). When Peter rebukes Jesus for saying such things, Jesus turns on him, 'Get behind me, Satan!

36. Heim, *Saved From Sacrific* , p. 62.

You are a stumbling block to me; for you are setting your mind not on divine things but on human things.'

Heim writes, 'This is a key text for our interpretation of Jesus' death.'[37] The text represents just the 'doubleness' that Heim has been tracing; the focus, on the one hand, on the critique of scapegoating in the New Testament, and on the other, Jesus' affirmation of his crucifixion as 'the necessary path for salvation,' even as he 'rejects the rationale of his persecutors at each step along the way.' Why is this sacrifice 'necessary'? Heim sums it up, 'the wrongness in the cross is precisely what Jesus aims to oppose and overcome in bearing it.'

Heim is adamant that early Christianity, including that which produced the documents of the New Testament, did not simply rehash and recycle the old sacrificial scheme in a new and more far-reaching way. But why is this different? Many passages from the New Testament rely on sacrificial language without reservation to describe the meaning of Jesus' death, but this sacrifice is different, not 'putting new wine into old bottles.' In other words, we should not be fooled by this language into thinking that this is part of the same old sacrificial system of scapegoating violence. Why?

According to Heim, sacrificial systems demand that something be given up in order for peace to be achieved. You ransom something in order to get something back. In other words, sacrifice is a dynamic of exchange. However, when God steps into the breach, Heim claims, the entire process is disrupted:

> God offers a ransom not only to get the captives out of the place of the scapegoat, but to act from that place, the place of utter abandonment...When God, who cannot be silenced and who will not take vengeance, stands in that place, the web of sacrifice collapses [38]

Does it really collapse? God could react to the injustice with rightful violence, but such would only fuel the fires of retribution. At the opposite extreme are victims who are simply quashed by violence and whose voices are forever silenced. For Heim, such a fate as this is avoided through the resurrection, by which 'the voice of the victim overcomes the silence of death, but without violence or retribution.'[39]

37. Heim, *Saved From Sacrific* , p. 152.
38. Heim, *Saved From Sacrific* , p. 162.
39. Heim, *Saved From Sacrific* , p. 164.

Heim calls this process a 'startling reversal' of the ancient and expected processes of sacrificial dynamics, but is it really a reversal? Summing it up near the end of his book, he writes,

> The sacrificing of Jesus was the work of sin, but the overcoming of that scapegoating death is the work of God. Sacrifice is the game the powers of this world were playing with Jesus, and apparently winning, according to the old rules. God's victory broke the hold of this game itself ...it is as if the prison where torture took place becomes a hospital.[40]

Yet, in the footnote attached to the quote above Heim himself acknowledges the slipperiness of the interpretation of the cross he has claimed. It is exceedingly difficult for the ancient dynamics of scapegoating *not* to be immediately reinscribed into the system that Heim describes as 'victory.' He writes, 'One could look at representations of Christian glory on the cross and see this as a representation not of victory over sacrifice, but of the sacrifice itself. God's victory *is* the dying.'[41]

What happens if we draw on Heim's theological reconstruction of sacrifice and weigh it over against the dangers I have outlined with respect to sacrifice and war-culture? Will Heim's work help us to resist war-culture's colonization of Christian understandings? Reinscribing scapegoating sacrificial dynamics into Christianity, for Heim, is akin to 'entering the passion story on the side of Jesus' murderers.' Yet, as the second epigraph at the beginning of this chapter poses the question, 'how can anyone believe that blood stains can be removed by the shedding of more blood?' I frankly find Heim much more compelling and convincing in his discussion of the dangers and prevalence of such reinscription in various strands of Christian tradition in sacred text, theology and Christian practice, than in his attempts to differentiate within the various sounds of the 'stereophonic' gospels a positive interpretation of Jesus' death as sacrifice

Heim is to be commended for his careful and serious treatment of the problem of scapegoating sacrifice infecting Christian texts, traditions, doctrine and practices. But I remain dubious as to whether his work to differentiate sacrifice is, in the final analysis, convincingly

---

40. Heim, *Saved From Sacrific* , p. 310.
41. Heim, *Saved From Sacrific* , p. 310.

'different.'[42] Part of the problem has to do with the way Heim critiques sacrifice as a mechanism of exchange. Fair enough, sacrifice does represent and enact the 'giving up in order to get back.' But blood sacrifice is equally about the power of merging, being joined together in that which is seen as the life force, blood. Sacrificial refle - es attempt to unite community members together in an atmosphere of sanctity *and* to separate them from evil, frequently working along both lines simultaneously.[43] God 'stepping into the breach' does not break this sacrificial reflex, it only reifies and reinscribes i

For Heim, Jesus' death is the necessary element that precedes God's step; the outcome of the sacrifice may be different (i.e., the continuing life of the voice through resurrection), but the necessity of this sacrifice (i.e., Jesus' death) remains. As he says, 'the free, loving "necessity" that leads God to be willing to stand in the place of the scapegoat is the way to unmask the sacrificial mechanism.' Elsewhere he writes that the 'sacrificial necessity that claims Jesus as a sinful mechanism for victimization,' is only revealed and overcome through additional 'necessity of sacrifice.' In other words, the 'price' to unconditionally refuse scapegoating is Jesus' death.[44] Thus, as I analyze Heim's logic, scapegoating sacrifice has been criticized only to have the blood sacrifice of Jesus' necessary death reinscribed. The system of exchange remains in place.

The 'stereophonic' melody lines Heim would have us differentiate blend together only too well, leading to great difficulty in distinguishing the diverse musical phrases Heim would have us hear. For instance, we might compare Heim's analysis with a recent editorial in a popular Christian publication, *The Lutheran*. A pastor writes about the way the 'traditional emphasis on atonement' has blocked out the 'subversive' element of Jesus' death as a religious leader who was silenced because of the threat he posed to the established order. This pastor seems to be quite aware of the sacrificial scapegoating mechanism in the Gospels that Heim wishes to emphasize and critique. 'We can't avoid reading that Jesus was considered a

42. Other thinkers criticize Heim as having conflated diverse sacrificial operations into one scapegoating mechanism. See Ben Fulford, 'Saved From Sacrifice: A Theology of the Cross,' *Modern Theology*, 24. 2 (April 2008), pp. 311–13.

43. See Nancy Jay, 'Sacrifice as Remedy for Having Been Born of Woman,' *Women, Gender, Religion: A Reader*, Ed. Elizabeth A. Castelli (ed.), (New York: Palgrave, 2001), p. 182.

44. Heim, *Saved From Sacrific* , p. 114.

threat to society by those who felt responsible to maintain peace and security,' the pastor writes. Jesus was killed by the state for just this perceived threat. But such awareness does little to impact this author's simultaneous emphasis on the necessity of Jesus' sacrifice as part of a cosmic plan. He continues,

> When I was young, I was taught that God loves me and that Jesus died for me. I was reminded to be thankful that God sent Jesus to die for my sins...during Lent and into Holy Week we lift up the death of Jesus as something he didn't deserve. He was innocent of all charges...He died so we might be saved. He paid the ransom. God was pleased with Jesus' sacrifice [45]

Heim would have us believe that Jesus' death on the cross is God's way of disrupting scapegoating sacrificial reflexes (Jesus' descent into hell resulting in the prison turned into a hospital), but for *The Lutheran's* author, highlighting Jesus' resistance to scapegoating sacrifice doesn't stop ongoing sacrifice at all. On the contrary, Jesus' necessary sacrifice is reified as a divinized exchange of ransom that pleases God. For the pastor the cosmic melody line of necessary sacrifice harmonizes perfectly with Jesus' 'subversive' (read: criticism of Rome's scapegoating system of empire) message and ministry. Heim and the pastor above share the same flaw in their logic: they criticize scapegoating sacrifice, only to reify it cosmically.

The question additionally may be raised whether Jesus' execution truly fits the Girardian pattern of scapegoat mechanisms; after all, such systems are said to unite communities in merged violence toward their victims. But is this the case with Jesus? The purpose of his execution more likely was to scatter and terrorize the community around him (though it might be said that this violence did unite the political elites/authorities behind it).[46] Heim seems to follow in the path of Walter Wink, who asserted that the cross exposes and defeats the powers.[47] For Heim this occurs through the resurrection, 'the voice continuing without violence or retribution.' But if indeed the cross does expose the deadly, unjust and oppressive nature of the Roman state, and if historical analogies to Jesus' cross continue to

45. George S. Johnson, 'Was Jesus Subversive? Considering the "other" Reason Jesus Died on the Cross,' *The Lutheran* (March 2008), pp. 28–29.

46. See Jack Nelson-Pallmeyer, *Jesus Against Christianity*, pp. 222–24.

47. Wink, *Engaging the Powers*. See pp. 145–55 for Wink's discussion of Girard.

reveal parallel historical realities, nevertheless piling sacrifice upon sacrifice seems an unlikely mechanism to interrupt this dynamic. Yet at its deepest core, the myth of redemptive violence inculcates the subconscious belief that more violence is the only realistic and effective antidote to the reality of violence.

In contrast to this myth, as Christine Gudorf has noted, God 'stepping into the breach' of sacrifice doesn't *cure* sacrifice. If anything, the violence of sacrifice is like a narcotic, anesthetizing and distracting us from examining and growing in awareness regarding the true roots of the conflict. Sacrifices should be averted in favor of digging into the realities behind the frustration giving rise to conflict in the first place; the key is not additional sacrifice, but deeper examination and greater awareness.[48] The notion that sacrifici l scapegoating systems may only be overcome through *bearing* the pain, loss and destructiveness they create is embedded in sacrificial systems themselves, those in war-culture *and* in Christianity (as well as other religions). To say as much is to glorify and mystify sacrificial dynamics as 'necessary,' cosmically approved and effective. This same cognitive framework is very deeply entrenched in our thinking.

Over a decade ago Elisabeth Schüssler Fiorenza articulated a clear warning against biblical texts and christologies that 'theologize kyriarchal suffering and victimization.' One strong prong of her critique was aimed at sacrificialism in biblical texts, and the book of Hebrews in particular came under her examination. She wrote,

> By ritualizing the suffering and death of Jesus and calling the powerless in society and Church to imitate his perfect obedience and self-sacrifice, Christian ministry and theology do not interrupt but continue to foster the cycle of violence engendered by kyriarchal social and ecclesial structures as well as by cultural and political disciplining practices.[49]

In contrast to Schüssler Fiorenza, Heim emphasizes the importance of Hebrews for his own argument, 'The whole history of

48. Christine Gudorf, *Victimization: Examining Christian Complicity* (Philadelphia, PA: Trinity Press International, 1992).

49. Elisabeth Schüssler Fiorenza, 'Ties that Bind: Domestic Violence Against Women,' *Women Resisting Violence: Spirituality for Life* (Maryknoll, NY: Orbis Books, 1996), p. 50. Schüssler Fiorenza defines 'kyriarchy,' as 'the pyramid of interstructured oppression (that) specifies women's status in terms of the class, race, country or religion of the men to whom they 'belong.'

sacrifice is reinforced in the cross, and the importance of the cross is that it is a supersacrifice. [50] Hebrews articulates 'the sacrifice to end sacrifice'; the 'one needful sacrifice' of Christ is meant to stop the nature of sacrificial violence.[51] At this point I have to ask, does this logic make any sense?

Heim's simultaneous critique and reinscription of sacrifice in Christianity may be compared with another recent book that also addresses the dangers of sacrificial imagery and logic in Christian texts and tradition. In *Abraham's Curse: The Roots of Violence in Judaism, Christianity and Islam*, Bruce Chilton is profoundly aware of the destructive links between sacrifice and war-culture.[52] He powerfully traces the interpretive threads of the *Aqedah* (the story of the [near] sacrifice of Isaac by Abraham) in Judaism, Christianity and Islam, and along the way emphasizes the deep connections between interpretations of *this* narrative of sacrifice, and the rise of sacrificial warrior culture and ideology. Yet Chilton is much less sanguine with respect to the book of Hebrews in the New Testament than is Heim. By the time of the vision of the book of Hebrews, Chilton tells us, early Christian proclamation of Abraham's offering of Isaac linked the notion of the 'super-sacrifice' of Christ with the 'mysticism of suffering' that united believers with Christ. The book of Hebrews presents the crucifixion of Jesus as 'the one sacrifice God always wanted.'[53] Prior understandings of sacrifice as a celebratory feast quickly were superseded in the West through focus on sin's connection to sacrifice. In contrast to celebratory understandings, ultimately, Hebrews' theology of Christ's eternal sacrifice became incentive for martyrs to emulate his death. Thus, by the time of the rise of the modern nation state, the rhetoric of Hebrews was captured by nations in secular form. Young soldiers were offered immortal national remembrance in exchange for their willingness to shed (and to give their own) human blood. Chilton writes,

> Unless you understand the theology of martyrdom, like it or not, you can never comprehend early Christianity or the capacity of Christians in every age to seek martyrdom, whether on the mass

50. Heim, *Saved From Sacrific*, p. 157.

51. Heim, *Saved From Sacrific*, p. 159.

52. Bruce Chilton, *Abraham's Curse: The Roots of Violence in Judaism, Christianity and Islam* (New York: Doubleday, 2008).

53. Chilton, *Abraham's Curse*, pp. 80–94.

scale of the crusades and the First World War, or on the personal
scale of Sir Thomas Moore, Dietrich Bonheoffer and Martin Luther
King, Jr.[54]

If sacrificial frameworks in Stone Age myth necessitated the offering of children, by the time of the Middle Ages the cognitive frame
demanded that blood must be shed in order for conflict to be resolved. As a result of this mindset, countries with a deep history of
Christianity are imbued with 'a culture of bloodshed,' and over the
centuries, have displayed an astonishing capacity to motivate their
young to war. This dominant sacrificial frame 'releases impulses
in the lives of nations which have proved more powerful than the
technological and political developments that in the end only serve
cultural purposes.'[55] Chilton concludes, 'The Christian veneration
of martyrs has proved to be the single most influential incentive to
self-sacrifice among world religions over the centuries. [56]

Even more, over time the sacrificial framework evolved, so
that the martyr became more than a passive victim. By the time of
Constantine, Roman soldiers were praised in hagiographies next to
victims of persecutions, and artists portrayed Abraham armed with
a sword rather than a knife. Thus, once again, we see the dual nature
of sacrifice, as martyr becomes *both* victim *and* warrior. Violence has
become 'ennobled.'[57]

The significance of the *Aqedah* for Christian history has to do with
Christian interpretation of Jesus as the ideal sacrifice Isaac never
quite reached. Christ's suffering became the incentive for martyrdom, with devastating consequences: 'No period of Christian history has ever been exempt from the attractions of Abraham's curse,
or from the conviction that offering young life in a holy cause is
noble.'[58]

Chilton's trenchant critique of the destructive cycles of sacrificia -
ism in Judaism, Islam and Christianity is indeed powerful. Yet, in
his book's final chapter, Chilton looks to additional threads within
each of these three religious traditions in order to search for resources that may disrupt and even correct abusive religious sacrificial

54. Chilton, *Abraham's Curse*, p. 90.
55. Chilton, *Abraham's Curse*, p. 99.
56. Chilton, *Abraham's Curse*, p. 203.
57. Chilton, *Abraham's Curse*, pp. 118–40.
58. Chilton, *Abraham's Curse*, p. 205.

dynamics. For instance, as he explores the interruptive possibilities within Christianity, Chilton interprets Jesus' words in Gethsemane as a challenge to the notion of the necessity of suffering sacrifice ('Carry this cup on, away from me!' Mk 14.36). He writes,

> Jesus discerns, during his final night in Gethsemane, that truly taking up his cross is not an automatic duty, but is only accomplished by means of his conscious appraisal that his death will benefit others, even as it fulfills his own purpose and personality, in revealing God's kingdom.[59]

In this way Chilton would draw a distinction between 'automatic martyrdom' ('acquiescence to an abstract command'), and 'Jesus' strategic choice.' Weighed over against his powerful and insightful critique of the *Aqedah* and its religious interpretations in the previous 200 pages of the book, his final chapter ends on a weak and somewhat indecisive note with these words,

> It is time for us, whether believers or not, to come down to the place of promise, where we can see that no moral value attaches to sacrificing any human life for any cause, with the possible exception of one's own.[60]

These final words reflect Chilton's attempt to rescue interpretation of Jesus' sacrifice unto death as in some way positive and worth emulation. In this final assessment, Chilton describes Jesus' self sacrifice as *his* choice, a noble choice, because Jesus is 'fully aware of emotions and doubts running through him,' but nevertheless 'made a choice to offer his life for his sheep.' Chilton continues with the argument that this martyrdom is somehow different, because it is not mere display, but an honest confrontation with one's own emotional state and external conditions. Once again, I fear, sacrificial violence has been analyzed and critiqued only to be, at the end, as with Heim, reinscribed.

One of the most compelling passages in Heim's book is his retelling of a friend's daydream. The friend remembers an incident from her childhood, when in the third grade, she was a part of a group that scapegoated an eight year-old boy, 'too pretty' and 'who probably didn't smell like the others.' Even in the third grade, the friend confesses, she knew she was doing something wrong by

59. Chilton, *Abraham's Curse*, p. 211.
60. Chilton, *Abraham's Curse*, p. 224.

participating in the daily torment of this boy, yet she was too afraid of being ostracized herself to do anything different. But as the day-dream continues, another child enters into the story, not someone with super powers, or different in any significant way, except that he was 'absolutely without fear.' Why? We don't really find out. Standing by the scapegoated child on the playground, he looks out at the tormenting group and says, 'Now we're going to play something else.' The friend concludes, 'And we all followed him, and we played. I can't remember what we played, just the huge feeling of relief in my chest.'[61]

In a somewhat disconnected second scene, the friend has another flash of memory. The same boy who started the new game is now cruelly hung on a chain link fence by older children who have made him the new scapegoat. Heim wishes to draw a connection between these two scenes, as if the second must inevitably follow from the first, but one wonders: must it? Some careful distinctions are in order here. This is not to refute the idea that standing before a scapegoating dynamic and refusing to participate *may in fact* lead to becoming the object of violence oneself. But if we theorize in such a way so as to present this as the dominant, inevitable or necessary human expectation with respect to conflict (as Girard and so many Christian theologians do), we only increase the likelihood that this dynamic will be repeated over and over again. Are there not also many examples in history when resistance to scapegoating has *not* resulted in violence?

Even the Bible contains narratives along these lines, such as the story of the Hebrew midwives who commit civil disobedience against the Pharaoh by refusing to kill Hebrew babies! (Exod. 1.15-22).[62] We need deeper analysis of power relations having to do with social status, class, economic power, gender, ethnicity, race and other markers of identity, power and privilege, and their role in inter-personal, social and political conflicts, as well as analysis of a wide variety of just peacemaking tactics, if we are to understand how and why resistance strategies create positive change in some contexts and are responded to by violence and repression in others.[63]

61. Heim, *Saved From Sacrific* , p. 225.
62. Wink, *Engaging the Powers*, p. 244.
63. See Perry Bush, 'Violence, Nonviolence and the Search for Answers in History,' in J. Denny Weaver and Gerald Beisecker-Mast (eds), *Teaching Peace:*

In fact, analyses of violence and strategies for direct nonviolent action underscore a whole variety of consequences that result from resisting scapegoating violence, and an increasing diversity of tactics with which to challenge violence. Glen Stassen and Michael L. Westmoreland-White define violence as 'destruction to a victim by means that overpower the victim's consent.'[64] Their careful defin-tion not only addresses the violence of war, but also encompasses violence that results from structural and systemic practices such as poverty, racism and sexism. It additionally incorporates the authoritarian character of dominating violence that strives to overpower the consent, judgment and human rights of its victims. According to these writers, resistance to violent structures *does* include persuasion that takes place through witnessing others' nonresistant action or martyrdom. But this is only one tactic among others, not the single or perhaps even the most important or effective tactic. Additional strategies to resist and promote change include argument, and nonviolent coercion through strike, boycotts, political action, or through various forms of collective pressure including ostracism and passive resistance. Moreover, just peacemaking strategies to decrease war represent further development of proactive and reactive strategies to reduce violence and its consequences. In other words, the naming of and resistance to systems of sacrificial scapegoating violence include a whole spectrum of strategies and practices.

Yet much Christian theology shares with war-culture the assumption that to resist sacrificial violence inevitably leads to consequential violence as the 'necessary' or inevitable conclusion. Even theologians of nonviolent soteriologies struggle with this temptation, such as J. Denny Weaver:

> The ultimate character of his [Jesus'] mission produced an ultimate response, namely killing him...Jesus did not relish dying, and he did not want to die. Apparently he could have saved his

Nonviolence and the Liberal Arts (New York: Rowan and Littlefield, 2003). Also see, Ched Myers' work on Jesus and the disciples' nonviolent direct action as portrayed in the Gospel of Mark. *Binding the Strong Man: A Political Reading of Mark's Story of Jesus* (Maryknoll, NY: Orbis Books, 1988). See Chapter Five for more in depth exploration of Just Peacemaking Theory.

64. Glen Stassen and Michael Westmoreland-White, 'Defining Violence and Nonviolence,' in Weaver and Beisecker-Mast, *Teaching Peace: Nonviolence and the Liberal Arts* (New York: Rowman and Littlefield, 2003), pp. 17–38.

life (Matthew 26:53), but that would have meant failing his mission. He chose to die rather than fail his mission.[65]

Does this theological exposition strengthen theorizing that posits violence and suffering as the only way to create positive change? In contrast to this thinking, note the simplicity and ease with which the child in the daydream says, 'Now we're going to play something else,' and the bubble is burst – in a way not dissimilar to the story from the Gospels Heim told earlier, when Jesus deflated the scapegoating intent of the group determined to stone the woman.

We need to pay closer attention to the body of literature that has emerged in recent decades exploring and outlining strategies for successfully countering potential and actual violence with actions that do not require the injury or death of any party, yet, as Wink notes, 'people not only have been kept ignorant of past nonviolent efforts, but often are unable to recognize them when they are happening right under their noses.'[66] Perhaps the most striking example of such narratives are those that run counter to American assumptions about the necessity of total war against the Nazis as 'the good war.' Our overly simplistic assumptions about the necessity and inevitability of violence to meet the threat of fascism is, in fact, unsettled when we explore the array of historical examples from the period of World War II demonstrating that '…nonviolence *did* work whenever it was tried against the Nazis.' From Bishop Kiril of Bulgaria, to Rumania's refusal to surrender Rumanian Jews, to Finland, Denmark, Norway, even in Italy, 'friendly noncompliance [was] more frustrating [to Nazi generals] than any other form of resistance, and [they] had no effective means to counter it.'[67] Again, the point here is not to argue against coercion, including the force of arms, in every instance. Nor is the point to argue against those

---

65. J. Denny Weaver, 'The Nonviolent Atonement: Human Violence, Discipleship and God,' in Brad Jersak and Michael Hardin (eds), *Stricken by God? Nonviolent Identification and the Victory of Christ* (Grand Rapids, MI: Eerdmans, 2007), pp. 352–53.

66. Wink, *Engaging the Powers*, p. 243. See also Glen Stassen *et al*, *Just Peacemaking* (Cleveland, OH: The Pilgrim Press, 1998).

67. Wink, *Engaging the Powers*, p. 255. Perry Bush's chapter noted above in Weaver and Beisecker-Mast, *Teaching Peace*, includes a more extensively developed argument that raises questions about assumptions regarding World War II as 'the good war.'

powerful historical instances in which visible suffering led to a huge impact in changing social injustices (such as occurred in many instances in the Civil Rights Movement in the U.S.). Instead, I am trying to shed light on the operations of that deeply embedded cognitive framework in U.S. culture, 'the myth of redemptive violence,' and its connections to Christian theology in U.S. War-culture. Essentializing the need for sacrificial suffering and death in war-culture is empowered by the same essentializing in Christian theology regarding the need for Jesus' suffering and death for salvation.

In fact, according to the 'narrative Christus Victor' theory of atonement developed by J. Denny Weaver, the problem with so many portrayals of atonement is precisely their emphasis on the *need* for Jesus' death, whether it be to satisfy God's honor or wrath, to reveal or teach something to humanity, or to display God's love.[68] In contrast to Heim, who understands Jesus' primary mission as dying to expose and overcome the scapegoat mechanism, Weaver insists that God did not will or need Jesus' death for any reason.[69] But even Weaver's efforts to outline a nonviolent atonement are complicated by the depth of contradictory images in sacred text. Weaver finds himself in the tricky position of working through a nonviolent soteriology utilizing scriptural imagery from the book of Revelation, a text deeply rooted in the experiences and images of war and state terrorism.

A strong element of suspicion is required in the presence of so many diverse soteriological accounts that either require Jesus' death or reinscribe sacrific as the 'necessary' solution to realities of human sin and social and structural violence. Weaver's question (who 'needs' Jesus' death?) should be placed before every proposed framework as a way to trace troubling dynamics of sacrifice and the essentializing of violence in Christian atonement. Not only outright sacrificial models, but also reinscribed sacrificial theories or models of Christian salvation will only maximize war-culture, especially as we find it in the U.S. context.

---

68. J. Denny Weaver, *The Nonviolent Atonement* (Grand Rapids, MI: Eerdmans, 2001). Also see 'The Nonviolent Atonement: Human Violence, Discipleship and God,' in Brad Jersak and Michael Hardin (eds), *Stricken by God? Nonviolent Identification and the Victory of Chris* (Grand Rapids, MI: Eerdmans, 2007).

69. Weaver, *Stricken by God*, p. 352.

II. The Meaning of Jesus' Life and Death: Surrogacy and Sacrament

A powerful tension is alive in contemporary Christian theology be-tween those theologians who assert that there is power and meaning in the suffering and death of Jesus for followers and communities; and those who wish to lay stronger emphasis on the importance of Jesus' life and ministry (or resurrection) as salvific. A snapshot of this tension may be seen through comparison and contrast of two Womanist theologians, Delores S. Williams and JoAnne Marie Terrell. For Williams, Jesus' 'ministerial vision,' captured in his lan-guage about the Kingdom of God, *does not* point to death; in other words, the Kingdom of God does not require one's death in order to become actualized. The primary significance of the cross is its pow-er to reveal the depth of sin 'in its most desecrated form.' Williams is adamant that the meaning of the cross is *not* about Jesus' conquer-ing of sin. Instead, the overcoming of sin occurs in the Gospels when Jesus journeys 'into the wilderness' to be tempted by the devil, and learns resistance. She concludes,

> The resurrection of Jesus and the Kingdom-of-God-theme in Jesus'
> ministerial vision provide black women with the knowledge that
> God has, through Jesus, shown humankind how to live peacefully,
> productively and abundantly in relationship. Humankind is there-
> fore redeemed through Jesus' life and not through Jesus' death.[70]

Williams highlights the way traditional soteriological models confer cosmic approval on the surrogacy experiences of black wom-en. *Penal substitutionary* models of atonement reify the unjust substi-tutionary patterns of black women's labor. Just as Jesus 'stands in' to receive punishment rightfully assigned by God to sinful human beings, so black women have been coerced into surrogacy roles. With their labor, nurturance and sexuality, black women 'stand in' for white women and/or men. As the field slave, the hard labor of the black woman was expected to rise to the level of any man's. As the 'mammy' the domestic slave cared for the children of white families at the expense of caring for her own. Finally, her body was not her own, and the slave thus was coerced into sexual relations

70. Delores S. Williams, 'Black Women's Surrogacy Experience and the Christian Notion of Redemption,' in Marit Trelstad (ed.), *Cross Examinations*: Readings on the Meaning of the Cross Toda, in Marit Trelstad (ed.), (Minneapolis, MN: Fortress Press, 2006). See also, Delores S. Williams, *Sisters in the Wilderness: The Challenge of Womanist God-Talk* (Maryknoll, NY: Orbis Books, 1995).

or raped outright, thus acting as the sexual surrogate for the white wife of the slave owner. Williams further traces the way these relations from the period of slavery continued in antebellum times and into the present era.

Therefore, through her excavation of the institution of surrogacy, Williams shows how social arrangements are ingrained and substantiated by way of theological assumptions. The argument I make in this book is similar: war-culture rests upon a sea bed of cultural values that are naturalized and absolutized by way of religious assumptions. The necessity of war and the 'inevitable' suffering that ensues (and in addition the positioning of such suffering as a 'necessary sacrifice'), not to mention the assumed 'nobility' associated with the ability to wage war and become formed as a warrior – these are cultural givens that are assumed to be natural, 'just the way things are.' Religious assumptions have played a strong role in the process of just such reification, naturalization and sacralization.

But to return to the tension between Williams and Terrell: if Williams draws back from willingness to assign anything positive, hopeful or encouraging about the death of Jesus, Terrell's writing moves in a different direction altogether. For Terrell, 'there is power in the blood.'[71] She emphasizes the countless generations who have found meaning and hope by seeing their own stories of unjust suffering mirrored in the story of Jesus in the Christian Gospels. 'Jesus was God *incarnate*, who lived, struggled, and died in suffering solidarity with society's victims.'[72] For Terrell the key component to analyze in sacrificial stories and schemes is the possibility of agency. The problem is *imposed* sacrifice, not sacrifice that is *chosen* for the sake of a higher good. In fact, the conscious choosing of sacrifice may even be 'sacramental.' Furthermore, a sacramental notion of sacrifice has saving significance for African American women and helps them to channel pain into service for the community. In the sacramental understanding of sacrifice Terrell envisions a 'holistic spirituality,' that aims to foster human freedom. Unlike Williams, she refuses to give up on the idea of sacrifice

71. JoAnne Marie Terrell, 'Our Mothers' Gardens: Rethinking Sacrifice,' in Marit Trelstad (ed.), *Cross Examinations: Readings on the Meaning of the Cross Today*, (Minneapolis, MN: Fortress Press, 2006). Also see, JoAnne Marie Terrell, *Power in the Blood? The Cross in African American Experience* (Maryknoll, NY: Orbis Books, 1998).

72. Terrell, 'Our Mothers' Gardens,' p. 42.

particularly the notion of sacrifice as the surrender or destruction of something prized or desirable for the sake of something with a higher claim, a potentially salvific notion with communal dimensions that got lost in the rhetorical impetus of the language of surrogacy.[73]

Thus, Terrell describes Jesus and the martyrs of the church as 'empowered, sacramental witnesses, not victims who passively acquiesced to evil.'

Terrell's work underscores the importance of Jesus as the 'Co-Sufferer.' In Jesus, Christians see and experience the reality of a God who fully embraces humankind, especially in any instance of suffering and injustice. As Martin Luther would put it, it is precisely at those moments when humans feel most abandoned and most at risk ('My God, my God, why have you forsaken me?') that God, in ways unperceived and unknowable to us, is most deeply present. Theologian Dori Grineko Baker describes a similar theological assertion that arose when she attempted to profoundly listen to the narratives spoken by adolescent girls about their life struggles: 'God is mysteriously omnipresent, but not magically omnipotent. Although we cannot explain it, God *is* at work within human tragedies to create healing potential. God may not fix things, but neither does God abandon us.'[74]

At the same time, questions emerge in connection with what Terrell has asserted, beginning with Terrell's discussion of agency with respect to sacrificial acts. What differentiates certain forms of self-sacrifice from others, and what may justify them, according to Terrell, is the idea that individuals freely destroy or surrender something for the sake of a higher good (in this sense Terrell's analysis is similar to Chilton's). Yet, in a culture such as ours, with such deeply embedded cognitive frameworks as the heroic nature of self-sacrifice, and the sacred tenor of suffering that follows, not to mention the necessity of sacrifice for the payment of sin, to what degree is such agency truly possible? How will we distinguish between sacrifice that is enacted as a result of capitulation to such schemes and sacrifice that is 'freely chosen?' Moreover, as theological critics of sacrifice have pointed out, all too often sacrificial mandates are

73. Terrell, 'Our Mothers' Gardens,' p. 49.
74. Dori Grinenko Baker, *Doing Girlfriend Theology: God-Talk with Young Women* (Cleveland, OH: The Pilgrim Press, 2005), p. 40.

directed to the least powerful and most marginalized of any society. Determining 'agency,' then, is fraught with complexity.

Second, the idea of 'sacramentalism' associated with sacrifice, also is problematic. Terrell suggests that sacramentalizing suffering may help assist the victims of suffering to channel their pain in positive ways. Yet is it not also likely that such sacramentalization justifies and rationalizes the social circumstances that create this suffering in the first place? Moreover, the dynamic of 'sacramentalism' is exactly akin to that which I am criticizing in this chapter, the problem of absolutizing or divinizing the 'necessary sacrifices' through which war and war-culture are justified and rationalized. Nevertheless, the question that I think resides beneath Terrell's desire to retain the notion of sacramentalism is an important one. The losses due to suffering seem insurmountable and unbearable; without some way of placing them into a transcendent frame of meaning, can we withstand their presence in our lives? This question is taken up later in this chapter and also in Chapter Five.

Excursis on Sacrifice: Nancy Jay's Anthropological Analysi

While rituals, practices and meanings of sacrifice diverge across chronology and context, the logic of sacrifice tends to operate in two ways simultaneously.[75] According to anthropologist Nancy Jay, the logic of sacrifice: 1) joins people together in community and 2) separates them from impurity, disease, evil, sin and other dangers. In other words, sacrifice is integrative and at the same time expiatory or differentiating. She writes,

> Joining and separating…are problematic because sacrifice is never so neatly one-sided. …Scholars have discussed communion and expiation as if they were wholly separate kinds of action, but their interdependence, both logical and ritual, is a regular feature of [even] unrelated sacrificial traditions [76]

Jay examines sacrificial logic and ritual in diverse ancient societies, Greek, Nuer and Israelite, and concludes that though completely disconnected from one another, all three sacrificial systems evince two aspects of resemblance: first, in unrelated traditions, the distribution of the victim's flesh 'indexes the alimentary community.' In

75. Nancy Jay, *Throughout Your Generations Forever*.
76. Jay, *Throughout Your Generations Forever*, pp. 17–18.

other words, those who eat the sacrificial meal together are formed into a social group and separated from others not belonging to the group. Second, a connection or association with 'femaleness' must be expiated through the sacrificial system. For the Nuer, the female principle is associated directly with evil; for the Greeks, childbirth and death both create pollution that must be abated by way of sacrifice; and lastly, among the Isrealites the uncleanness of menstruation and childbirth are related to pollution generally speaking.[77]

Jay's project is to explore the significance of sacrificial logic and ritual in the practices of unrelated communities. At the same time, she examines the development of theories of sacrifice that attempt to provide a universal framework for sacrificial practices. Overall, she summarizes, sacrificial theories have tended to fall into two different categories. 'Social contract theories' of sacrifice emphasize the sacrificial act as in some way overcoming an original violent state of male human nature. Freud, Hobbes and Girard all fit into this first category. In her critique of Girard, Jay shows how he grounds all community and culture on a male control of male violence. The role of sacrifice (and the sacred) are to redirect the liquid flow of hostility between enemy brothers whose mimetic desire always ends in reciprocal violence. Sacrificial rituals, thus, are a kind of 'booster shot' in Girardian theory, providing a small injection of violence (the attack on the scapegoat) in order to prevent a total loss of control. Girard assumes the necessity of sacrifice, given the unquestioned foundation of a universal human nature, which upon further examination, is determined by biologically-given male violence.

In other words, Girard's theory depends on a 'dispositional' understanding of human nature, in which violence and evil are universally rooted. In contrast, 'situationist' perspectives on the reality of evil seek to explore a variety of external determinants of behavior, to try to understand, for instance, how seemingly 'good' people may be formed into torturers of other humans. One famous case involves scholars who investigated patterns of hatred, bias and scapegoating in the World War II era. According to psychologist Phillip Zimbardo, 'dispositional bias' led psychological researchers such as Adorno, Levinson and others, to try to identify various personality factors underlying behavioral hatred toward Jews and other minority groups during World War II. But this same propensity to

77. Jay, *Throughout Your Generations Forever*, pp. 28–29.

locate violence in human nature was later criticized. It failed to take notice of important political, economic, societal and other historical processes that also deeply influenced the development of this channeled behavior of hatred and violence on the part of so many.[78] Dispositional frameworks miss important contextual characteristics that contribute to violence and evil. And Girard's model, based on such a dispositional framework, thus, is too narrow in scope to fully map out the complex and diverse realities of violence and evil in human individuals and societies.[79]

In addition to 'social contract theories' of sacrifice, Jay analyzes 'Durkheimian' constructions of sacrifice. In these theories, sacrifice is less about the joining and separation of social groups, and more about addressing the dichotomy between the sacred and the profane, a 'great gulf that can only be crossed by a victim in death.' Like the first category, however, Durkheimian theories of sacrifice rely upon constructions of an eternal human nature, 'separating consciousness from mortal individuals and making it unitary and transcendent.' The problem with such constructions is that they inevitably tend to represent those in power, who are likely all to be men.

According to Jay, the logic and rituals of sacrifice not only issue into a useful way to control religious meaning, but are equally effective in centralizing channels of communication with transcendent powers (who, of course, provide legitimation for the social order). Thus, sacrificial systems work to legitimate a world in which male domination (as the foundation of human nature) is essentialized and eternalized. Sacrifice becomes coterminous with patriarchal civilization; domination is 'sacrificially maintained.[80]

---

78. Phillip G. Zimbardo, 'A Situationist Perspective on the Psychology of Evil: Understanding How Good People are Transformed into Perpetrators,' in A.G. Miller (ed.), *The Social Psychology of Good and Evil* (New York: Guilford, 2004).

79. According to historian Jon Pahl, 'Girard never addresses violence and religion in American culture, and consequently fails to recognize the hybrid forms of religious violence as they have emerged in civil and cultural religions.' See Jon Pahl, *Empire of Sacrifice: The Religious Origins of American Violence* (New York: New York University Press, 2010), Chapter One, 'Rethinking Violence and Religion in America,' pp. 13–34. See also Chilton's critique of Girardian theory, 'Sacrificial Mimesis,' *Religion* 27. 3 (Jl 1997), pp. 225–30.

80. Jay, *Throughout Your Generations Forever*, p. 150.

In conclusion, Jay claims that universal theories of sacrifice are not the most helpful tool for deconstructing and analyzing sacrificial frameworks, patterns, rituals and social arrangements. Better understanding may be achieved by raising key questions about the relationships between the logic and rituals of sacrifice, social organization and gender. We should ask questions such as the following: How does sacrifice work to form social groups and their boundaries? Who is included, and who excluded? What is the relation of childbearing women to sacrificial practices? How does sacrifice operate so as to provide intergenerational continuity between men? To what degree do sacrificial logic and practice facilitate social reproduction (and minimize the significance of sexual reproduction)?

Jay believed that by the end of the twentieth century, blood sacrificial religions were on the wane in a world of increasing industrial production, markets, and scientific and technological development. She wrote in the conclusion of her book,

> Blood sacrifice does not even make sense in contemporary industrial society, where separate individuals, joined in temporary, voluntary association, are thought of as basic units of society; where social institutions are not conceived as integrated by descent, real or metaphorical.'[81]

Writing before the terrorist destruction of the World Trade Center's twin towers, Jay found it difficult to imagine that the maintenance and reproduction of domination by way of rhetoric and rituals of blood sacrifice could be sustained into the twenty-first century in places such as the United States. But as I attempt to demonstrate in this book, these frameworks powerfully live on. The electrical conduit of sacrifice, sacralized by way of its connections with Christian sacrificial frameworks, energizes both the status of U.S. warriors and war-culture in the United States and masks all-too-real systems of control and destructive power.

III. Sacrificialism: The Tie that Binds Economics with War-Culture

Christian theology has not yet fully come to grips with the problematic nature of sacrificialism in Christianity and its impact on Western life and thought. The depth of embedded sacrificial cognitive frameworks and their resulting subconscious existence in our lives makes

81. Jay, *Throughout Your Generations Forever*, p. 150.

them exceedingly difficult to unearth and examine, much less criticize. Yet Jay's work demonstrates the importance of questions we must pose in the face of sacrificial constructions. Analyses of power, class, race, gender and more are required in order to expose the way dominating actors utilize sacrificial logic to demand or justify the sacrifice of the dominated. We need to counter the essentializing of violence as the sole antidote to conflict. Here I discuss a third response to the problem of sacrifice represented by yet another group of theologians. A school of Latin American Liberation theologians has been working on the problem of sacrificial cognitive frameworks with respect to 'economic religion' and 'its fascination both with its promises and its demands for sacrifices.' Brazilian theologian Jung Mo Sung explores neoliberal economics and the problem of sacrificialism in Christianity and society.[82]

Sung outlines the belief structure that undergirds neoliberal economics. This, of course, is a belief structure largely held by those who have 'won' in the economic system, in other words, those who hold capital. In 'the theology of the new economic order' the market is 'the way and the truth' leading to abundant life. 'Original sin' consists in any pretension having to do with directing the market from outside in order to address economic and social evils. 'The proud' consist of those groups such as labor unions, ecclesial movements, political parties of the left and so forth, all who stand guilty of encouraging such market manipulation from outside. They only delay 'the arrival of paradise,' the benefits of the market coming fully into existence. The market is omniscient and omnipotent. To love is to defend one's self-interest in the market and 'to avoid the temptation to do good' by meddling in market dynamics. Finally, in order to allow the market to arrive at its full potential, we must endure and enact those 'necessary sacrifices' along the way demanded by market laws.

In this way, Sung describes two sides of one economic coin. On the one side is the 'redeeming progress' of the market coming fully into being. Commodities go to where there are a greater number of votes or dollars. On the other side of the coin, however, are the suffering and death of millions of people, the 'necessary sacrifices' for

---

82. Jung Mo Sung, *Desire, Market and Religion* (London: SCM Press, 2007). Other theologians who are working on these issues include Franz Hinkelammert, Ivone Gebara, Elsa Tamez and more.

this same progress. These sacrifices may take the form of employment cuts, higher costs of living, austerity programs and more, all of which supposedly promise a better future, greater competitiveness and freedom for the flow of capital. In addition, just as we saw earlier in the proclamation that 'the sacrifices that war brings are good for people,' a parallel justification occurs in this economic system of belief. In the place of a strong collective social responsibility for the welfare of all, the owners of capital put forth an argument to justify the lopsided economic reality from which they benefit: economic sacrifices in the long run are good and healthy for the general public. This is a 'shame-blame game that hides a shifting of burdens from the strong to the weak,' 'an undeniable sign that rationalizing ideologies are actively at work.'[83] Moreover, the tie between this 'economic religion' and war is further undergirded by belief that war brings economic benefits. Yet even in the case of World War II, which many people assume was the economic engine that ended the Great Depression in the United States, economists warn us against such naïve thinking. While economic gains did come in the early stages of the war, when the United States was still selling goods but was not yet a combatant, the situation changed significantly once the United States entered the war. As one economist observes,

> While overall economic output was rising, and the military draft lowered unemployment, the war years were generally not prosperous ones. As for today, we shouldn't think that fighting a war is the way to restore economic health.[84]

Yet Michael Novak has gone so far as to directly provide the theological framework for the assumption that sacrifice is a natural and necessary element in neoliberal market practices. 'If God so willed his beloved Son to suffer, why would He spare us?' In response to such thinking, Sung writes,

83. Bob Goudzwaard with Julio de Santa Ana, 'The Modern Roots of Economic Globalization,' in Julio de Santa Ana (ed.), *Beyond Idealism: A Way Ahead for Ecumenical Social Ethics* (Grand Rapids, MI: Eerdmans, 2006), p. 118.

84. Tyler Cowen, 'The New Deal Didn't Always Work, Either,' *The New York Times*, Economic View, 23 November 2008. See also Robert Higgs, *Depression, War and the Cold War* (Oakland, CA: Independent Institute, 2006), and Ronald L. Friesen, 'War and Peace in Economic Terms,' in J. Denny Weaver and Gerald Beisecker-Mast (eds), *Nonviolence and the Liberal Arts* (New York: Rowman and Littlefield, 2003). Chapter One addresses 'military Keynesianism,' the analysis of military spending as an economic stimulant.

> The transcendentalized market provides to the exercised violence
> in the name of the market laws a purity that allows it to be per-
> ceived as something positive and creative: the economic religion.

Sacrificialism has led to the idea of the inevitability of inequality
and social exclusion (these realities become 'necessary sacrifices').
Those who are the beneficiaries of current market systems 'are receiving what they fairly deserve,' while the poor are seen either as
guilty for their poverty or inexcusably inefficient. Yet the incentive
structure of capitalism, with its emphasis on the idea of maximiz-
ing personal consumption, is less than 200 years old. What *is* of
course much, much older are the sacrificial cognitive frameworks
that undergird this structure and animate it. Thus, Sung concludes,
theologians must grapple much more seriously with the sacrificial
constructions at the heart of Western Christianity itself. 'Sacrificial
logic underlies the sacralization of a social system of human works
and institutions; this logic has the capacity to reverse the notion of
good and evil.'[85]

Sung would not have us do away with markets in their entirety;
his emphasis is not on the inherent evil of the market itself, but the
evil of the sacralization of markets, the market as idol, what he calls
'the transcendentalization of the market.' When we associate the
market with the capacity to solve 'by unconscious automatism' all
social and economic problems, we have elevated the market to a
form of religion. More to the point of this chapter, what energizes
and enlivens such transcendentalization is the logic of 'necessary
sacrifices.' For Sung, the economy must exist for the life of all people; the religion of neoliberal economics, in contrast, preaches that
people exist for economic laws based in the accumulation of wealth,
and that sacrifices even to the present have not been effective, because too many still persist in failing to accept the inevitability of
market laws.[86] Sung continues with a trenchant criticism of the impact of sacrificial constructs within Christian tradition itself

> We know that the market absorbed its sacrificial theology from
> a determined historical configuration of Christianity. It is obvi-
> ous that sacrificialism was and is present in many other religions
> and societies. The influence of Christian sacrificial theology in the
> mentality of the West is also undeniable. In the struggle against
> the culture of insensitivity that marks our time, it is fundamental

85. Sung, *Desire, Market and Religion*, p. 72.
86. Sung, *Desire, Market and Religion*, p. 94.

that we show that human suffering, particularly the suffering of the poor and excluded, is not part of God's demand for salvation. We need living practices and witnesses to show that what God wants is "mercy, not sacrifice" (Mt. 9.13) [87]

I wish at this juncture to return to the tension I outlined earlier between Womanist theologians Williams and Terrell. As a result of her unflinching examination of the power of theological frameworks to reify and naturalize the social injustice of black women's surrogacy, Williams has arrived at the position of outright jettisoning sacrificial frameworks as having to do anything with salvation. In contrast, Terrell's thinking may be compared to what Jung Mo Sung has called 'a left-wing sacrificialism' – in other words, the requiring (or sacramentalizing) of sacrifices in the struggle for a society without sacrifice. A contradiction is at the heart of Christian suffering experience: those who suffer, such as those women described by Terrell, experience the contradiction between their ongoing suffering reality and the proclamation of a God who desires salvation. Yet far too often Christianity has claimed that God cannot save us without sacrifice, without some sort of suffering in order to pay for sin or otherwise mitigate the reality of evil. Sacrificial theologies transform suffering into a kind of payment or necessity that is exacted by God, or required or inevitable given a world of human sin.

Sung is part of a body of liberation theologians that reject such understanding. They seek a different theology, a god 'who wants change.' Yet far too often, the change that does occur 'seems so little.' Where is the Kingdom? A crisis of *utopia* emerges, a profound existential intensity. Some liberation theologians return to the theology of sacrificialism at this point. They speak of the Kingdom of God as a *utopia*, 'a horizon that makes it possible to leave behind and postpone (sacrifice) everything, even one's own child/life/–' (you fill in the blank).

For Sung, the return to sacrificialism at this juncture is to fall into a pretension of modern reason: the belief in the possibility to construct a perfect society within history, in other words, a theology of progress. This pretension inevitably leads to sacrifici l demands. Therefore, in view of the dangers of sacrificialism, Sung suggests an alternative interpretive frame. We should redefine *utopia* as the condition for us to be able to elaborate theories of action, even while

87. Sung, *Desire, Market and Religion*, p. 98.

we insist on the historic non-attainability of the Kingdom (or to translate *basilea* more inclusively, 'God's intended world').[88] God's intended world always remains ahead of us, as goal and criterion for judging all contemporary attempts at greater justice-making.

Seeking Ways Forward

One place to begin, to follow Sung and Jay's admonitions, is with a theory of action (as opposed to a theory of sacrifice) to address suffering experience. Some 35 years ago, Dorothee Soelle reminded us that we must seek the causes of suffering in order to eliminate it, and the meaning of suffering in order to discover our humanity.[89] Soelle came out strongly against 'Christian masochism and sadism,' in other words, religious interpretation of suffering as punishment, training or expiation. Like Delores S. Williams, Soelle was worried about the alliance between repressive theism (God requiring sacrifice and suffering in order to teach or save us) and repressive society (the supposedly 'necessary sacrifices' in social arrangements sacralized by theological assumptions). For Soelle, seeking the causes of suffering meant investigating a phenomenology of suffering. She described 'affliction' as involving three distinct elements: 1) physical pain; 2) psychological pain, the sense of being poured out, numbed, imprisoned; and 3) social degradation, the abandonment, ridiculing or scapegoating of the sufferer.[90] Yet Soelle was concerned not only with the propensity of sadistic ecclesiastical structures and doctrine, she equally criticized the prevalence of human apathy, our desire to avoid, repress or separate ourselves from our own suffering or the suffering of others.

> People stand before suffering like those who are color-blind, incapable of perception and without any sensibility. The consequence of this suffering-free state of well-being is that people's lives become frozen solid.[91]

88. This is Schüssler Fiorenza's translation of the Greek phrase from the New Testament, *basilea tou theou.*

89. Dorothee Soelle, *Suffering* (Trans. Everett Kalin; Minneapolis, MN: Fortress Press, 1975).

90. Soelle draws upon the phenomenology of Simone Weil for her typology of suffering. See Weil, 'The Love of God and Affliction,' *Waiting for God* (New York: Harper, 1951).

91. Soelle, *Suffering*, p. 38.

Soelle drew upon a 'historicized' interpretation of Jesus' passion and resurrection to find a way beyond theological sadism/masochism on the one hand, and frozen human life on the other. What is important about Jesus' passion is our realization that Jesus' experience is one that may happen to anyone. We might compare Soelle's thinking with Terrell's insight, with regard to the depth and meaning Christians have found in Jesus as 'Co-sufferer.' What must our response be? A first step is to lament, to express ourselves, to grieve, to ask 'why?' What then of the narratives of Jesus' resurrection? Soelle wrote that a 'historicized' resurrection may be described as those historical moments and places where humans somehow find it possible to continue to love and affirm life, even in the midst of suffering and uncertainty. I appreciate Soelle's beautiful delineation of the resurrection for its very modesty. Victimization, violence and suffering continue, yet despite this reality, we as humans struggle and sometimes manage (with God's help) to continue to love, heal and affirm l fe.

Here Soelle again finds company with Terrell, in her emphasis on finding a way through suffering to love, affirmation and service for the flourishing of all. Yet it also should be noted that Soelle, unlike Terrell, does not link this way through to sacrifice. A key nuance further emerges. For Soelle, suffering in and of itself is not the issue: the key is whether we will *work* on and with suffering. As humans we will suffer; suffering is inevitable in human experience (thus suffering is *not* glorified in and of itself). The question is, as opposed to masochism, sadism or apathy, will suffering become our *passion*? In other words, will we perceive, express ourselves, weep?

> To meditate on the cross means to say good-bye to the narcissistic hope of being free of sickness, deformity and death. Then all the energies wasted on such hopes could become free to answer the call to respond to suffering.[92]

This is to reject apathy as a response to the reality of suffering. But Soelle takes this even further, for not only does she reject apathy and 'human frozenness,' she advocates action and involvement. For Soelle, the only meaningless suffering is that which occurs when people can no longer *work* on suffering, that is, when suffering has destroyed all human ability and power.[93] Suffering is not to be

---

92. Soelle, *Suffering*, p. 131.

93. Tom Beaudoin in this respect underscores the importance of 'the penitential role of theology' as described by Johannes Baptist Metz. In the face of

borne, tolerated or endured – none of these reactions changes the reality of suffering; instead suffering changes as Christians affirm life, though suffering indeed accompanies it; and as they work on suffering and 'hold it open for the promised future.'[94]

Theological schemes that attempt to interpret suffering as a kind of vindication of the power of God through powerlessness, or that encourage willingness to suffer as central to Christian identity, or that posit a kind of righteousness behind the reality of suffering, or that interpret Jesus' suffering as a necessary sacrifice or scapegoat for sin – all move in the direction of theological sadism. In contrast, Soelle explores what she describes as a paradoxical freedom to *work* with suffering to expand love. She reflects on the last letters of those condemned to die by the Nazis, and is struck by these same letters' lack of bitterness or anger, and also by the expression of a deep love for those the writers are leaving behind. 'Facing death they know they may not avoid, they demonstrate concern for others, a deep knowledge of the connection between sorrow and joy, and a desire to impart a mission to those who remain.'[95] This is work with salvific and humanizing potential.

Liberation theologian, Jon Sobrino, has also reminded us that theology begins with honesty toward reality. 'It is extremely difficult to see and hear reality, to let it be without manipulation.'[96] In a world of structural injustice, institutionalized violence and institutionalized concealment of both injustice and violence, such honesty is hard to come by. In the context of U.S. War-culture and its trumpet call regarding the necessity and valor of sacrifi e, Christian interpretation of the life and death of Jesus as sacrifice has played a destructive role, and has made it more difficult for us to see our reality as citizens of the U.S. honestly and fully. Given our context

suffering that has destroyed human ability and power, the role of theology is exposure to catastrophe and its survivors. We must 'think of faith only in the face of those challenges, and in so doing, hand over everything about the previous theological life that fed into the theology that helped create a profoundly intolerable situation for human beings.' Tom Beaudoin, *Witness to Dispossession: The Vocation of a Post-modern Theologian* (Maryknoll, NY: Orbis Books, 2008), pp. xii–xiii.

94. Soelle, *Suffering*, p. 107.

95. Soelle, *Suffering*, pp. 135–41.

96. Jon Sobrino, *Where is God? Earthquake, Terrorism, Barbarity, and Hope* (Trans. Margaret Wilde; Maryknoll, NY: Orbis Books, 2004), p. 29.

of war-culture in the United States, I do not believe it is wise or ethically defensible to attempt to rehabilitate theological sacrificial frameworks in our efforts to speak about and understand the meaning and nature of Christian ethics and practice. At the same time, given the centrality of sacrifice in Christian texts, tradition, history and practice, I realize that such a movement away from sacrifice is far from a simple or easy task.[97] Nevertheless, a way forward does emerge if we take seriously Nancy Jay's insistent questions posed to sacrificial structures and logic; and when we take into consideration Jung Mo Sung's recommendation that we redefine *utopia* as the condition for us to be able to elaborate theories of action, even while we insist on the historic non-attainability of God's intended world. One way forward is to continue to peel back the layers of sacrificial constructions where we find them, in our search for greater truth and honesty about ourselves. If Sung aptly criticized not the market in and of itself, but the 'transcendentalization of the market,' our work to excavate the layers of sacrificial theologies and constructions of war-culture similarly 'detranscendentalizes' war-culture. I close this chapter with one such attempt.

Sacrifice and Commemorating Hiroshim

On the 50th anniversary of the dropping of the atomic bombs on Hiroshima and Nagasaki, the Smithsonian Institution attempted to mount an exhibition in commemoration and as an act of honest remembering. The story of this attempt is recounted in a beautiful and haunting book, *Hiroshima in America: A Half Century of Denial*, by historian Greg Mitchell and psychologist Robert Jay Lifton.[98] They describe the Smithsonian as 'America's national museum

97. I am struck and sobered by Bruce Chilton's assessment regarding what he sees as the impossibility and inadvisability of trying to do away with sacrificial dynamics. As I understand Chilton, it seems that he is suggesting that the best we can do is try to steer sacrifice toward more generous and less violent frameworks, the celebratory feast in place of blood rituals of sacrifice The ethical analysis of this chapter arrives at a different conclusion. Given the dangers and destructiveness of sacrificial frameworks uniting theology and war, a responsible ethics not only will analyze and critique such frameworks, but search for ways beyond and outside them. See 'Sacrificial Mimesis,' *Religion*, 27.3 (1997), pp. 225-30.

98. Greg Mitchell and Robert Jay Lifton, *Hiroshima in America: A Half-Century of Denial* (New York: Avon Books, 1995).

and repository of memory.'[99] We learn that by the late 1940s the Smithsonian came into possession of the *Enola Gay*, the plane that carried the atomic bomb over Hiroshima, but the plane was never publicly exhibited. Director of the Air and Space Museum, Martin Harwit, led the effort to put together four different displays to provide visitors to the Smithsonian with an opportunity to remember, to ask questions and to reflect on the meaning and consequences of these events. The four displays would explore: 1) the final months of the Pacific war; 2) the decision to drop the bomb; 3) the devastation of Hiroshima and Nagasaki; and 4) the postwar legacy of the nuclear arms race. At the same time, from their earliest planning, museum experts knew that this would not be a plan without controversy. As project manager Tom Crouch articulated the stakes at risk in one internal memo, 'Do you want to do an exhibition intended to make veterans feel good, or do you want an exhibition that will lead our visitors to think about the consequences of the atomic bombing of Japan?'[100]

Even before a first script for the exhibition was completed, internal memos were leaked to various veterans groups in the United States. The sparks of what would become a firestorm of reaction ignited. Part of the response had to do with the challenge of what Mitchell and Lifton describe as 'the official narrative' regarding the decisions and history leading to Hiroshima. The 'atomic cover-up' initiated by government officials before, during and especially after Hiroshima encouraged a tendency in the United States, the authors claim, that increasingly has connected secrecy with national security, and encouraged Americans not to think critically, demand information or engage in debate. 'We got used to putting the gravest problems, military and social, in the hands of experts and political leaders who claimed to have them under control.'[101]

Repeatedly, U.S. government from the time of the bombing forward, had publicly endorsed a casualty estimate for a planned invasion of Japan at 500,000 to 1 m American soldiers. The ideology of the 'necessity' of the bomb to save one million American lives became sacred text in the intervening decades; at the same time, the deaths of the Japanese were considered a reasonable sacrifice,

99. Mitchell and Lifton, *Hiroshima in America*, p. 277.
100. Mitchell and Lifton, *Hiroshima in America*, p. 279.
101. Mitchell and Lifton, *Hiroshima in America*, p. 335.

especially in light of the loss, pain and suffering Americans had suffered during the war. In contrast to this sacrificial logic, the museum intended to include information from more recently declassified government documents that disputed this 'official narrative.' They also intended to show declassified images that would provide many Americans with their first glimpse of the scope and nature of the atomic devastation.

Veterans were especially concerned about the last section of the exhibit on the bomb's legacy and the nuclear arms race; according to them, this would 'tarnish the Hiroshima mission.'[102] The controversy heated up further during the summer of 1994. On 10 August, 24 members of Congress sent a letter of protest to the Smithsonian secretary, calling the script 'narrow and biased,' and based on 'political correctness.' *The Washington Post* printed a blistering editorial. Authors Mitchell and Lifton note that even after the entire episode was over, when they tried to interview museum officials about what had taken place, many refused to speak about the series of events for fear that they might lose their jobs.

Additional media outlets began weighing in. *Newsweek* admonished the museum for daring to challenge 'the inescapable logic of the decision to use the bomb.' *The Wall Street Journal* chalked up the museum's intentions as the result of 'academics unable to view American history as anything other than a woeful catalog of crimes and aggressions...' The White House said nothing publicly but watched closely. Speaker Newt Gingrich called for the exhibit's cancellation and said that the Smithsonian had become 'a plaything for left-wing ideologies.' Perhaps the tenor of the protest was best described in the language of a letter written by Secretary of Veterans Affairs Jesse Brown to Smithsonian Curator Harwit, asserting that to question the righteousness of the decision to drop the bomb would dishonor all who served their nation in the Pacific.

Eventually, the exhibit was completely scaled back. Only the plane, *Enola Gay*, a plaque identifying it and a video of the crew recounting their experience would be included. The Secretary to the Smithsonian, Michael Heyman, described the decision at a press conference, saying that the museum had made a 'basic error':

102. Mitchell and Lifton, *Hiroshima in America*, pp. 282–283.

> In this special anniversary year, veterans and their families expected a tribute to their *valor* and *sacrific* . They were not looking for analysis and frankly, we did not give enough thought to the intense feelings such an analysis would evoke[103] (italics mine).

The sacred canopy of World War II veterans' 'necessary sacrifice' played a decisive role in these events. Not only did the unquestioned sacrificial framework enable continued secrecy and confusion of facts regarding this important history, it also contributed to what Lifton and Mitchell call 'psychic numbing ...a diminished capacity or inclination to feel.' They sum it up with these powerful words, 'If we can speak of an age of numbing, especially for Americans, it begins with Hiroshima.'[104]

The Smithsonian attempted to help the nation enter into profound address of a complex, painful and difficult chapter of our history, in a way that moves past the familiar tropes of American exceptionalism, and outside the 'black and white' thinking of sacrificial logic. Yet, if anything, the cementing of the 'official narrative' of Hiroshima and the mortar of those same characteristics of 'valor' and 'sacrifice' assigned to American soldiers of World War II are further reified in another very important and even more recent receptacle of memory. This is, of course, the World War II memorial on the national mall of Washington D.C., whose construction was completed and celebrated in May, 2004. The official website describes the memorial as:

> a monument to the spirit, *sacrific* and commitment of the American people to the common defense of the nation and to the broader causes of peace and freedom from tyranny throughout the world.[105] (Italics mine)

A central exhibit, 'Freedom wall,' decorated with white stars on a blue background (representing the American deaths that occurred in World War II), is emblazoned with words that reference the sacrificial framework, 'Here we mark the price of freedom.' Twenty four bas-relief panels commemorate various battles, the contributions of women and medics, various forms of weaponry, and especially scenes of liberation and victory. While there is one panel celebrating

103. Mitchell and Lifton, *Hiroshima in America*, p. 295.
104. Mitchell and Lifton, *Hiroshima in America*, p. 337.
105. National World War II Memorial website, http://www.wwiimemorial.com/default.asp?page=facts.asp&subpage=intro, accessed 29 March 2008.

the B-17 war plane, there is no mention of either the massive fir -
bombing of cities on the Allied European or Pacific fronts, or the
dropping of the atomic bombs, though one panel does commemorate the experience at Pearl Harbor.

We can learn a lot from studying this recent exercise in memorialization in the U.S. context. Perhaps one of its most important
functions is to determine what may be questioned, what may be
discussed, and what is definitively placed *off* the table of examination. If the search for greater honesty about ourselves requires peel-
ing back the layers of sacrificial logic, this memorial has the effect
of tying our hands behind our backs. We are invited to honor those
who participated in the war and especially, to mourn and honor
those U.S. military who died, but we are not invited to question or
ponder further. Ultimately, this memorial continues the process of
reification of a particular national identity, an identity that comes
from war, and from a deep cognitive framework regarding belief
in the redemptive nature of violence and the necessity of sacrifice
to achieve freedom and justice.[106] And in fact, isn't this precisely the
cognitive framework heard by so many U.S. citizens every Sunday
when they attend churches in our land?

Postscript

> Good morning. This weekend, families across America are com-
> ing together to celebrate Easter…during this special and holy time
> each year, millions of Americans pause to remember a sacrifice
> that transcended the grave and redeemed the world…On Easter
> we hold in our hearts those who will be spending this holiday far
> from home – our troops…I deeply appreciate the sacrifices that
> they and their families are making…On Easter, we especially re-
> member those who have given their lives for the cause of freedom.
> These brave individuals have lived out the words of the Gospel:
> "Greater love has no man than this, that a man lay down his life
> for his friends…"
>
> President George W. Bush, Easter 2008[107]

106. See Deborah D. Buffton, 'Memorialization and Selling War,' *Peace
Review: A Journal of Social Justice* 17. 1 (Jan–Mar 2005), pp. 25–31.

107. 'President's Radio Address, Easter 2008,' The White House: President
George W. Bush, http://georgewbush-whitehouse.archives.gov/news/
releases/2008/03/20080322.html, accessed 4 January 2010.

Thus the President of the United States continued to utilize the cognitive framework of sacrifice up to the end of his term, making a smooth elision between Christianity and war to sacralize the tragic loss of young life in the final months of his presidency. Yet this is a much bigger problem than just this president and his language. In fact, the language of sacrific was equally shared by Hillary Clinton, Barack Obama and John McCain in their campaign speeches during the 2008 presidential campaign. In particular, in the case of Clinton and especially Obama, such language was meant to stave off attack that they lacked 'national security credentials.' Even as Obama ran on a platform of having been against the Iraq war from the beginning of his campaign, his language about the necessity of war and the losses of war as heroic sacrifice is actually little different from that used by President George W. Bush. For instance, in a speech specifically laying out his resistance to the Iraq war and intention to remove the troops, Obama said,

> The sacrifices of war are immeasurable…As we stand at the beginning of the fifth year of this war, let us remember …the thousands upon thousands of families who are living the very real consequences and immeasurable sacrifices that have come from our decision to invade Iraq. We are so blessed in this country to have so many men and women like this – Americans willing to put on that uniform, and say the hard goodbyes, and risk their lives in a far off land because they know that such consequences and sacrifices are sometimes necessary to defend our country and achieve a lasting peace.[108]

I fear that such language, dangerously close to the discourse of martyrdom, will do little to challenge or change the deep roots of 'the necessity of war-as-sacrifice' as sacred and normalized in the U.S. context.

So what of the questions that were raised in the introduction of this chapter? If root understandings of sacrifice in Christianity are bound to become ammunition in a doctrine of the necessity of war and war-culture, what must our response be? I remain uneasy regarding theologies that criticize sacrificial social dynamics only to reinscribe sacrifice cosmically and in Christian practice. Lifting the

108. 'Remarks of Senator Barack Obama on the Iraq War,' Barack Obama, Senator for Illinois, http://obama.senate.gov/speech/070321-remarks_of_sena_11/, accessed 2 April 2008.

lid on the box of sacrifice reveals unending associations, practices and operations that animate war-culture, impede deep thinking and analysis of the causes and consequences of violence, rationalize destructive social structures, and glorify suffering. Finally, it is impossible to remain uncritical within a sacrificially-oriented Christianity, especially in a war-culture such as the United States.

Moreover, it would seem that the quest for a nonviolent and sacrificially-free soteriology requires continued attention to the complex interplay of sacrificial frameworks and practices in Christianity *and* national identity and action. Chapter Five explores the possibilities involved in advocating a shift from a theology of sacrifi e to a theology of work. In addition, as Williams and Sung so powerfully demonstrate, and as the Smithsonian example also illustrates, continued excavation and genealogy of the operations of sacrifice in many different settings and practices is perhaps our best way forward if we are to better understand the reality of U.S. War-culture, and discern the appropriate moral responses to our reality. Jon Sobrino perhaps says it best:

> In the United States, the empire is conceived in religious categories. Like a divinity, it possesses ultimacy and exclusivity...also like divinity, the empire offers salvation...It demands an orthodoxy and a style of worship, and above all, like Moloch, it must have victims to live on.[109]

In the U.S. context, we must find ways to expose and question this framework of blood sacrifice uniting war-culture, nationalism and Christianity. Even more, we must struggle our way to cognitive and theological frameworks that support life and flourishing, instead of glorifying suffering, sacrifice, violence and death. Our true salvation (God's intended world) depends upon it.

109. Sobrino, *Where Is God?* p. xiv.

Chapter Five

Detranscendentalizing War

There probably can never be full recovery of memory, but in order to escape the miasma of war there must be some partial rehabilitation, some recognition of the denial and perversion, some new way given to speak that lays bare the myth as fantasy and the cause as bankrupt. The whole truth may finall be too hard to utter, but the process of healing only begins when we are able to at least acknowledge the tragedy and accept our share of the blame.

— Christopher Hedges[1]

Introduction

By the end of America's first total war, the Civil War, the Christian sacrificial archetype had fully merged into American civil religion. Both the martyred president and the war dead with whom he was inextricably linked, were understood as those whose sacrificial deaths were '... the last full measure of devotion,' making possible 'a new birth of freedom.' The mythic symbolism connecting a cosmic interpretation of Abraham Lincoln's untimely death with the sacrifice of Jesus for salvation entered the nation's bloodstream, as the words from Lincoln's own law partner, William H. Herndon, demonstrated:

> For fifty years God rolled Abraham Lincoln through his fiery furnace. He did it to try Abraham and to purify him for his purpose ... making him the noblest and loveliest character since Jesus Christ.[2]

1. Chris Hedges, *War is a Force that Gives Us Meaning* (New York: Anchor Books, 2002).
2. Quoted in Robert Bellah, 'Civil Religion in America,' *American Civil Religion*, Russell E. Richey and Donald G. Jones (eds.), (New York: Harper and Row, 1974), p. 32.

Of course, from its earliest inceptions American nationalist identity emphasized Hebraic religious themes, such as America as 'the new Israel,' carrying out 'the errand into the wilderness,' the 'elect nation' as 'the shining city on the hill,' etc. However, this 'second great trial' of the United States (as Robert Bellah has described it), the experience of the Civil War, was the mortar that cemented Christian sacrificial constructions and the symbolism of war in nationalist identity. As one scholar has written,

> In [the Gettysburg Address], Lincoln symbolically died, just as the Union soldiers really died – and as he himself was soon really to die. By his words, he gave the field of battle a symbolic significance that it had lacked. For us and our country, he left Jefferson's ideals of freedom and equality joined to the Christian sacrificial act of death and rebirth.[3]

3. Robert Lowell, 'On the Gettysburg Address,' *Lincoln and the Gettysburg Address,* Allan Nevins (ed.), (Illinois: Urbana, 1964), 88–89, quoted by Bellah in *American Civil Religion,* pp. 31–32. One might note that Lincoln's thinking about the nature of the Civil War operates on more than one level in the Gettysburg Address. If one significant theme has to do with sacrificial death and rebirth, Lincoln's words also give evidence of his thinking about the Civil War as the payment of a debt to God by the nation as a whole for the sin of slavery. Along these lines, note in the following quote from the Address the notion that the immoral shedding of blood and gain of wealth through slavery creates a debt that only can be met with the additional shedding of blood. 'Yet, if God wills that it [the war] continue until all wealth piled by the bondsman's two hundred and fifty years of unrequited toil shall be sunk, and until every drop of blood drawn with the lash shall be paid by another drawn with the sword, as was said three thousand years ago, so still it must be said "the judgments of the Lord are true and righteous altogether."' However, unlike the theme of sacred sacrifice, the trope of the suffering of war as the consequence of righteous jeremiad did not take hold in the collective American psyche. For studies that explore these and other Judeo-Christian religious themes in American self-representation and politics, see Mark A. Noll and Luke E. Harlow (eds), *Religion and American Politics* (New York: Oxford University Press, 2007); Rosemary Radford Ruether, *America, Amerikkka: Elect Nation and Imperial Violence* (London: Equinox Publishing 2007); and William G. McLoughlin, *Revivals, Awakenings and Reform: An Essay on Religion and Social Change in America, 1607–1977* (Chicago, IL: Chicago University Press, 1978). Robert Bellah wrote about the 'three great trials' that have faced U.S. citizens over the course of U.S. history in *The Broken Covenant: American Civil Religion in Time of Trial* (Chicago, IL: University of Chicago Press, 1992, 1st edn).

Historian Drew Gilpin Faust claims that Lincoln's assassination was 'the ultimate death – and became in many ways emblematic of all the losses of the war.'[4] Comparison of Lincoln to Christ echoed through countless other funeral sermons, and brought to a climax the notion that individual Union and Confederate soldiers alike participated 'in the war's divine purpose, realized through the sacrifice of the one for the many.' America's purposes were tied to God's. Yet if the 'sacred significance' of this war, for leaders such as Frederick Douglass, was the freedom of slaves bought at such a high price, in reality, the emancipationist goals of the war largely would go abandoned for at least a century. Instead, notions of divine sacrifice became grist for rationalization of the increasingly powerful nation's expansionist tendencies. As Horace Bushnell, clergyman and theologian, preached in his sermon following the Union defeat at First Bull Run in 1861, the United States was justified in claiming its status as a redeemer nation because it had been 'hallowed' by 'rivers of blood.' He continued, 'Ours be it also, in God's own time, to champion … the right of this whole continent to be an American world.' National expansion was justified by the need to compensate for the high cost of so much death.[5]

In today's terms, the loss of life experienced in the Civil War would amount to approximately six million dead.[6] One in five men died during this period of U.S. history, leaving the nation, particularly in the South, with a 'harvest of death,' and every household mourning. Even more, almost half of those who died remained unknown, the details of their dying and burial never recovered for their families and loved ones.[7] One Union chaplain, observing the mass pit burials required to manage the unbelievable numbers of dead, remarked that such burial was similar to the ways farmers cover winter vegetables to protect them during the season of frost; however, 'the vegetables really get more tender care.'[8] Most important, this was a deciding moment in U.S. history in which 'sacrifice and the state became inextricably intertwined.'[9]

4. Drew Gilpin Faust, *This Republic of Suffering: Death and the American Civil War* (New York: Knopf, 2008), p. 156.
    5. Faust, *This Republic of Suffering*, p. 191.
    6. Faust, *This Republic of Suffering*, p. xi.
    7. Faust, *This Republic of Suffering*, p. 267.
    8. Faust, *This Republic of Suffering*, p. 74.
    9. Faust, *This Republic of Suffering*, p. xiii.

Such unimaginable loss demanded a response, some kind of rationale to assure that so many lives had been given to a high enough cause. The symbolism of sacrifice quickly was reified through the same types of memorialization we already have examined. Not only was the nation hallowed for further expansionism through the need to find meaning in this massive loss, the obligation of so many dead led to huge national changes with respect to remembering, honoring and numbering the dead. In the largest federal program undertaken up to that time, following the Civil War the task was mounted to account for the dead and give them a proper burial. But the federal obligation (and funds) only extended to Union soldiers; in the South, women's and religious associations came together to raise money, buy land for cemeteries and gather their dead that 'had been left to rot as a matter of policy.' Land for the National cemeteries such as the Gettysburg National Cemetery and the Arlington National Cemetery was set aside. However, even in these national cemeteries, racial segregation remained the norm; when the reinterment program finally was completed in 1871, 30,000 black soldiers were re-buried in 'colored' areas in the new national cemeteries, apart from the white soldiers.[10] Not all the dead were equally 'grievable.'

Memorial Day became a yearly ritual event in the nation. In the twentieth century, the Tomb of the Unknown Soldier (following World War I) and the eternal flame lit in memory of another martyred president were additional layers that deepened and strengthened the cognitive framework of the sacrifice of the one for the many. Following the Civil War, Memorial Day became an important yearly national ritual for rededication to 'the martyred dead, the spirit of sacrifice and the American vision.'[11] As one scholar has described it, 'The Memorial Day rite is a cult of the dead.' But this cult symbolically connects and thereby elevates human sacrifice by identifying it with Christian understandings of the meaning of Jesus' death as sacrifice for humanity. In this way, the emphasis on the sacred nature of the losses of war are given divine sanction, those who sacrifice are promised the reward of eternal life, and all this is analogized to the Christian God who gave his life for all.[12] In

10. Faust, *This Republic of Suffering*, pp. 236–37.

11. Bellah, *American Civil Religion*, p. 33.

12. W. Lloyd Warner, 'An American Sacred Ceremony,' *American Civil Religion*.

particular, the public school system in the United States became an important context for these rituals.

In the midsize town in which I live, this cultic activity continues, including and perhaps especially in the public school system. The local elementary school where my children attend does not recognize International Peace Day, initiated in 1981 by the United Nations to 'commemorate and strengthen the ideals of peace both within and among all nations and peoples.'[13] However, since the inauguration of the Iraq War, Veterans Day has taken on increased significance in the school calendar. Each year local veterans are invited to come to school and share breakfast with the children; in preparation all the children are instructed by their teachers to write letters thanking the veterans. The first year my daughter attended this school, she reported to her father and me that her teacher required her to 're-write her letter.' 'Why?' I asked. In her first letter she had asked the veteran to help stop the war in Iraq. Such a request was not in keeping with the 'thankfulness we owe our veterans,' her teacher told her. The unquestioned sacred nature of military service bleeds into divine sanction for war itself as something that may not be questioned, much less protested.

Chris Hedges, the foreign correspondent who for 20 years covered the armed conflicts in El Salvador, Bosnia, Argentina, Israel/ Palestine, Kuwait, and more, writes the following:

> While the excesses carried out in the name of the nationalist cause are forgotten or ignored, the myth of the nation has a disturbing longevity. It lies dormant, festering in the society, nurtured by boys' adventure stories of heroism in service to the nation, the monuments we erect to the fallen, and carefully scripted remembrances until it slowly slouches back into respectability.[14]

One does not have to be an absolute pacifist in order to take seriously the deadly connections between war-culture and cognitive sacrificial structures influenced by Christianity; in fact, I would not describe myself as such. However, becoming aware of these deadly links *must* arouse our deep suspicion about assumptions we commonly make in the United States about war, the ways in which our leaders decide to go to war, the means by which the American

13. *International Day of Peace*, www.internationaldayofpeace.org/, accessed 8 December 2008.
14. Hedges, *War is a Force*, p. 61.

public is aroused to support war, and the religious and nationalist frameworks undergirding the social, political, economic and military structures we have built and continue to nurture and expand (at the expense of many other needs) to support the war-culture in which we live.

But such questioning leads to serious consequences, for once we begin to understand and interrogate these destructive connections, the cognitive 'transcendentalization' of war and war-culture begins to dismantle in our minds. A new kind of consciousness or awareness about our reality begins to dawn upon us. This is not necessarily a comfortable awareness or consciousness, because it is attended by many new questions. 'Detranscendentalizing' war and war-culture unsettles formerly unquestioned assumptions and values. How then should we think about what soldiers do? How will we describe their deaths if not as sacred sacrifice? Moreover, how will we understand the nation, its purpose, and our connection to it? What will we do differently with respect to decision-making regarding conflict and the use of armed force

Finally, the exploration of these links also forces the question about the relationship of Christian following to American civil religion. What will it mean to uncouple Jesus' death on the cross from the powerful national narrative of Christ's sacrificial death as the archetype for the necessary sacrifices made in war to preserve 'the American way of life'? Detranscendentalizing war-culture means taking up these important questions, destabilizing some dominant frames of understanding, and reemphasizing others.

Honestly Assessing the Plurality of Images of Christian Redemption

It has been documented that the evangelical Christian community in the United States quickly unified in support of the Iraq War. While evangelical theology may not unequivocally advocate war, its depiction of the problem of evil and understanding of the God-given responsibility of the state to punish wrongdoing, easily slide into the rhetoric of fighting; overall evangelicals tend 'to find conflict normal, seek to distinguish good and evil, create out-groups that are labeled "evil" (or at least unsaved), and are willing to support the state when it fights to deter evil and to spread religious and political freedom.' Apocalyptic biblical literature and prophecy, especially focusing on conflicts, natural disasters and war, have an important emphasis in the evangelical community as God's historical revelation, and as signs of Christ's Second Coming: 'In this act of return, Jesus Christ is not the gentle prophet of peace (so often portrayed by liberal Christians), but the strident warrior-king who comes to defeat the Antichrist.'[15]

In the preaching and teaching of evangelical leaders such as Rick Warren, pastor of the California mega-church, Saddleback, Christian traditions of nonviolence are overshadowed by the gospel narratives that describe Jesus cleansing the Temple with force. War would seem to be the natural state of affairs not only between nations, but between Satan and Christ, and evil only will be overcome in the end times when those who have chosen Christ enter into his kingdom of everlasting peace.[16] In addition, as we already have seen, *sacrificial, penal substitutionary, satisfaction* and *christus victor* understandings of atonement further undergird this theological worldview, and add to the presumption *for* war by linking the necessity of Christ's sacrifice for salvation with the necessity of the sacrifices of war for temporal order.

Such a clear and predictable moral worldview may be comforting in the way it explains a complex and fraught world. This theology posits acceptance of war as normal and moral, and at best limits and at worst ridicules hopes for reconciliation and the possibility of a more peaceful world through non-warring means. For the time being, war is the way the world works, order achieved through violence is necessary, and for the most part, peace belongs to a far-distant future when Christ will reign. But the supposed 'normalcy' of a kind of Christianity that supports state-sponsored war is itself a cultural and historical construction that begs interrogation.[17] For many who hold these views, the ambiguity promoted by liberals (religious and otherwise) is to be rejected. But I wonder if more theological ambiguity isn't precisely what we need.

Chapter Two's exploration of the abuse of the rhetoric of sacrifice in the post-9/11 period of U.S. politics and culture concluded

15. James K. Wellman, Jr, 'Is War Normal for American Evangelical Religion?' in James K. Wellman, Jr (ed.), *Belief and Bloodshed* (New York: Rowman and Littlefield, 2007), pp. 195–207

16. Wellman, 'Is War Normal for American Evangelical Religion?', pp. 206–207.

17. Wellman, 'Is War Normal for American Evangelical Religion?', p. 208.

with recommendations that I wish to return to and explore more deeply in this final chapter. The second Bush Administration provided a prime example of the way that the rhetoric, justification and explanation regarding 'the necessity of sacrifice' combined with a veil of religious mystification and glorification, manipulating public interpretation and approval for war. One way to counteract such a dynamic is to encourage deeper theological interpretation of primary religious symbols themselves, in order to increase awareness regarding just how the discourse of sacrifice functions and is vulnerable to abuse and manipulation in the public and political realm.

Let me propose at least two ways we might go about this theological task. First, I suggest a return to the plethora of images, theories and metaphors for salvation in Christian history and tradition to counteract the focus on 'sacrifice' as the one necessary and indispensable method through which salvation is interpreted and accomplished. Second, we can mine the repository of work from biblical scholars and theologians to (re)discover many unanswered questions and fascinating trajectories of exploration regarding what may be known historically about Jesus' death, the events leading to it, and the many meanings Christians derived from it, from Jesus' earliest followers on. I will make brief comments on each of these pathways in what follows.

Not only students at liberal arts colleges such as where I teach, but parishioners sitting in the pews of Christian churches across the country, tend to be woefully uneducated and unaware about the depth, breadth and complexity of 'soteriology' (the study of Christian salvation) in Christianity. In one course that I teach, 'Jesus Saves? Salvation Metaphors in Christian Thought,' I regularly observe students' disbelief, then amazement, as they gradually become aware through our study of some (not all!) of the major metaphors of Christian salvation, regarding the sheer diversity of Christianities they encounter. It is as if these students become aware of a central, deeper and more ambiguous internal conversation within Christianity itself regarding the meaning, the mechanics, and the consequences and unanswered questions involved in what Christians call 'being saved.'

In the early centuries of Christianity, as church councils came together to hammer out agreement with respect to central Christian doctrines, when it came to theological exposition of Christian salvation, the pluralism one sees from the earliest times in Christianity largely was left intact.[18] And in the course of Christian history, Christian claims, understandings, poetic images and theoretical explanations of salvation have only grown further.

We have already explored a few metaphors that play a dominant role in U.S. Christian culture and politics, especially the overriding influence of *penal substitution*, which portrays Jesus as the scapegoat stepping in to receive the rightful punishment from a wrathful God in the place of sinful humanity. This is one of the latest major images of salvation to take hold in the history of Christianity, coming into full expression with the development of forensic understandings of law and justice during the period of the Western Reformation. Ironically, this relatively late flowering of salvation theology, *penal substitution*, then later became the dominant doctrine of much fundamentalist and evangelical Christianity in the United States, and remains so. This seems at odds with other central tenets of fundamentalism, that suggest that what is most important is returning to the 'fundamentals' of early Christianity and eschewing later Christian theological developments as misguided or less authentic.

In fact, at least eight different 'clusters' of salvation images may be identified in New Testament documents alone, including *sacrifice, victory, divinization, satisfaction, exemplary models, penal substitution, restoration of human faculties,* and *healing*.[19] And this list further can be augmented to include models that developed over the course of Christian history, such as those in more recent decades resulting

---

18. Of course, one must start a study of these councils with questions about the true degree of consensus or the imposition of orthodoxy/kyriarchy imposed in such procedures.

19. I follow Paul Fiddes' typology of salvation images from *Past Event and Present Salvation: The Christian Idea of Atonement* (Louisville, KY: Westminster, 1989). In contrast, H.D. McDonald, in *The Atonement of the Death of Christ in Faith, Revelation and History*, identifies no fewer than sixteen distinct salvation metaphors, images and theories in the history of Christianity (Grand Rapids, MI: Baker Book Hose, 1985). Yet again, John T. Carroll and Joel B. Green focus on five New Testament 'constellations,' (*The Death of Jesus in Early Christianity*, Peabody, MA: Hendrickson, 1995). Finally, though a much earlier resource, I find L.W. Grensted's history to be particularly useful because not only does Grensted outline different models of Christian salvation, but also helpfully demonstrates lines of continuity and disagreement between theological thinkers, so that we see just how writers built upon and reacted to earlier understandings. See, *A Short History of the Doctrine of the Atonement* (Manchester: University Press, 1920).

from the work from a wide variety of liberation theologians. What are the consequences of such multiplicity? The many diverse theological voices across the ages challenge current univocal and repressive U.S. patterns in Christianity regarding *penal substitution*. To demonstrate the insight that comes from seriously engaging with these multiple voices, I turn to the example of Anselm of Canterbury from the eleventh century.

Anselm's commitment to *fides quaerens intellectum* (faith *must* seek understanding) led to his development of the treatise, *Cur Deus Homo* (*Why God Became Human*), in order to respond to what he saw as misleading and mistaken dominant soteriological patterns reigning in his own time.[20] In particular, what held sway among people of Anselm's era was the salvation narrative of *ransom*, which held that human beings through their own willful sinfulness had become enslaved by the devil. Briefly, the *ransom* theory of atonement portrayed the act of salvation as a kind of divine trick. Satan attempts to lure Jesus into his lair just as he has all humans, who as a result of their sinfulness are easily led astray into enslavement. However, Satan makes the fatal mistake of failing to recognize Jesus' sinless and divine nature at one with his human nature. Artists influenced by this soteriological theory portrayed Satan as a huge fish swallowing the divine bait.[21] Yet the devil has no right to the sinless one, and chokes on the line.

Satan's error breaks the power of his hold on humanity and opens the door to the reestablishment of humanity's right relationship with God. Though the medieval language can be a bit of a barrier, eventually liberal arts students are captivated by the series of logical criticisms Anselm levels at the soteriological pattern of *ransom*. And all this is to lend weight to the salvation reconstruction Anselm wishes to recommend, the theory of *satisfaction*, a theory which itself is deeply influenced by feudal practices and values, the dominance

20. Anselm of Canterbury, '*Cur Deus Homo*, (Why God Became Man)', *A Scholastic Miscellany: Anselm to Ockham*, Eugene R. Fairweather (ed.), (Philadelphia, PA: Westminster Press, 1956).

21. As Kathryn Tanner notes, this imagery is associated with Gregory of Nyssa. See Tanner, 'Incarnation, Cross, and Sacrifice,' *Anglican Theological Review* 86 no 1 (Winter 2004): 35–56. Gregory of Nyssa, 'The Great Catechism,' in Philip Schaff and Henry Wace, (eds.), *Nicene and Post-Nicene Fathers*, Vol. 5 (Peabody, MA: Hendrickson Publishers, 1994), see especially Chapter 24, at p. 494.

of the Norman Empire and the gradual changes in Anselm's culture favoring legal understandings of justice.

For contemporary readers, the point of appreciating Anselm only secondarily has to do with the specific claims he makes regarding *satisfaction* theories of atonement as more persuasive than earlier notions of *ransom*. In fact, scholars have demonstrated that both Anselm's criticism of *ransom* and his development of *satisfaction* are very closely intertwined with his own dependence upon the Norman Empire of his time.

For instance, Anselm's depiction of human sin as a cosmic disruption of God's honor makes little sense apart from its social embeddedness in relations between feudal lords and their vassals. The restoration of God's honor as symbolic of salvation also must be seen within the centralizing, consolidating powers of hierarchical order in the Norman Empire. Consequently, one cannot study Anselm without becoming aware of just how deeply various soteriological constructions are influenced by their context and chronology; it finally is impossible to seriously analyze or understand *satisfaction* apart from the feudal structure of Anselm's society and all the ensuing sets of relations, values and practices that follow.[22]

To see this in action, we can turn to one focal point in the treatise: Anselm's illustration of the inner workings of *satisfaction* by way of a fable. There was a king who was sinned against by every member of the population of one of his cities. Only one man, of the same race of the others, did not participate in this undefined sin. All the rest rightly were condemned to death. However, the man without sin stepped forward to perform a service 'sure to please the king greatly.' As a result, the king granted all the people of the city absolution from every past fault, ' … because of the greatness of this service.'

Anselm's fable as an analogy for soteriology does not make immediate sense outside of his context. One has to understand feudal/vassal relations in order for the story to work, and the qualities of loyalty, service, obligation and reward that these social relations require. We see as much by paying attention to exactly *what* it is about this service that is so 'pleasing,' and that repairs the breech in honor. Anselm writes,

22. See Joerg Rieger, 'Resisting and Reframing the God-Human: Christology and Empire in the Middle Ages,' *Christ and Empire: From Paul to Postcolonial Times* (Minneapolis, MN: Fortress Press, 2007).

> Nothing that man can suffer for God's honor, freely and not as
> an obligation, is more bitter or harder than death. Nor can a man
> give himself more fully to God than he does when he surrenders
> himself to death for His honor.[23]

In the feudal society of Anselm's time, the loyal subject who dies
in order to protect the honor of the lord or king truly is an object of
emulation and praise. Anselm translates this social value to cosmic
levels when he defines the 'pleasing service' offered by Christ as his
death. But *Cur Deus Homo* not only is important for the ways it demonstrates the social grounding of all soteriological constructions. At
the same time, the end result of the theological interchange between
Boso and Anselm in *Cur Deus Homo* reveals more than Anselm perhaps intended.

Anselm attempted to answer the question of soteriology (why
the God-human?) definitively, once and for all, but the fact remains
that his treatise leads to theological terrain and possibility beyond
his control. Specifically, the joy of studying Anselm's theological ar-
gumentation is the resulting germ of awareness we gain regarding
the incompleteness of all human attempts at soteriological construction. While Anselm criticized *ransom* on the basis of its supposed
'irrationality' and negative portrait of a weakened God who has to
resort to divine trickery with the devil, his own reconstruction opens
the door to seeing all soteriological development as an ongoing and
unending process. Just as Anselm submitted the image of *ransom* to
intellectually rigorous critique and analysis, so may we investigate
and evaluate Anselm's reconstruction, and in fact, every proposed
image, theory and metaphor for salvation in Christianity.

In my mind, this leads to at least three important consequences:
first, the ongoing theological conversation/debate regarding soteriology suggests the need for modesty with respect to any ultimate claims made for theological theories, images and metaphors.
Second, the example of Anselm's brilliant theological argumenta-
tion suggests a model for a way forward: the use of every intellectual resource possible in the service of openness. Not only must
we acknowledge the flaws in dominant theological models, we also
must demonstrate willingness to think things through again in hope
and preparation for something new. Finally, Anselm's criticism and
reconstruction of soteriology illustrate the importance of exploring

23. Anselm of Canterbury, 'Why God Became Man,' pp. 161–67.

and revealing the connections between soteriology and culture, not only of Anselm's time, but every era. The door thus is thrown wide open to investigate and challenge U.S. Christianity's 'captivity' to *penal substitutionary* models of salvation.[24]

Moreover, even while this same criticism begins with theological analysis, it *also* reaches beyond the specifically theological to investigate those substitutionary models of salvation embraced by the nation itself in its rhetoric about 'the necessity of the sacrifice of war for salvation,' with salvation here understood variously as democracy, security, the free market, etc. As I have argued throughout this book, what is incumbent in this current moment is analysis that both incorporates the theological material, and widens the scope of inquiry to explore just how particular theological claims, models, understandings and practices inform and are themselves influenced by social, cultural, political and economic realities. Theological claims regarding the ultimacy or supremacy of *penal substitutionary, sacrificia* or any model of soteriology may not be isolated from concurrent exploration of the real operations and functions of this same theology in the layers of our cultural, political, religious and economic life. These debates are 'transdisciplinary.'[25] Thus, a return to and deeper focus on the multivalency of a wide diversity of soteriological voices in conversation and debate with one another is an important way forward in our attempts to destabilize the dominance of *penal substitutionary* patterns in U.S. popular Christianity.

At the same time, in addition to attending to the multiplicity of soteriological voices in Christianity, a second pathway forward may be identified. This second trajectory has to do with ongoing historical investigation regarding Jesus' death. Many followers of Christianity tend to take it for granted that Jesus' cross and death always have been central features of Christianity. But, 'it took Jesus a thousand years to die.' According to art historians, images of the crucified Christ did not begin regularly to appear in religious settings until the tenth century.[26] Of course, in some noncanonical gospels, such as the Gospel of Thomas, there is no passion narrative at

---

24. Dr. Joel Green coined this phrase.

25. Rieger, *Christ and Empire*, p. 6.

26. Rita Nakashima Brock, Rebecca Ann Parker, *Saving Paradise: How Christianity Traded Love of This World for Crucifixion and Empire* (Boston, MA: Beacon Press, 2008), p. ix.

all.[27] Additionally, historical critical biblical scholars underscore the diversity of canonical biblical material with regard to the portrayal of Jesus' death on the cross.

One example is the passion narrative from the Gospel of Luke. Luke's placement of the tearing of the temple curtain in his narrative raises interesting questions about how to interpret Jesus' death. Is it to be understood essentially as an atoning act? In contrast to Mark's Gospel, in which the tearing of the curtain occurs immediately after Jesus' death and the confession of the centurion ('Truly, this man was the Son of God'; Mk 15.39), Luke places this element of the passion narrative in a different location, before Jesus' death, as 'darkness came over the whole land' (Lk. 23.44). This may suggest God's judgment upon God's people; as one scholar summarizes, 'Luke does not share Mark's view that Jesus' death brought about atonement for sin ... For Luke, Jesus dies the death of a righteous martyr who has suffered from miscarried justice; his death will be vindicated by God at the resurrection.'[28] Even further, other scholars believe that Luke was motivated to respond to charges of Jesus as less than heroic, demonstrated by his cry of dereliction from the cross as portrayed in Mark: 'My God, my God, why have you forsaken me?' (Mk 15.34). Accordingly, Luke drew upon Socratic ideas of 'the noble death,' and dealt with the 'embarrassment' of a lack of heroic stoicism in Mark's Gospel by deleting those overly emotional verses, and instead depicting Jesus as calm, in control and innocent of all charges. In Luke's portrayal of Jesus death, then, less emphasis is placed on any necessary atoning function of Jesus' death, in favor

27. Elaine Pagels traces the history of the Gospel of Thomas, and its differences from the Gospel of John and other examples of early Christian thought. *Beyond Belief: The Secret Gospel of Thomas* (New York: Random House, 2003). Some New Testament scholars dispute elements of Pagels' findings: See Arland J. Hultgren, 'The Gnostic Gospels and Current Popular Views of Jesus,' *Reformed Review* 59 no 3 (Spring 2006): 283–91.

28. Bart D. Ehrman, *The New Testament: A Historical Introduction to the Early Christian Writings* (New York: Oxford University Press, 2008), p. 135. Also see Dennis D. Sylva, 'The Temple Curtain and Jesus' Death in the Gospel of Luke,' *Journal of Biblical Literature* 105 no. 2 (1986): 239–50. At the same time, other New Testament scholars insist that the leitmotif of the necessity of Jesus' suffering remains preserved in the Lucan narrative as much as in Mark's Gospel. See, Joel B. Green, 'Jesus on the Mount of Olives (Luke 22: 39-46): Tradition and Theology,' *Journal for the Study of the New Testament* no. 26 (1986), 29–48.

of seeing Jesus as a role model: like Socrates, Jesus dies as a self-contained, heroic martyr.[29]

Overall, scholars more and more demonstrate that Christian documents and history portray not a univocal portrait, but a wide array of diverse emphases and interpretations regarding the centrality and meaning of Jesus' death. For instance, yet other theologians have reflected on the wealth of images in early Christianity centuries, not of death, martyrdom or sacrifice, but of paradise. But in contrast to many contemporary Christian notions about heaven as some sort of home-world completely apart from the planet Earth, these early Christians understood 'heaven' as a paradise on earth, 'the world's luminosity' blessed and permeated by the Spirit of God. Such images of paradise, not as an alien escape from the earth, but a renewed and regenerating earth and humanity, are reflected in the beautiful image from the New Testament book of Revelation: the river of the water of life, flowing from God through the middle of the street of the city, surrounded by the tree of life producing fruit and leaves for the healing of the nations (Rev. 22.1-3).[30]

Reclaiming the image of paradise is not to escape from the harsh realities, fears and struggles in the real world. If war and conflict characterize the world and cosmos until the second coming of Christ, as is the case in the evangelical theological world view described above, retrieval of images of paradise from Christian history neither promotes an other-worldly retreat from the world's problems, nor forestalls the possibility of greater peace by placing it into the distant future of a second coming. The key has to do with revisioning what we think 'paradise' includes. Such a process means that we must:

> let go of the notion that paradise is life without struggle, life free from wrestling with the legacies of injustice and current forces of evil. Assuredly, we are in a world in which the struggle continues. However, it is also true that we already live on holy ground, in the presence of God ... Our spiritual challenge is to embrace this reality: histories of harm are all around us, forces of evil operate within and among us, and yet ... the risen Christ is with us on the

29. Greg Sterling, '*Mors Philosophi*: The Death of Jesus in Luke,' *Harvard Theological Review* 90 no. 4 (Fall 2001): 383–402.

30. See, Barbara Rossing, *The Rapture Exposed: The Message of Hope in the Book of Revelation* (New York: Basic Books, 2004), pp. 154–57.

road, the Spirit rises in the wind, the rivers of paradise circle the earth ... another Christianity is possible.[31]

Recall Jung Mo Sung's redefinition of a theological vision of *utopia*: claiming the possibility to imagine and elaborate theories of action, recognizing the historic non-attainability of the totality of the Kingdom in the here and now, and remembering that God's intended world always remains ahead of us, as goal and criterion for judging all contemporary attempts at greater justice-making.

We might call this a 'collaborative eschatology,' in other words, a shift in traditional ways of theologizing about the ultimate working of God's purposes in history, and the role human beings play in these events. Our realism about the world's conflicts and violence does not have to lead us to resignation regarding war as moral and normal, and just peacemaking as romantic, or a distant hope related to a far-off future.

In various settings in recent years, New Testament scholars N.T. Wright and John Dominic Crossan have reflected on and debated the question of the historical warrants for Jesus' resurrection and its theological consequences. Though these two scholars disagree on much with respect to historical explorations of beliefs, narratives, early understandings and religious interpretations of 'resurrection,' they do agree that the Christian doctrine of resurrection far too often has been 'co-opted' by post-Enlightenment conservative Christianity.[32] Why? These Christians reduce the theological import of resurrection by focusing on an overly narrow question: 'Do you or do you not believe that Jesus came bodily out of the tomb?'

As Crossan goes on to say,

> They've reduced it to "Do you or do you not believe that Jesus came bodily out of the tomb?" and then that means that a camera could have picked up Jesus, as it were. And that's all they want to talk about. If they take resurrection to mean just that, then they say I can't be a Christian. I think that is awful ... Because it [the resurrection] does point to something concrete in the world – changing the world, not just changing me subjectively.[33]

---

31. Brock and Parker, *Saving Paradise*, p. 417.

32. Robert B. Stewart (ed.), *The Resurrection of Jesus: John Dominic Crossan and N.T. Wright in Dialogue* (Minneapolis, MN: Augsburg, 2006), p. 22.

33. Stewart, *The Resurrection of Jesus*, p. 31.

For Crossan, the 'collaborative eschaton' begins with Jesus' proclamations in the gospel narratives that the Kingdom of God has begun. In the healing of the sick, the sharing of common meals with those who have been healed and the announcement of the Kingdom in the midst of this world, 'God has already acted and is waiting for us to react, to collaborate, to cooperate, to get with the divine program.'[34] When Jesus says that 'his Kingdom is not of this world' (Jn 18.36), Crossan takes him to mean that this kingdom runs counter to the history of civilization itself. Judea, a province of the Roman Empire where Jesus was born, is a good example of the excesses of 'civilization' because it follows the pattern of all imperial projects: piety, war, victory (through violence), then peace. This is the way empires come and go throughout history. As Crossan says, 'It is only a question of who has lost it, who has got it, who wants it and who is next.'[35] But, he insists, the program of Judaism into which Jesus is born, and the vision inaugurated by Jesus and continued by his followers, runs a different course entirely: first covenant, justice, then peace – or peace through justice in this world by nonviolence. Thus, the collaborative eschaton is the radical shift from violence and injustice to nonviolence and justice, a shift that involves both God and humankind in collaboration.

Detranscendentalizing war and war-culture in the context of the United States means taking up intellectual work and activism to detach Jesus' death on the cross from the powerful national narrative of Christ's sacrificial death as the archetype for the necessary sacrifices made in war. A return to the multiplicity of soteriological images, metaphors and theories, all in conversation and debate with one another across the ages, provides a useful critique in the face of monopolizing and consolidating emphasis on *sacrificia penal substitution* as the one emphatic way to salvation religiously and politically. Likewise, the diversity of biblical, historical and theological Christian documents regarding Jesus' death, and investigation into developing meanings of eschatology, also shed light on reductive interpretations that conflate unending war with Christian theology regarding Jesus' death, resurrection and second coming. But in addition to attending to biblical and noncanonical Christian

---

34. Stewart, *The Resurrection of Jesus*, p. 179.
35. Stewart, *The Resurrection of Jesus*, p. 184.

texts and theological frameworks, U.S. cultural and political frames of meaning also require investigation and critique.

How Will We Speak About the Death of Soldiers If Not as a 'necessary sacrifice'? Politics and Grievin

If the [discipline of the] humanities has a future as cultural criticism, and cultural criticism has a task at the present moment, it is no doubt to return us to the human where we do not expect to find it, in its frailty and at the limits of its capacity to make sense. We would have to interrogate the emergence and vanishing of the human at the limits of what we can know, what we can hear, what we can see, what we can sense.

Judith Butler[36]

During World War I in Europe, what began as unabated enthusiasm for war soon collided with deep disillusionment that rose out of the actual experience of war's mass destruction and death. As the war began, 'the Myth of the War Experience' provided the lens for interpreting war through focusing on patriotism, a deeper search for life's meaning, desire for adventure, and tropes of masculinity. However, this interpretation all too soon crashed with devastating realities, such as the battle of the Somme in 1916, when over 400,000 British men died.[37]

We do well to pay close attention to what developed out of this extreme experience of cognitive, emotional, material and spiritual dissonance. In Germany, Greek ideals melded with Christian frameworks to create a derealized grounding from which the actual experience of war would be confronted and transcended. In 'the cult of the fallen soldier,' Greek values of harmony, balanced proportions and controlled strength – all manifested and celebrated as aspects of youth – meshed with popular Christian piety. The deaths of young soldiers were justified as a sign of military commitment, and glorified as a type of idealized inner control required to obey a high ideal. At the same time, popular exclamations, such as 'Now we are made sacred,' juxtaposed the sacrifice of soldiers with the death and resurrection of Christ.[38]

36. Judith Butler, *Precarious Life: The Powers of Mourning and Violence* (New York: Verso, 2004), p. 151.

37. George Mosse, *Fallen Soldiers: Reshaping the Memory of the World Wars* (New York: Oxford University Press, 1990), p. 68.

38. Mosse, *Fallen Soldiers*, pp. 74-75.

In this way, the passion of Christ became an analogy for the experience of the nation as a whole: through these sacrificial deaths of the most worthy citizens, Christ was understood to illuminate the very world, such that war itself was interpreted as a strategy for Christological revelation. Suffering as a purifying force was recommended to the troops in the trenches; more widely, suffering was advised to the nation as a whole, to lead to a stronger and purified Germany, 'encased in armor.'[39] Here the older and more traditional theology of war (serving God and Christ by fighting for the father/motherland/monarch), evolved into a different but no less lethal combination: archetypal religious rhythms of death and resurrection intertwined with advocacy of war and aggression.

Most importantly, this popular piety grew into an important resource that could be manipulated to overcome fear of death itself. Eternal life, assured to those who had sacrificed themselves for the nation, now outweighed any value of the importance of living in the here and now. 'The expectation of an eternal and meaningful life – the continuation of a patriotic mission – not only seemed to transcend death itself, but also inspired life before death.'[40] The corresponding growth of war memorials and cemeteries for the war-dead cemented and extended these same frameworks. These sites became popular destinations and shrines of public worship and pilgrimage in Europe following the war, and the development of commercial measures, such as cheap tours for mourners, enabled increasing numbers of civilians to participate in the growing cult.[41]

The actual experience and dread of war thereby was 'cleansed,' or we might say, thrust into the distance. And once this took place, it was all too easy for the 'Myth of the War Experience' successfully to refocus the memory of war. Not long after, at the time of the rise of National Socialism in Germany, Nazis reinvigorated this cult and made their own martyred dead central in its observance; the 'Myth of the War Experience' had become a useful tool through which the suffering memory of millions was exploited for militarily aggressive political ends.[42]

By this time the destructive capacity of assigning sacrificial categories to the military and to the nation should be all too clear in

39. Mosse, *Fallen Soldiers*, p. 77.
40. Mosse, *Fallen Soldiers*, p. 78.
41. Mosse, *Fallen Soldiers*, p. 92.
42. Mosse, *Fallen Soldiers*, p. 106.

our minds. But the question is, what should we do about it? A new way of thinking is required, one that makes it possible to speak and think of the deaths of soldiers outside of these sacrificial frameworks. Moreover, the identity and representation of the nation itself also must be rethought. We must seek new awareness regarding the processes through which these same sacrificial constructions mystify our thinking about the true nature and meaning of the losses of war. What is called for is deeper analysis of loss and grieving, and greater honesty about the dynamics of power that sacrificial frameworks hide so neatly from view.

The experience of loss has the possibility to reveal our very 'inscrutability' to ourselves. The mystery of grief is such that, when my beloved has died, my own identity is thrown into question. At the same time, bereft of that one, exactly what it is that I have lost also remains a mystery to me. Loss reveals to us the reality of our interdependence and frailty as humans, and is expressed in our vulnerability. As humans we are vulnerable, that is, we are dependent upon and at risk of possible danger from those who surround us, at our very beginnings and throughout our lives.

The instability and 'unknowingness' of grief tempts us to try to banish it entirely, or cut it as short as possible. Yet Judith Butler reflects on the possibility of grief as a resource for politics itself. Grief is a mode of knowing that comes in the form of a sense of dispossession – Who am I and what has this made of me? What is left of me? What is it in the Other that I have lost? Grief is that trace of my inevitable human connection to others. Going further, Butler asks, 'Can this insight lead to a normative reorientation for politics?'

> To grieve, and to make grief itself into a resource for politics, is not to be resigned to inaction, but it may be understood as the slow process by which we develop a point of identification with suffering itself ... This then might lead us to evaluate and oppose the conditions under which certain human lives are more vulnerable than others, and thus certain human lives are more grievable than others.[43]

Butler's insight may be juxtaposed with Jon Sobrino's theological writing on 'connatural knowledge.' For Sobrino, the knowledge that comes for Christians by way of the cross means a break with customary forms of epistemology. The 'wonder' associated with

43. Judith Butler, *Precarious Life*, p. 30.

knowing through the cross is a highly qualified sort of wonder – to put it succinctly, this knowledge is a form of grief, or sorrow. A cognitive bridge opens between grief before the cross of Jesus, and grief in the face of so many analogical historical crosses throughout history. Sympathy and knowledge of our own and others' vulnerability are born. Moreover, as with Butler, for Sobrino the knowledge arising from this sorrow 'cannot rest on contemplation,' but issues into action. Specifically, it has the potential to become *agape*, as 'the person who feels sorrow in the face of another's misery tries to overcome it by bridging the distance between the self and the other's misery.'[44]

This is not to recommend suffering and sorrow as a new form of education; instead, as Soelle would say, it is to acknowledge that 'what happened to Jesus could happen to anybody.' Or along with Butler, we may say that 'loss follows from being socially constituted bodies, attached to others, at risk of losing those attachments, exposed to others, at risk of violence by virtue of that exposure.'[45] Yet, as we shall see, not everyone shares the same risk of exposure; dynamics of privilege and power embodied in the structures of the nation, the global economy, sex, race, ethnicity and religion all play a role in determining who is the most vulnerable.

Butler reflects on the quality of mourning in the United States following the 9/11 attacks, and the social dynamic through which a forestalled U.S. grief in this era became a usable resource in the drive toward war. What occurred in this era was a strange kind of grief, an abbreviated form of mourning that extended only so far, and no further. Once again, as with other processes of memorialization, we might consider what occurred in the months and years following 9/11 in terms of public forms of grief. *The New York Times* published individual obituaries for all those who died in the World Trade Center Towers. At the same time, the flag-draped caskets of the dead bodies returning from the fields of war in Afghanistan and Iraq through the Dover Air Force Base were off limits to photographers.[46] Meanwhile, the U.S. Department of Defense mounted a

44. Jon Sobrino, *Christology at the Crossroads* (trans. John Drury, New York: Maryknoll, 1985), pp. 198–200.

45. Butler, *Precarious Life*, p. 20.

46. Prohibition of photographs of such caskets became public policy in the U.S. during the presidency of George H.W. Bush, and remained so until the policy was changed during the early months of the Obama presidency.

concerted effort *not* to tally the numbers of war-dead among the citizens of Afghanistan and Iraq, and in fact during the post-9/11 era regularly disputed the numbers of dead reported by various non-profit and health organizations.

I regularly ask groups, 'How many soldiers have died in the Iraq and Afghanistan wars?' Most people are able to come up with a number that is fairly close to the official tally from the U.S. government, over 5,800 by 2011. However, a second question, 'How many Iraqi and Afghan people have died?' more often than not leads to uncertainty and a dawning realization among U.S. citizens that they have little idea. In a recent classroom of undergraduates, when I posed these questions, students guessed that the number of Afghan/Iraqi dead might rise to perhaps 30,000. None knew of the report from the Bloomberg School of Public Health at Johns Hopkins University in cooperation with other health agencies, that counted the number of war-related dead in Iraq from 2002–2006 at 650,000.[47]

How shall we examine and account for what we know and what we fail to know or recognize? Butler describes a process of 'derealization' that took place in the United States following 9/11. The loss of certain lives amounted to a perception of an attack on national sovereignty – these lives publicly were grieved and memorialized. In contrast, other lives were reduced to pure evil, and in still other cases, the deaths that occurred as a result of the wars were poorly marked or not at all. Butler asks,

---

47. Gilbert Burnham, Shannon Doocy, Elizabeth Dzeng, Rihadh Lafta, Les Roberts, 'The Human Cost of the War In Iraq: A Mortality Study, 2002–2006,' Bloomberg School of Public Heath, Johns Hopkins University, School of Medicine, Al Mustansiriya University, Center for International Studies, Massachusetts institute of Technology, Cambridge, Massachusetts, Baghdad, Iraq, http://i.a.cnn.net/cnn2006/images10/11/human.cost.of.war. pdf, accessed 28 February 2009 . See also, Madelyn Hsiao-Rei Hicks, M.D., M.R.C.Psych., Hamit Dardagan, Gabriela Guerrero Serdán, M.A., Peter M. Bagnall, M.Res., John A. Sloboda, Ph.D., F.B.A., and Michael Spagat, Ph.D., 'The Weapons That Kill Civilians –Deaths of Children and Noncombatants in Iraq, 2003–2008,' *The New England Journal of Medicine*, 16 April 2009, Vol. 360, pp. 1585–88. This study claims that from March 2003 to March 2008, a total of 91,358 civilians were killed specifically as a result of armed violence. Women and children were in the largest numbers of victims with respect to the use of air attacks and mortars, while precise methods of gunfire and torture tended to result in larger number of male civilian deaths.

How is it that certain lives will be highly protected, and the abrogation of their claims to sanctity will be sufficient to mobilize the forces of war; other lives will not find such fast and furious support and will not even qualify as "grievable"?[48]

Deeper examination into these issues reveals that the public obituary is 'an act of nation-building,' and the inequitable distribution of grief we have seen in the post-9/11 period all too well served 'the derealizing aims of military violence.' In this process of derealization, certain narratives moved front and center while other story lines were repressed, reduced or erased. Such normative frameworks determine which bodies are somehow more human than others, that is, worth protecting and mourning.[49]

The process of derealization by which the deaths of so many Iraqis were relatively absent from U.S. consciousness, momentarily was disrupted by the public outburst of grief and protest from the Iraqi journalist who threw his shoes at George W. Bush during his last visit to Iraq as President of the United States. This man, Muntadhar al-Zeidi, now in his 30s, spent the better part of the decade of his 20s as a journalist in Iraq with the job of chronicling Iraqi war-death. However, though the video clip of the flying shoes circled endlessly on news outlets, much less media attention addressed the cry of grief aimed at the president along with the shoes. 'This is your farewell kiss, you dog! This is from the widows, the orphans and those who were killed in Iraq.' At his defense trial, al-Zeidi explained that his actions had not been pre-meditated, but erupted uncontrollably as President Bush lauded his own accomplishments in the war at this end of his presidency. 'I was seeing a whole country in calamity while Bush was giving a cold and spiritless smile,' al-Zeidi testified. 'He was saying goodbye after causing the death of many Iraqis and economic destruction.'[50] Butler writes,

Our ability to respond with outrage depends upon a tacit realization that there is a worthy life that has been injured or lost in the

48. Butler, *Precarious Life*, p. 32.
49. See Judith Butler, 'Survivability, Vulnerability, Affect,' *Frames of War* (London: Verso, 2009).
50. Sinan Salaheddin, 'Iraqi Shoe-Thrower Reveals Motive,' Associated Press, 21 February 2009, *AOL News*, http://news.aol.com/article/iraqi-police-bomb-kills-4-wounds-11-in/342834?icid=sphere_newsaol_inpage, accessed 28 February 2009.

context of war, and no utilitarian calculus can supply the measure
by which to gauge the destitution and loss of such lives.[51]

Nevertheless, in contrast to al-Zeidi's insistence that Iraq's devastating losses not be papered over, in the United States sacrificial
rhetoric and frameworks played an important role in the process of
derealization, controlling the framing of certain losses and minimiz-
ing or altogether erasing others. If the lopsided allocation of grief
meant a tendency to repress or minimize the reality of the death
of so many Iraqis and Afghans, then the naming of the loss of U.S.
soldiers as 'a necessary sacrifice' foreclosed the possibility for exploring the deeper 'unknowingness of grief' created through this
experience of death. Instead these losses were transformed into a
type of mystified moral credit or honor. The personal questions cus-
tomarily posed in grief, 'What have I become? What is left of me?
What is it in the other that I have lost?' – initially focused on those
who died in the World Trade Center Towers and the other attacks of
9/11. However, a wider communal grief taking in the deaths of soldiers and civilians of Afghanistan and Iraq only began to be raised
at the level of the general public as American military deaths in Iraq
began seriously to mount before the 2006 elections in the United
States. Indeed, political questions that inevitably follow from the
personal – 'Why this death? Why this loss?' – tended to be followed
by the concomitant response, '*It was a necessary sacrifice.*

Thus the possibility of deeper reflection regarding the given human condition of vulnerability to the other, deep dependence upon
the other, and responsibility to/for the other, was truncated. As a
result, it would seem that consciousness regarding the other (in this
case, the deaths of so many Afghans and Iraqis *together with* a serious accounting for the deaths of more than *5,800* U.S. soldiers), remained on the periphery of national awareness and concern for far
too long, at least for a number of years following the initiation of the
wars in Afghanistan and Iraq.

Released in 2007, the documentary film, *Body of War*, captures the
national shift that began to occur once citizens of the U.S. realized
how badly the war was proceeding in the pre-2006 period. The film
follows 25 year-old veteran, Thomas Young, upon his return to the
United States after being severely wounded and paralyzed just a

51. Butler, 'Survivability, Vulnerability, Affect,' p. 54.

few days into his first military tour in Iraq.[52] Immobilized from the chest down, Thomas finds that all the former values and rationalizations he assumed about himself, the United States and war have dissolved into a deep and pervasive 'unknowing.' He has to rediscover and recover everything, including a new sense of his own and the very nation's identity. He had enlisted just a few days after 9/11, hearing President Bush's threatening call from the top of the pile of wreckage, 'Those who did this will hear back from us very soon!' Then Thomas was determined to defend his country and strike back. In his current state of grief, he finds he has to question everything; nothing can be taken for granted.

The pathway to some semblance of wholeness is slow, agonizing and painful. In one scene, Thomas wheels himself into the living room where his wife created a kind of shrine from the military mementos he received at the time of his injury: a folded flag, a Purple Heart, a letter of thanks signed by the President. Slowly Thomas gathers up these items, places them in a box and deposits the carton in a hall closet. 'I don't need these things to know what I lost,' he says. 'I have to live with it every day.' And the losses, indeed, are considerable; loss of two-thirds of his bodily movement, of sexual function, loss even of the ability to cough on his own. But perhaps just as devastating for Thomas is the new confusion he experiences about the political implications of his situation. Profound individual grief leads to the need to completely reconceptualize his former perspectives about patriotism, trust in the national leaders, and certainty regarding the evil of those who are declared the enemy.

Though many U.S. citizens, like Thomas, at first quickly aligned to the derealizing narrative of the abrogation of national security, sanctity and sovereignty, and the concomitant 'necessary' response of war-as-sacrifice, dissenting voices may be discerned along the way of this post-9/11 history. Rowan Williams, now Archbishop of Canterbury in the UK, was in New York City on 9/11, and in refle - tions on the experience, written less than a year later, described the vulnerable power expressed in final communications, as those in the upper floors used cell phones to contact loved ones from the Towers before they fell. In the months following, a rabbi collected the same

---

52. Ellen Spiro and Phil Donahue, *Body of War*, Docudrama Films and New Video, 2007.

words of those final communications and chanted them at a window every morning as a kind of sacred text, a kind of prayer.[53]

The reflections of these individuals represent an important minority voice during this period as they articulated the depth, power and wonder of love, and affirmation of life, even and perhaps especially in those moments when there is nothing to be done. In addition, voices such as these insist on the important insight we might gain through our grief following the fall of the Towers regarding fellowship with brothers and sisters across the globe – we are not invulnerable; the destiny of the world is a shared one. As Williams put it, 'the trauma can offer us a breathing space; and in that space there is the possibility of recognizing that we have had an experience that is not just a nightmarish insult to us but a door into the suffering of countless other innocents, a suffering that is more or less routine for them in their less regularly protected environments.'[54]

Butler as well comments on a new awareness of vulnerability arising from this loss that for some in the U.S. had distinct political implications: the end of 'First-worldism,' understood as the right to be free from the very real vagaries of suffering, free from vulnerability to others (not only personally but politically as well), and free from the need of others for one's own wellbeing (including the need for others not only personally, but also in the community of nations). The end of First-Worldism involves what Butler describes as 'the loss of the prerogative, only and always, to be the one who transgresses the sovereign boundaries of other states, but never to be in the position of having one's own boundaries transgressed.'[55]

A year after 9/11, one novelist put the question regarding the end of First-Worldism this way: 'will we learn to live unhoused from our towering isolation, or try to build it up again and crawl back into it?'[56] In this way we see how a deeper grief leads to a re-examination of the structures of power and privilege that undergird notions of prerogative, sovereignty, and freedom from transgression of one's boundaries. Yet acknowledgement of alterity from minority voices

53. The story of this rabbi is recounted in the documentary film, *Faith and Doubt at Ground Zero*, Helen Whitney, 'Frontline,' *PBS*, 2002.

54. Rowan Williams, *Writing in the Dust: After September 11* (Grand Rapids, MI: Eerdmans, 2002), p. 59.

55. Butler, *Precarious Life*, p. 39.

56. This quote comes from Madison Smart Bell, novelist and Professor of Creative Writing at Goucher College, Baltimore, MD.

such as these largely was repressed in favor of a narrative reasserting dominant First-World impermeability, ably assisted by the rhetoric of 'the necessity of sacrifice,' and its foreclosure of a deeper and more reflective grief.

A political theology of the cross adds to this analysis. Pastoral theologian, Sharon Thornton, writes about the way the personal and political collide in the cross in ways that deeply challenge the derealizing narrative from the post-9/11 period:

> In Jesus' experience of death on the cross, the significant issues of public and private life come together. Economics, politics, religion, dreams and the demise of dreams, the meaning of sickness and health, who is on the inside and who is on the margins, the meaning of dominating power and an alternative expression of vulnerable power – all these and more come together at the foot of the cross. The cross is a political symbol of reality in all its starkness and ambiguity. It represents inflicted death by criminal actions and the tenacious power of life under such extremes … Jesus' suffering on the cross invites us to view suffering not as private pain alone, but as part of the historical and communal fabric within which our lives are formed.[57]

A political theology of the cross does not allow us to sit comfortably with Christian religious commitments, because its first demand is that we ask who is on *this* cross and why. 'What happened to Jesus might happen to anyone' –as well as being a statement that emphasizes Jesus' shared humanity with all humans, also leads to a second step with respect to all historical analogies to the cross, to inquire about the social, religious, political, economic, and cultural dynamics that led to *this* one being nailed to *this* cross.

Even more, this second step involves self-criticism as we begin to assess our own explicit and implicit values and assumptions, and as we dare to interrogate just whose 'burden is multiplied by the way we go about our business.' This self-criticism disallows the narrowness of perception embodied in so much national memorialization that glorifies certain losses/crosses while glossing over or ignoring entirely others. Moreover, it leads to the need for criticism of social and political structures, the ways we are entangled in them and the processes through which we derive our very identities

---

57. Sharon Thornton, *Broken yet Beloved: A Pastoral Theology of the Cross* (St. Louis, MO: Chalice Press, 2002), pp. 115–16.

and cognitive structures for thinking and valuing from them. As Thornton writes,

> Only by listening to those who have a quarrel with us and by engaging in such self-critical activity can pastoral care and theology address the historical and contemporary practices that continue to wound and divide people ... Pastoral theology begins with confessing its collusion in harm and its inability to "save itself" as it seeks to participate in a tradition of *fides quaerens intellectum*, perhaps better understood for today as *pain seeking understanding*.[58]

To raise such questions is neither to excuse the horrific and destructive acts of 9/11 or terrorism generally speaking, nor to lapse into guilt. Instead, a political theology of the cross assists in decentering unilateral and defensive structures in order to ask about the ways our national perceptions and representations are formed and enacted. For Butler, this process involves resisting cycles of revenge that pose as justice. Legal redress for wrongs committed should be pursued, but for a different end,

> taking stock of how the world has become formed in this way precisely in order to form it anew, and in the direction of non-violence ... Our collective responsibility [is] not merely as a nation, but as part of an international community based on a commitment to equality and non-violent cooperation ... we seek to re-create social and political conditions on more sustaining grounds.[59]

Thus, a wider and deeper frame of reference and descriptive power is called for in the face of the sacrificial and binary characterizations that so dominate the post-9/11 United States. As we saw in Chapter Two, potential or actual war seems always to correspond with black and white divisions, the 'enemy' as evil, irrational, inhuman, aggressive, etc., versus 'us' as morally good, reasonable, charitable and peace-loving. Victimage rhetoric glorifies and mystifies 'the ultimate sacrifice' made by members of the U.S. military, and simultaneously effectively shifts 'collateral sacrifices' of war (i.e., the deaths of Iraqis and Afghanis) off the table entirely. As the theorists above already begin to suggest, the way to resist such tendencies involves what communications scholar Robert Ivies calls, 'nonconforming solidarity through the expression of the unity of humanity.' In other words, the task of resistance to sacrificial binaries has to do

58. Thornton, *Broken yet Beloved*, p. 116.
59. Butler, 'Survivability, Vulnerability, Affect,' p. 16.

with rehumanization of all the parties involved in and affected by war: soldiers, enemies, noncombatants, citizens.

Rehumanizing discourse avoids 'reciprocal recrimination,' that is, the communicative strategy that simply reverses the declaration of attributes. The rhetoric from anti-war dissenter Ward Churchill, a professor at the University of Colorado, may be explored as one example. Churchill's response to 9/11, blaming Americans for the World Trade Center Tower attacks, only fed into the strength of the Bush Administration's strategy by reversing the binary categories, instead of challenging the overall characterization strategy. As Ivies puts it, 'negative tactics of dissent … are susceptible to recapture within the strategic framework of political authority.'[60] Churchill's volatile language and blaming of Americans merely reversed the order of culpability first utilized by the Bush Administration, and consequently, his developed and detailed criticisms of U.S. foreign policy and the war on terrorism easily were sidestepped and ridiculed. Ivies concludes, 'his critique failed to move the democratic contestation of ideas productively forward.'[61]

Reversing or shifting the blame fails to challenge dominant habits of thinking and perceiving; as a result, deeper collective thinking is discouraged. In contrast to this mirroring, Ivies describes democratic communication as 'artful speaking in the democratic idiom … contesting opinions robustly but respectfully, that is, with respect for the diverse views and plural interests of a strong and inclusive – open and vital – democratic public.' He concludes, 'the stories we tell each other can either promote humanizing dialogue or reiterate dehumanizing monologues.'[62]

Tantalizingly, Ivies suggests that what we really need at this moment in U.S. history are 'humanizing rites of peace' to resist the reductive and polarizing effect of so much political discourse. Writer Paul Fussell comes to mind from the WWII era as one powerful voice who spoke simultaneously as an army lieutenant in a rifle platoon, and as a thoughtful critic suspicious of the nation's wartime rationalizations. Ivies speaks almost longingly of the hope for 'rehumanizing news of the day,' and of drama, poetry, art, literature and

60. Robert L. Ivies, *Dissent from War* (Bloomfield, CT: Kumarian Press, 2007), p. 114.
61. Ivies, *Dissent*, pp. 125–29.
62. Ivies, *Dissent*, p. 92.

music that emphasize peaceful relations domestically and interna-
tionally alike. He decries the general lack of any peace curricula in
our schools and universities, never mind public monuments that
celebrate and memorialize peaceful reconciliation and non-violence.
Finally, he wonders, what about 'the Sunday sermon of redemption
by means other than vicarious sacrifice?' These are the 'rites' we
need if we are to make any sustained change of habituation in our
dynamics as a nation, more toward a presumption for peace and
away from a presumption for war, if we are to move away at all
from 'the cruel cycle of deliverance by violence.'[63]

A Theology of Soldiers' and Citizens' Work: Toward Deeper Rehumanization

Both Cindy Sheehan and Mrs. Galvez relied on sacrificial language
in their attempts to find some sort of meaning in their sons' deaths.
Toward the end of the first decade of the twenty-first century, even as
increased numbers of Americans became more and more suspicious
about any justifiable moral criteria that could rationally endorse the
Iraq and Afghanistan Wars, the same sacrificial language continued
to be used to explain and justify the deaths of soldiers, albeit with
some slight twists. For instance, by 2009, when PA resident Staff
Sgt. Mark C. Baum, 32, was killed by small arms fire after responding to an Improvised Explosive Device attack, the local newspaper
from his hometown reported his wife, Heather's, description of him
as 'a hero, a good man.' His mother-in-law explained further, 'He
believed in what he was doing.' But then she continued, 'He wasn't
always happy with the politics – nobody is – but he believed in what
he was doing.' As U.S. citizens increasingly became disenchanted
with the Iraq War, one began to see greater attempts at separating
individual heroism and accomplishment from declarations about
the fulfillment of a worthy national mission that merits the sacrifice
of these deaths.

Nevertheless, the 'official narrative' from representatives of military institutions remained more or less the same. Thus, tellingly, in
response to Sgt. Baum's death, the PA National Guard spokesperson reiterated the same sacrificial discourse we have seen too often.
As Maj. Gen. Jessica L. Wright, commander of the Pennsylvania

63. Ivies, *Dissent*, p. 93.

National Guard, said in a press release about Sgt. Baum, 'His bravery and dedication serve as a reminder of all of the sacrifices that are made each day to ensure that freedom and democracy prevail.'[64] In contrast to Maj. Gen. Wright, here Sgt. Baum's family took comfort in their loved one's personal characteristics; he was heroic and dedicated to the last in trying to protect those around him from harm. Nevertheless, now this personal praise was separated from any attempt to justify the politics that require sacrifices such as this young man.

Clearly, detranscendentalizing war and war-culture means resisting and challenging sacrific al descriptors for soldiers and the business of war alike. Yet, if we move away from describing the deaths of soldiers as 'a necessary sacrifice,' what will we call these losses? How will we understand what soldiers do? We need to search for language that can help us recapture the fullness, the precariousness, the vulnerability of the face of the other.

Soelle's beautiful words perhaps suggest an avenue forward. Recall her statement regarding the cross: 'To meditate on the cross means to say good-bye to the narcissistic hope of being free of sickness, deformity and death. Then all the energies wasted on such hopes could become free to answer the call to respond to suffering.' For Soelle, the question is, will we *work* on and with the realities of suffering? Conceiving of the call to respond to suffering as a form of *work,* or *labor*, may yield the benefit of demystifying and rehumanizing the forms of service and engagement to which humans dedicate themselves. In other words, searching for a way outside of the conundrum of sacrificial rhetoric, I suggest that we turn to a deeper theological construction of *work/labor*, and offer a few thoughts below as starting points for further theological endeavor.

A Theology of Work, not Sacrific

Conceiving of a theology of work or labor immediately brings to the surface a whole series of connotations. The words, 'work' and 'labor' are somewhat interchangeable, yet 'labor' also connotes the creative effort to bring new life into the world. When I was in labor with my first child, the midwife who supported me suggested, at

64. Catherine Meredith, 'Soldier from Quakertown Killed in Iraq,' *Morning Call*, 23 February 2009, http://www.mcall.com/news/local/all-quakertown-soldier-killed-0223-cn,0,7273624.story, accessed 23 February 2009.

one particularly difficult moment, that I think back to 'the hardest thing in my life I had ever accomplished' and use that moment as a way to gain strength and hope for the physical work involved in giving birth. My mind immediately leapt to some of the most difficult labor I had to date attempted in my educational pursuits. Though a very different type of work, the connection nonetheless helped immeasurably in that all-consuming moment!

Sacrificial rhetoric, as we have seen, mystifies exchanges and transactions; it calls things equitable that can never be equitable, and distances human beings from the realities of suffering and death that are occurring; it forestalls grief and promotes violence as the way to redemption, both religiously and politically. 'Sacrificial collateral' all too easily mutes the cry of the face of the other. In contrast, working on and with the realities of suffering is a humanizing endeavor indeed. In fact, we might develop a theology of work or labor to embrace hopefulness of natality, the bringing into being of something distinctive, something new, something that only occurs because people are coming together for the purpose of creation.[65] The turn to suffering experience as a site for increased focus and work, moreover, links this effort with what liberation theology calls 'the epistemological privilege of the oppressed.' If we want to understand the nature of justice more clearly, we must turn, not to the narratives of the 'winners' in history, but to those whose existence hangs in the balance, who are left out, ground up, or otherwise relegated to invisibility by the dominant structures that order human lives, communities and nations.

Theologies of work can assist in the important analysis of power structures that are called for by this reorientation. For instance, contemporary theologies of work or labor commonly include analysis of the cycle of *alienation* involved in so many economic and labor relations. In addition, these theologies explore the logic of *utility* all too prevalent in economic processes that encompass workers, the subjects of their work, and the world itself. A brief explanation of each of these terms follows.

First, alienation occurs through the division between the worker and her work's product; the worker has no role either in envisioning the possible results of her labor, nor does she plan or have the

65. Hannah Arendt, *The Human Condition*, Margaret Canovan, Introduction (Chicago, IL: University of Chicago Press, 1998, 1st edn).

option to use what she creates.[66] As a result the worker never really makes any progress, the cycle of work never changes, and the worker has little control of her time. Moreover, she is alienated from other workers, and isolated therefore not only from her product and her productivity, but also from her fellow humans. In addition, the Protestant work ethic that encouraged belief in labor as the will of God, and as the duty of the human person, easily enabled the shift away from the notion of meaningful work to a way of thinking about the concept of work as good regardless of its substance. In this way the cycle of alienation deepened: 'Religion has served to accommodate people to meaningless work.'[67] This dynamic of alienation and depoliticization may be extended to the work of soldiers when such divisions occur between themselves and their labor. The split between the reactions of Sgt. Baum's family and the National Guard's spokesperson to his death is a case in point. While the spokesperson linked his demise with the necessary sacrifice made for freedom and democracy, in contrast, the meaning of Sgt. Baum's death, for his family members, was alienated from any supposed military and political goals that took him to Iraq in the first place.

Second, the logic of utility exacerbates this same dynamic by converting all relationships into exchange relationships. As we have seen, sacrificial schemes require this logic, and rise to the surface over and over again as *the* dominant descriptor for soldiers' labor. Usefulness, efficiency, profit, and rationality operate as gods in much of modern work, resulting in the increasing instrumentalization of more and more of the human and/or other living participants and material components in any working system. One theologian elaborates four steps by which the logic of utility takes hold. First, intrinsic value is removed from the material world, and the world is revisioned as little more than a collection of usable resources. Such thinking leads to a second step, the instrumentalizing and casual pillaging of the natural world. A third step involves the elevation of human subjectivity to a divine level with respect to work; with the natural world reduced to usable resources, a decisive shift occurs in the way value is assigned. Thus, emphasis increasingly is placed on human acts of will, and human impact on the world of material

66. Dorothee Soelle with Shirley A. Cloyes, *To Work and to Love: A Theology of Creation* (Philadelphia, PA: Fortress Press, 1984), p. 56.
67. Soelle, *To Work and to Love*, p. 59.

things, as the primary way to assign value (thus usurping the role of God, who declared all things good). In the end, with the fourth step, labor magnifies to a 'Herculean' level, and any end other than self-interest combined with efficiency of means is regarded with hostility:

> People are reduced to commodities whose "usefulness" can be measured in terms of profit and efficiency, and who will be disposed of accordingly. The world of work has become total, seeking to obliterate all other accounts of the world. Absolute utility reveals itself as nothing but violent self-interest and nihilism.[68]

The theological critique of such work is that it is a form of curse in human life, expressing self-alienation and separation from others, the world and God. This critique of labor is needed to think through more deeply the work of soldiers, the everyday workers in the world of war and militarization. Describing their work and deaths as 'necessary sacrifices' neatly masks the commodified reality of soldiers' lives, as their labor and even the meaning of their lives are measured through the categories of 'efficiency' and 'usefulness' named above. In fact, soldiers may be described as belonging to the 62 percent of Americans who are 'working class,' that is, who belong to that class of citizens defined not primarily in terms of their income level, but in terms of the limited power and authority they have over their own work. As Joerg Rieger claims, 'the work that we do for a living shapes us to a large degree, and who holds the power over this work determines who ultimately benefits from it.'[69] Thus, beginning with an analysis of the work of soldiers, we inevitably find ourselves moving to other layers of our social structures, beyond soldiers as workers, to the means and ownership of the production of war and war-culture. Here we will find the true beneficiaries of soldiers' labor. In the end, a theology of work attempts to hold to account those systems that brutally instrumentalize human bodies and spirits. At the same time, we also need to examine and incorporate theologies of work that reconceive more hopeful portrayals of human endeavor.[70] For work also has the potential in

---

68. John Hughes, *The End of Work: Theological Critiques of Capitalism* (Victoria, Australia: Blackwell Publishing, 2007), pp. 219-20.

69. Joerg Rieger, *No Rising Tide: Theology, Economics, and the Future* (Minneapolis, MN: Fortress Press, 2009), p. 35.

70. David H. Jensen, *Responsive Labor: A Theology of Work* (Louisville, KY: Westminster John Knox Press, 2006), p. 41.

human existence to be experienced as a gift from God, and to be itself a means of thanks for the work God continues to accomplish.

'Good work' involves a variety of characteristics that reoccur across various theological accounts. Work provides opportunities for self-expression, for social relatedness and reconciliation with nature.[71] Human work should be deeply tied to the intrinsic value of the world, and of workers as human persons with dignity. Good work promotes increasing investment in workers, and encourages workers likewise to invest their skills and gifts in the workplace for the benefit of both management and labor.

In addition, though work is an important part of human identity, a theology of good work acknowledges the need for rest and for personal development apart from one's workplace. Humans are more than commodity-producing and owning creatures. The maintenance of a decent standard of living, combined with ecological sustainability of work practices, also are measures of the practices of 'good work.' When societies value workers as people, they will refuse to reduce people to the goods they produce, will value just wages, fair prices and honest trade, and will encourage worker ownership as an important way to discourage hyper-specialization and encourage collaboration and a shared stake in the profitability of the workplace.

Good work encourages counter-cultural practices that resist and attempt to transcend the dominant standard of utility. One theologian imagines some examples:

> the responsible craft of an artisan, the liberal arts vision of education as more than technical ... the corporate commitment to certain values even at the expense of personal interest, the gratuitous delight of child's play, the non-competitive relations of parental love, the Sabbath rest understood as more than mere recreation at the service of work, the transcendent logic of the liturgical and sacramental.[72]

Good work is connected to 'the Great Work,' joining with God to bring into being the New Creation. Thus good work is linked to the 'collaborative eschaton' described above. 'Work is ultimately an eschatological act.' Work has to do with our desire to be remembered,

71. These are the categories of a theology of work envisioned by Dorothee Soelle and Shirley A. Cloyes, *To Work and to Love*.
72. Hughes, *The End of Work*, pp. 230–31.

and to make a lasting difference in the world. If eschatology may be defined as ' ... believing in a future that is life-giving and not only about death,' then work has to do with the challenge each of us faces to consider what we want to leave behind. Play, surprise and the Spirit all are eschatological elements of work. At the same time, good work is connected to the politics that arise from a deeper and more reflective grief such as Judith Butler describes. Work involves both the *via positiva* and the *via negativa*. As theologian Matthew Fox writes,

> There is so much work to be done in our time, but it is primarily work on ourselves – work on our better selves (the *via positiva*) and work on our shadow selves (the *via negativa*). Once we start paying attention to the inner needs of our species, we will see that there is no shortage of work. There is work to be done on the inner needs of our communities as well, with their capacity for joy and celebration (the *via positiva*) as well as their need for sharing grief, anger, outrage and sorrow (the *via negativa*). Where are all the workers? They are among us. But we need to invite one another to this work.[73]

As we focus on this theology of 'good work' described above, it is important that we recognize how counter-cultural its values have become in the contemporary culture of the U.S. economy. According to one recent report:

> Large companies are increasingly owned by institutional investors who crave swift profits, a feat often achieved by cutting payroll. The declining influence of unions has made it easier for employers to shift work to part-time and temporary employees. Factory work and even white-collar jobs have moved in recent years to low-cost countries in Asia and Latin America. Automation has helped manufacturing cut 5.6 million jobs since 2000 ... "American business is about maximizing shareholder value," said Allen Sinai, chief global economist at the research firm Decision Economics. "You basically don't want workers. You hire less, and you try to find capital equipment to replace them."[74]

Just down the hallway from my office at the college, a bulletin board above the drinking fountain is covered with yellowing sheets

73. Matthew Fox, *The Reinvention of Work: A New Vision of Livelihood for Our Time* (New York: Harper Collins, 1995), p. 47.

74. Peter S. Goodman, 'Despite Signs of Recovery, Chronic Joblessness Rises,' *The New York Times*, 21 February 2010.

of newspaper tacked up over the last years, one sheet stapled over another, all bearing hundreds of small photographs of American soldiers who have been killed since the beginnings of the wars in Afghanistan and Iraq. Someone at the college (I don't know who) took up the responsibility over these years to make sure that the flesh-and-blood reality of these deaths would be a part of our daily life, even if in such a small way as pinning their photographs to a bulletin board. The young faces of these men and women look down on me every time I go for a drink of water. *How did you die, and what was your work?* I often wonder in front of these faces.

Indeed, there is so much human suffering in need of good work in the world for healing, reconciliation and new life. But sacrificial descriptors dehumanize soldiers and give voice to the lie of redemptive violence. The same frameworks mute the cry of the suffering of those who have been buried beneath the label of 'collateral damage' that this 'necessary sacrifice' requires. The sacred canopy of sacrifice prevents and mystifies the important analysis of political, economic and social systems that give rise to war and war-culture. Soldiers become enslaved to the cycles of alienation and reduced to objects of utility. And one can only wonder at the burdens this places on the soldiers themselves. Captain Dan Kearney, leading the 173rd Airborne Brigade Combat Team in the Korengal Valley of the Kunar province of Afghanistan, and attempting to 'subdue the valley' after seven years of air strikes and civilian deaths, found it hard going. 'After five months of grueling foot patrols up and down the mountains, after fruitless encounters with elders who smiled in the morning and were host to insurgents in the evening and after losing friends to enemy fire, Captain Kearney's men could relate to the sullen, jittery rage of their predecessors in the 10th Mountain Division. Many wondered what they were doing out there at all.' Captain Kearney described himself as 'Dr. Phil with guns,' with increasing numbers of his troops resorting to medications such as Prozac and other antidepressants in order to maintain some sort of equilibrium in an increasingly insane context. He described one soldier's bizarre behavior to a visiting reporter. 'Medicated,' Kearney said. 'Last tour, if you didn't give him information, he'd burn down your house. He killed so many people. He's checked out.'[75] Meanwhile,

75. Elizabeth Rubin, 'Battle Company is Out There,' *The New York Times Magazine*, 24 February 2008, http://www.nytimes.com/2008/02/24/magazine, accessed 23 March 2009.

a small number at the top of the social/economic ladder are grow-ing richer as a result of these enterprises; and overall, the increase in resources dedicated to war and war-culture shrinks social safety nets more and more.

A theology of work, not sacrifice, critiques the commodification and dehumanization of soldiers, insurgents and civilians alike, and searches for the roots of current forms of suffering, to ask just how we are implicated in this suffering as a result of 'the way we go about our business.' In other words, a theology of work analyzes the power dynamics that give rise to and control specific forms of human labor, including the labor undertaken by political and eco-nomic leaders, the structures of the corporate world inextricably in-tertwined with the production of the means of war, and the labor of members of the military. It investigates these dynamics to inquire about the true beneficiaries of war and war-culture. It also searches for the best ways to 'work on suffering,' to intervene and make a difference for the sake of everyone involved. A theology of work focuses broadly in its search for ways forward given the ongoing realities of injustice and conflict

A Theology of Work and Just Peacemaking

The shift advocated here from a theology of 'the necessity of war-as-sacrifice' to a theology of work can benefit from and has much to contribute to the ongoing development of Just Peacemaking Practices. In the 1990s 23 scholars worked for five years to develop a series of practical initiatives that have been historically demon-strated to diminish the prevalence of war. These 'preventive prac-tices' are 'historically situated, concretely observable, work together for peace, and are therefore ethically normative or obligatory.'[76] As these scholars and activists asserted, the problem with Just War tradition is its tendency to focus too narrowly and superficially on military action alone. As a result, Just War categories reinforce the myth of redemptive violence and fail to challenge the logic of sacri-ficialism. Instead of providing a way to probe to the roots of the con-flict, roots that often have to do with unjust and inequitable human economic, political, social and cultural systems, Just War tradition

---

76. Glen Stassen, 'The Unity, Realism, and Obligatoriness of Just Peacemaking Theory,' *Journal of the Society of Christian Ethics* 23.1 (2003): 175.

takes too narrow a view. Primary focus on the question of the justifi-ability of military action inevitably shortcuts a longer historical in-vestigation that would dig deeper into social, political and cultural realities. At the other end of the spectrum, pacifist traditions may lack clear and detailed pathways for specific ways to address spe-cific forms of injustice that over time, if left unaddressed, develop into militarism, terrorism, war, and other forms of conflict and vio-lence. At the extreme, pacifist frameworks can perpetuate isolation and withdrawal.[77]

Both pacifism and Just War tradition may be enhanced by a theology of work that closely aligns with just peacemaking initia-tives. While just peacemaking theorists underscore the importance of ongoing debates between Just War and pacifism regarding the justifiability of armed force, at the same time, just peacemakers em-phasize the opportunity these realistic and pragmatic practices of-fer to lessen the destructiveness of war and provide opportunities for preventing specific wars. These initiatives broaden the scope of analysis of injustices that give rise to conflict, and involve hard work over long and sustained periods of time both before and after actual armed conflict has erupted. Ten peacemaking practices include:

1. Support Nonviolent Direct Action.
2. Take Independent Initiatives to Reduce Threat.
3. Use Cooperative Conflict Resolution
4. Acknowledge Responsibility for Conflict and Injustice
5. Advance Democracy, Human Rights and Religious Liberty.
6. Foster Just and Sustainable Economic Development.
7. Work with Emerging Cooperative Forces in the International System.
8. Strengthen the United Nations and International Efforts for Cooperation and Human Rights.
9. Reduce Offensive Weapons and Weapons Trade.
10. Encourage Grassroots Peacemaking Groups and Voluntary Associations.[78]

---

77. For a powerful discussion about the commonalities and the sharp differ-ences between Just War tradition and pacifism, see David L. Clough and Brian Stiltner, *Faith and Force: A Christian Debate about War* (Georgetown, Washington DC: Georgetown University Press, 2007).

78. Glen Stassen (ed.), *Just Peacemaking: Ten Practices for Abolishing War* (Cleveland, OH: The Pilgrim Press, 1998, 2nd edn).

To briefly give an example of these initiatives in action, I turn to just peacemaking thinkers who have drawn upon the initiatives above to highlight the limitations in the argument of historian Jean Bethke Elshtain, who as we saw in Chapter Three, led a group of scholars, members of think tanks and activists in support of war following 9/11. This analysis demonstrates just how and why we need work that takes a longer and a deeper historical, political and theological critical view.[79]

One area of criticism of Elshtain involves analysis of the way Just War tenets were used in her argument for war. The criterion of 'just intent' in Just War tradition protects against the use of war as a form of political or social vengeance; yet, as the just peacemaking thinkers show, Elshtain's focus on punishment of terrorists was not sufficiently circumscribed by a criminal justice approach that treats terror as a criminal act. As a result, her advocacy for war failed to address the way that punishment can lapse into vengeance. Second, these analysts address Elshtain's attention to a second Just War criterion, 'noncombatant immunity.' Early on, Elshtain was cognizant of the need to avoid grievous harm of noncombatants in the implementation of the war in Iraq. However, as the war continued, she failed to address the reality of the overwhelming injuries sustained by the Iraqi people as a result of the course of the war, such as the 'devastation caused by the two-week period of "shock and awe,"' not to mention the overall scale of death and destruction that the Bloomburg report documents.

In fact, a longer and more incisive analysis of American history, especially post-World War II history, is essential to take into account all the variables leading to the Afghanistan and Iraq wars. As the just peacemaking thinkers write, 'Post-World War II policy has been significantly shaped by narrow economic interests, ... involving a U.S. role in coups in Iran, Guatemala, the Congo, Indonesia, among others ... to protect the interests of U.S. capital.' Though Elshtain's work overall has demonstrated criticism of U.S. consumerism and even at times, capitalism, she failed to connect this thinking to U.S. foreign policy supporting an invasion of Iraq.

---

79. Pamela K. Brubaker, Glen H. Stassen and Janet L. Parker, 'A Critique of Jean Bethke Elshtain's Just War Against Terror and Advocacy of a Constructive Alternative,' *Journal of Religion, Conflict and Peac* 2.1 (Fall 2008).

All in all, these thinkers conclude, the work to adequately address terrorism and the conditions that give rise to it involves three simultaneous tasks: analyzing and building security through international cooperation, bringing into clear view the lack of sustainable economic development that often gives rise to terrorism, and rejecting the paradigm of 'the War on Terror.' The terminology of 'War on Terror,' erodes the rule of law, diminishes respect for human rights, and hides questionable political purposes from view. It universalizes terrorism and thereby discourages analysis of diverse contexts and root causes that give rise to terrorist acts.

Finally, the authors recommend an ecumenical approach to counter-terrorism that is based in 'respect for human rights, international law, multilateral cooperation and the struggle for economic and social justice.' Counter-terrorism should be de-militarized, should address terrorism's root causes, should enlist faith communities to play a role in the prevention of conflict and building cultures of peace, and should draw upon religious institutions to emphasize the human condition of mutual vulnerability and need for security and reconciliation between enemies. Just peacemaking theory does not completely prohibit the just use of military force, but it does provide more serious constraints and outlines more specific strategies for addressing the reality of human conflict and violence in a way that goes beyond Just War tradition. This work must take place over the extensive periods of time, long before specific conflicts erupt and long after armed hostilities have ended [80]

In addition to underscoring the important impact these ten peacemaking initiatives have had in a world of conflict and war, one additional just peacemaking initiative should be advocated related to the themes of this book. This 'eleventh' initiative involves investigation and analysis to de-escalate and detranscendentalize war-culture, and disentangle the ethos and institutions of war from diverse cultural, political and economic realms. Moreover, the central component of detranscendentalization is to lay bare the logic of

---

80. It was reported in March, 2009, that the Obama Administration ordered speechwriters to cease using the terminology of 'the war on terror,' in favor of 'overseas contingency operations.' See Oliver Burkeman, 'Obama Administration says Goodbye to "war on terror,"' *guardian.co.uk*, 25 March 2009, http://www.guardian.co.uk/world/2009/mar/25/obama-war-terror-overseas-contingency-operations, accessed, 5 March 2009.

sacrificialism that unites the practices, history, rhetoric and theology of Christianity with U.S. nationalism in war-culture, and that mystifies analysis about war-culture's genealogy and architecture. One important goal of this initiative is to search for ways of speaking and acting outside of sacrificialism in both religion and the nation as a whole.

Why is this 'eleventh just peacemaking initiative' important? War-culture predisposes us *toward* war. Our ethical deliberation about war and conflict does not begin with a blank slate, but from the onset is profoundly influenced by all the permutations of war-culture that shape our acculturation and self-identity as citizens in the United States. In many diverse ways we are inclined to believe that violence is effective and masterful, that war-as-sacrifice is heroic, virtuous, and the ultimate duty for American citizens, and that the immensely superior military power of the United States can and will solve whatever problems we face. At the same time American citizens largely are oblivious to the interpenetrations of war-culture in our lives, and heedless regarding the destruction it wreaks around the world. War will save us, it will protect us, purchase our freedom and democracy, it is the normal (and even divinely sanctioned) state of affairs. These assumptions are deeply engraved in the American character. Thus, our moral analysis of conflict and war has to begin with honesty about our own context here in the United States. This honesty is all-important if we are to engage the important work of lessening the scope and destruction of war, as is the goal of just peacemaking practice. But much ethical work on war completely misses this point.

Additionally, while just peacemaking does highlight the importance of reducing the weapons trade, detranscendentalizing war and war-culture includes more extensive moral deliberation regarding the economics of war-culture, and the extent of U.S. dependence upon it. Thinking through the labor of soldiers, 'the workers,' must be accompanied by exploration of the true economic beneficiaries of war and war-culture, but the same dominant messages in our culture about the effectiveness, masterfulness and necessity of war-culture easily distract and otherwise prevent us from taking up these important questions. Focus on the labor of soldiers as the heroic labor they perform and the necessary sacrifice to secure the nation, is a deformation of and distraction from the economic reality of war and war-culture. In fact, the labor of soldiers provides economic surplus that goes to those who control and own the means of war and war-culture's production.

Thus, given the ubiquity and depth of U.S. War-culture, ethical deliberation must begin with a strong hermeneutic of suspicion regarding any judgment that recommends armed force. For instance, Christian ethicists have claimed that just peacemaking theory should more specifically address the realities of sin and collective egotism, and the possible use of force as a peacemaking practice.[81] Lisa Sowle Cahill calls for an additional practice to be added, 'one that directly refers to the necessary use of countervailing force to raise the profile of justice for those whom a given system has disenfranchised.'[82] However, such a recommendation, without being firmly grounded in clear-eyed acknowledgement of U.S. War-culture and its true beneficiaries, is susceptible to being reabsorbed into the arsenal of imperial power. The powers that be in war-culture clothe themselves in this very language, 'the necessity of inevitable violence to protect and increase justice' (such as we saw in the language from the Bush Administration with respect to the planned Iraq War). Moreover, social location matters here. Though, as Chapter One demonstrated, all our lives are intertwined with the machinery of war-culture, to the degree that our livelihoods directly depend on war-culture, it becomes increasingly difficult for us to honestly acknowledge and assess its destructive consequences, and the greater our temptation to fall in line with the official narrative of 'the necessity of war-as-sacrifice.

As Reinhold Niebuhr recognized, it is highly unlikely that the privileged voluntarily will relinquish forms of power. In fact, in the context of war-culture, the recommendation of coercive power as a supposedly 'countervailing force' more often than not serves as a screen for the increase of war-culture. Moreover, sacrificial ideologies, especially, we have seen, in the context of U.S. War-culture, blur incisive analysis of armed force as 'a last resort' to increase justice. In fact, the lurch toward violent forms of coercion is rationalized through sacrificial mechanisms that mystify the very realities of privilege and disenfranchisement Cahill would have us

81. Lisa Sowle Cahill, 'Just Peacemaking: Theory, Practice and Prospects,' *Journal of the Society of Christian Ethics* 23.1 (2003): 195–212.
82. Cahill, 'Just Peacemaking', p. 201.

more carefully address. Therefore, dealing with human sinfulness with respect to war must begin with de-escalating war-culture, and dissecting the practices of sacrifice that activate and sacralize frameworks and practices for war and war-culture within the national representation of the U.S. Any endorsement of 'the necessity of coercion or force,' even to raise the profile of justice for the disenfranchised, should encounter strong ethical suspicion, given the powerful cognitive framework in U.S. history and culture of 'the necessity of war-as-sacrifice.'

Along with moral criticism regarding the overarching power structures in war-culture, thinking through the ethics of armed force leads to deliberation regarding the work of members of the military. Developing an in depth theology of the work of soldiers is beyond the scope of this book. Nevertheless, a theology of work, not sacrifice, with respect to soldiers and the use of armed force, involves at least three steps.

First, detranscendentalizing the work of soldiers begins with disconnecting what they do from the language and ritual of sacrifice. Thus, we have to begin with greater awareness and critical attention to the sacrificial frames inextricably tied with war, that dominate U.S. historical recollection, national identity and representation. The importance and simultaneous difficulty of this beginning movement cannot be overstated, for this is to raise questions about the sacrality of U.S. War-culture. Articulating questions about war-culture's sacred canopy is likely to be interpreted as a form of national heresy, and inevitably evokes responses of anger, ridicule and denial, as examples from this book demonstrate. Only once the case has been convincingly made regarding the pervasiveness of war-culture's interpenetrations, is it possible for deeper awareness to emerge about the sacralization of war-culture in the United States (see Chapter One).

One important aspect of this first step is to reassess the acculturation of soldiers beginning in boot camp (or in a military educational institutions), in order to examine the way these systems promote psychological realignment away from individual, familial and communal forms of self-identification and consciousness, to what the U.S. army handbook calls 'unit cohesion.' Here precisely is where the language of sacrifice begins to take hold, as the soldier is acclimated to perceive what s/he does as a necessary sacrifice required for the

ongoing life of the nation.[83] This rationalization involves psychological consequences to which young soldiers have no way to consent
in informed ways. Examination of military sacrificial acculturation
reveals the connections between this realignment and the process
of alienation and commodification of soldiers. Again, analysis is
required to uncover the beneficiaries of these social and political
processes, in order to lay bare just how sacrificial dynamics uphold
given structures of power and control. Recall the introductory statistics about the economics of U.S. War-culture in Chapter One: in
2009 it was reported that the U.S. is responsible for 41.5 percent of
all global military expenditures; in contrast, the next largest spender
is China, at 5.8 percent. In addition, the United States is overwhelmingly the dominant salesperson of weapons to the rest of the world,
representing over 68 percent of total global sales. What should
we make of such utterly outsized and unbalanced global military
economics?[84] Emphasis on the sacrificial nature of the military use-
fully detracts from important investigation of the interpenetration
between the institutions of the military, the political establishment
and corporate worlds, but this precisely is where greater analysis
and clearer visibility is needed. Finally, de-escalating war-culture
reveals the need for stronger boundaries between military and civilian institutions (such as government and think tanks, corporations,
educational institutions, religious institutions, etc.) so as to protect
the balance of powers and mitigate against processes of legitimation
that mystify and normalize war and war-culture.

Just peacemaking initiatives come into play in the second step
of ethically addressing the work of soldiers and armed force. Just
peacemaking thinkers identify three different types of international
forces to intervene when humanitarian disasters occur:

1. Unarmed or lightly armed peacekeepers who help to maintain
   the peace after conflicted parties have reached agreement.

83. See Gwynne Dyer's chapter on boot camp in *War: The New Edition*
(Toronto and Ontario, Canada: Vintage Canada, 2005). In addition to exploring the psychological realignment to sacrificial self-identity, this investigation
also should search out the inculcation of other elements from 'the Myth of War
Experience,' including those tropes of masculinity, patriotism, the search for
adventure, and the drive for meaning.

84. Stockholm International Peace Research Institute Report, 'Recent Trends
in Military Expenditure,' 21 October 2009. Retrieved 21 Oct. 2009 from http://
www.sipri.org/research/armaments/milex/resultoutput/trends

2. Peace-enforcers, who protect international humanitarian contingents from attack.

3. Armed forces, who might be called upon by the consensus of the international community in extreme cases, such as genocide, nuclear buildups and state terrorism.[85]

Yet coercion includes activities far beyond the work of soldiers, since coercion also includes the pressure from government and voluntary organizations to encourage political actors to change policy. Boycotts, taxes, constraints on corporate entities, diplomatic tactics to address recalcitrant leadership, economic sanctions and more are examples of nonviolent coercion. However, though we tend to identify these kinds of practices as 'nonviolent,' Reinhold Niebuhr's insight regarding the unintended violence that may result from nonviolent coercive initiatives prevents any simplistic categorization along these lines.[86]

85. Stassen, *Just Peacemaking*, p. 163. Cahill underscores the importance of 'changing the framework of discourse' so that violent relationships and solutions are lowered to more of a secondary status, and 'nonviolent, cooperative, conciliatory and diplomatic' achieve primary status as plausible and serious political possibilities. Cahill, 'Just Peacemaking' pp. 208–209.

86. See Reinhold Niebuhr, *Moral Man and Immoral Society* (New York: Scribner, 1960). For an in depth analysis of the destructive consequences of UN economic sanctions approved through the UN Security Council, see W. Michael Reisman and Douglas L. Stevick, 'The Applicability of International Law Standards to United Nations Economic Sanctions Programs,' *European Journal of International Law* 9 (1998): 86–141. Economic sanctions have appeal because they tend to cause less internal political resistance than other strategies, and are relatively cheap to employ. However, their destructive consequences, especially on the lives of the poor, were devastating in the context of their usage in Southern Rhodesia, Iraq, Libya, Yugoslavia and Haiti. Moreover, as with violent military strategies, the destructive capacity of economic sanctions may be rationalized by way of sacrificial exchange frameworks. In one example, Southern Rhodesia in the early 1970s, the chairman of Zimbabwe's African National Council declared in a statement before the UN Security Council that sanctions should not be weakened despite their destructive consequences: 'pain was a price for freedom.' As the authors conclude, 'The ease with which these self-authorized affirmations and waivers of others' human rights were accepted by a United Nations ostensibly bent on protecting human rights manifested a troubling disregard for the welfare of "non-combatants."' See, pp. 100–101. For further discussion of these issues also see John Howard Yoder, *The War of the Lamb: The Ethics of Nonviolence and Peacemaking*, Glen Stassen, Mark Thiessen Nation, and Matt Hamsher (eds), (Grand Rapids, MI: Brazos Press, 2009), Chapter Six, 'Just War and Nonviolence: Disjunction, Dialogue, or Complementarity?'

This second step, and any (even highly limited) reconsideration of the use of armed force, must thoroughly address the haunting question: is it possible to do the work of killing without losing one's soul? Military memoirs tend to rebuff and ridicule such questions, but given the rise of mental, emotional and spiritual distress experienced by members of the military following tours of duty in any war zone, we must take seriously the fact that the normalization of war and war-culture has led to repression and denial of the consequences of participation in war.[87] The simplistic labeling of killing as the heroic and necessary sacrifice soldiers make deflects from serious and honest analysis of these acts and their consequences. For instance, Chairman of the Joint Chiefs of Staff, Navy Admiral Mike Mullen, emphasized that the problems plaguing war veterans from Afghanistan and Iraq will exist for generations to come. Veterans caught in the destructive cycles of homelessness, family strains, psychological problems, and suicide, are a population in distress that the United States should expect to be dealing with *for 60 to 70 years*.[88] Sacrificial exchange dynamics in the discourse of Just War deliberations, as various 'goods' are traded for others in a calculus of 'expendability,' easily mask or otherwise glorify these destructive patterns. *Killing diminishes the human soul.* Stanley Hauerwas writes, 'When we kill, even when we kill in a just war, our bodies rebel ... War is a mighty practice, a power that destroys those

87. Among other recent memoirs, see Colonel Jack Jacobs and Douglas Century, *If Not Now, When? Duty and Sacrifice in America's Time of Need* (New York: Berkeley Caliber, 2008), pp. 135–36. The authors write, 'The freedom that we enjoy today has been purchased with the blood and sacrifi e of countless men and women who were doing the right thing, what they were supposed to do, when they needed to do it.' Here is the prototypical reliance on sacrificial justification which 'purchases' freedom through war. Yet immediately following, the authors seem to discount the rationale of 'the necessary sacrifice' and instead emphasize that the real reasons soldiers fight and die are their loyalty and love for fellow soldiers: 'So the great irony is that individual effort in battle is not the act of logic but an act of love... Soldiers fight for each other, safe in the conviction that the love of comrades trumps the fear of death, that the pain of one's wound is nothing compared to the unendurable agony of failing one's friends.'

88. Robert Burns, 'Admiral Says War Veterans Will Suffer for Years,' Associated Press, 3 April 2009, Common Dreams.org, http://www.common-dreams.org/headline/2009/04/03-2, accessed 5 March 2009.

ennobled by the force of war.'[89] In one study of soldiers returning from the fields of war in Iraq, 40 percent reported either directly killing or being responsible for killing while deployed. Fully 77 to 87 percent of soldiers in combat infantry units indicated directly firing upon combatants, while 14 to 28 percent reported responsibility for the death of noncombatants. Psychologists involved in this study underscored that killing, perhaps more than any other war-related trauma, was 'a potent ingredient in the development of mental health difficulties,' including Post Traumatic Stress Disorder, alcohol abuse, anger and relationship problems.[90] A theology of work, not sacrifice, searches for ways to work on human injustice and suffering outside of these dynamics of exchange and sanctification of death and destruction. Moreover, the dynamics of exchange in Just War deliberations frequently leave out economic analysis. Ethical deliberation should focus on the connection between an increasing U.S. arms trade and the need for opportunities to demonstrate the effectiveness and necessity of military technological prowess. Moral questions also should be applied to the growth of secondary corporate contracting as a major facet of war and war-culture. Such analysis leads to the rise of a third emphasis in a theology of work, not sacrifice

In the face of the threat of war, a theology of work strenuously exerts itself in the task of rehumanization. Jon Sobrino asks, 'How does Jesus go on humanizing this imperial world? Most fundamentally he challenges us to give priority to mercy.'[91] Rehumanization may be defined as a re-emphasis on human precariousness and precarity. In other words, rehumanization requires the value of human interdependency, and the analysis of human failure to live up to

89. Stanley Hauerwas, 'Sacrifici g the Sacrifices of War,' *Criswell Theological Review*, n.s. 4.2 (Spring 2007): 77–96, 94.

90. Maguen, Shira, Barbara A. Lucenko, Mark A. Reger, Gregory A. Gahm, Brett T. Litz, Karen H. Seal, Sara J. Knight and Charles R. Marmar, 'The Impact of Reported Direct and Indirect Killing on Mental Health Symptoms in Iraq War Veterans, *Journal of Traumatic Stress* 23.1 (2010): 1–5. Ethnic minority status and female gender were significant predictors of depression and PTSD symptoms, while younger age, lower education, male gender and being single were indicators of alcohol abuse. Lower education, female gender and being married or in a relationship all were predictors of relationship problems.

91. Jon Sobrino, *Where is God? Earthquake, Terrorism, Barbarity, and Hope* (Maryknoll, NY: Orbis Books, 2004), p. vxiii.

this value. In the inclusive egalitarian nature of the human person, one life always is intimately linked with other life – this is the reality of human precariousness. My existence not only is finite, but requires vast social and economic needs to be met for its sustenance. As Butler says, 'one's life is always in some sense in the hands of another.'[92] The 'social network of hands' required for the continuance of any and every human life means that unless this life would be grievable to us if lost, it really ceases to be life; it is something other than life. This is the nature of all human life (and nonhuman life as well).

In contrast to the precariousness of life, precarity connotes something different. Precarity is that set of political conditions by which some human populations suffer from lack of requisite social and economic supports, and are thus more significantly exposed to injury, violence and death.[93] As we have seen, those whose lives are less grievable face increased burdens of poverty, injury, abuse and violence. Thus, the enactment of rehumanization means reconsideration of the realities of bodily vulnerability and interdependence, and what Butler calls 'the differential allocation' of political precarity.

I have learned firsthand how difficult it is to perceive precariousness and precarity of life with respect to those who we consider 'our enemies.' The college students I teach, having little firsthand experience of the devastation of war, except through those friends and relatives who have been deployed, find it difficult to imagine at a deep level what it would be like for one's life to be so fragmented and at risk. I have turned to memoirs by survivors of war, especially those written by individuals whose countries the U.S. fought against, as one way to break through this lack of awareness. In one class we read *A Dimly Burning Wick: Memoir from the Ruins of Hiroshima*, by Sadako Teiko Okuda, in which the author describes eight days immediately following the dropping of the Hiroshima bomb, when she searched the city for her missing nephew and niece. Each day she travels closer and closer to the epicenter of the blast:

> I didn't know where I was or how I had come to the place where I found myself, but we had come to a place more terrible than any other, near the center of the explosion … Before me was a wasteland, barren but for the dead bodies that filled virtually every inch

92. Butler, 'Precarious Life, Grievable Life'; Butler, *Frames for War*, p. 14.
93. Butler, *Frames for War*, p. 25.

of the ground. I wanted to scream but the only sound that escaped my mouth was a deep moan. Behind me, a soldier was pouring fuel oil over a pile of dead bodies and was setting them alight. My nostrils were filled with a sickening stench as body parts were set on fire. I heard a sound too ghastly for words. As charred corpses burned and burst open, the internal organs exploded, boiling on the galvanized iron sheets on which they lay. Tearing my attention away from that horrific sight, I saw right in front of me an older child, who perhaps a few days ago had been in middle school but who now was collapsed on the ground, covered in blood. Before I could act, an old person tripped and fell on him, trembled two or three times in something like a convulsive fit, and then ceased to move. It was complete and utter hell on earth...[94]

Rehumanization relies on human imaginative power to stand against the tide of violent sacrificialism that rationalizes violence and destruction as necessary and inevitable. In the face of so many pressures to turn away, or excuse the violence of war as a regrettable but unavoidable exchange demanded by the needs of security, the process of rehumanization involves *metanoia*, turning back around to honestly assess the consequences of our actions and to grieve the loss of life, not only of those we know, or are connected to by kinship or country, but in addition the loss of life of others who seem all too distant and even dangerous. Such grieving is difficult, and we would rather not, since it brings home to us the reality of our own lives' precariousness and the possibility that we, too, might experience the precarity to which so many others have been exposed.

This movement may be linked theologically with the intentional turn to 'the underside of history.' In the narratives of Judaism and Christianity, we see the divine emerge precariously, over and over again, in the lives of those whose existence is deeply conditioned by the reality of political precarity. From Moses, taking the side of slaves being beaten by their overlords, to the cries of the prophets regarding the easy trampling of the poor and oppressed, to the story of the birth of Jesus to his unwed mother and life in a family of 'construction workers,' the work of God in the world is biblically imaged primarily not through 'top-down' portrayals, but through very different means that call into question all our ways of

94. Sadako Teiko Okuda, *A Dimly Burning Wick: Memoir from the Ruins of Hiroshima* (trans. Pamela Bea Wilson Vergun; New York: Algora Publishing, 2008), pp. 55–56.

exercising power, security, well-being and relationship.[95] If dominant structures of wealth, omnipotence, success and control shape the primary images of God in contemporary U.S. Christianity, then our intentional turn to the narratives of those who have been most marginalized and most damaged by war and war-culture reframes our perceptions not only about war and the nation, but also about the very being of the divine and the concomitant meaning of human life and relationship.

In the process of rehumanization we may find courage to dream of different and more hopeful responses to threats against our security. When the group 'Poets against the War' came together to protest the coming Iraq War in 2002, Coleman Barks, a renowned translator of the Near-Eastern poet Jalal al-Din Rumi, wrote his own prose poem, and it stands as a beacon to this good work of rehumanization in the world facing the threat of war. In the poem, Barks implores President Bush to reconsider the war, and to imagine what it would be like for the first missile strike to result in the deaths of his 'closest friend, Laura ... and twenty five other family and friends.' Then Barks suggests an entirely different way of dealing with this threat:

> ... Now imagine some
>
> other way to do it. Quadruple the inspectors. Put a thousand and one U.N. people in. Then call for peace activists
>
> to volunteer to go to Iraq for two weeks each. Flood that country with well-meaning tourists, people curious about
>
> the land that produced the great saints, Gilani, Hallaj, and Rabia. Set up hostels near those tombs. Encourage peace
>
> people to spend a bunch of money in shops, to bring rugs home and samovars by the bushel. Send an Arabic translator with
>
> every four peace activists. The U.S. government will pay for the translators and for building and staffing the hostels, one hostel for
>
> every twenty visitors and five translators. Central air and heat are state of the art, and the hostels belong to the Iraqis at the end
>
> of this experiment. Pilgrims with carpentry skills will add studios, porches, ramadas, meditation cribs on the roof, clerestories,

95. Rieger, *No Rising Tide*, pp. 80–81.

and lots of subtle color. Jimmy Carter, Nelson Mandela, and my
friend, Jonathan Granoff at the U.N., will be the core

organization team. Abdul Aziz Said too has got to be in on this,
who grew up in a Bedouin tent four hundred miles

east of Damascus. He didn't see a table until he was fourteen.
Shamans from various traditions, Martin Prechtal,

Bly, and many powerful women, Sima Simar, Debra, Naomi, Jane.
I offer these exalted services without having

asked anybody. No one knows what might come of such potlatch,
potluck. Maybe nothing, or maybe it would show some

of the world that we really do not wish to kill anybody, and that
we truly are not out to appropriate oil reserves...[96]

In addition to the reality of mass death Barks hoped might be
avoided through a rehumanizing means of intervention in Iraq,
one sad irony raised by the poem above relates to the speed and
seeming thoughtlessness by which thousands of years of the culture
Barks so values was 'sacrificed' by the U.S. military as yet another
aspect of collateral damage, when the Iraq National Museum was
left unprotected and was looted during the initial invasion. Though
by 2008 about 700 artifacts had been reclaimed, overall between
3,000 to 7,000 pieces remain missing, including up to 50 that are considered to be of the greatest historic importance, from collections
that chronicle 7,000 years of the Babylonian, Sumerian and Assyrian
civilizations.[97]

Detranscendentalizing the Nation

Machiavelli favored the people as a reliable 'foundation' for power princi-
pally because they did not demand much ... Among the most important
elements in the political education of the citizenry was the promotion of
a religion that emphasized sacrifice: inevitably the city or state would be

96. Coleman Barks, 'Just this Once,' *Winter Sky: New and Selected Poems,*
1968–2008 (Athens, GA: University of Georgia Press, 2008), pp. 33–37. See the
Appendix for the full text of this wonderful poem.

97. Bushra Juhi, 'Iraq Museum Reclaims 700 Stolen Artifacts,' *National*
Geographic, 28 April 2008. As Juhi summed it up, 'Iraqi and world culture officials have struggled to retrieve the treasures with little success.' http://news.
nationalgeographic.com/news/2008/04/080428-AP-iraq.html, accessed 19
April 2009.

at war and would have to defend itself by expanding its power over other
states or cities.

Sheldon S. Wolin[98]

Even given attempts to deestablish theologies and politics based on sacrifice, one wonders if any truly meaningful transformation of the war-culture in which we live is possible, especially given the ease with which this 'Moloch' beckons sacrificial actors to its work. Wink's analysis of the myth of redemptive violence remains as salient as ever; the notion that we must kill in order to preserve what is good in the world is ' ... the spirituality of militarism.' By divine right the state claims the authority to order citizens to the ultimate sacrifice of their lives, and to utilize violence to cleanse the world of evil (though the allocation of sacrificial mandates remains highly unequal). The enemies of the United States are a 'cancer' to be surgically destroyed; such was the description used by UN Ambassador Susan Rice in her defense of the Afghanistan surge of 30,000 additional troops in December, 2009, when she justified increased military force through her description of the Taliban forces in Afghanistan as a 'tissue' hospitable to the 'cancer' of Al Qaeda.[99] These frameworks enable uncritical violence and mask the deep interpenetrations of war-culture in the United States at large.

As psychologist Lawrence Leshan warns us, 'This is very hard for us to admit – war is very attractive to human beings.'[100] Along the way of writing this book, I have been brought up short time after time by various attempts to describe just this dynamic, the attractiveness of war, and its compelling character. James Hillman has conjectured that the ultimacy of the battle itself calls forth a kind of sublime love that outshines all other less intense forms of affection. He writes,

> The *extremis* of battle renders plain and naked the inability to escape. Battle becomes the paradigm of the ethical, of altruism, of

98. Sheldon S. Wolin, *Democracy Incorporated: Managed Democracy and the Specter of Inverted Totalitarianism* (Princeton, NJ: Princeton University Press, 2008), p. 152.

99. Walter Wink, *Engaging the Powers: Discernment and Resistance in a World of Domination* (Minneapolis, MN: Fortress Press, 1992), p. 26. Ambassador Rice used this language on *The Rachel Maddow Show* on 2 December 2009. http:// www.msnbc.msn.com/id/26315908/, accessed 12 March 2009. Revd Maurice Charles pointed out this language to me.

100. Leshan, *The Psychology of War*, p. 117.

love. No other love can be equal. It is a love sublime, a love in terror. It is unspeakable. The veteran does not, cannot talk about these moments because it was so terrible and because it was so loving.[101]

In Hillman's mind, it is precisely the terror, ugliness and inescapability of the ultimate moment in battle that calls forth the most sublime ethical response, as he recalls a cryptic admonition from Levinas, 'being reveals itself as war.'[102] Is this why human beings return to war again and again?

As Jean Bethke Elshtain ponders the question, she muses over the attraction to war in comparison with the alternative: 'a sterile peace.' In other words, the promise of war to give meaning, to offer opportunities for the demonstration of courage and ultimate action, the attractiveness of quick, forceful, seemingly masterful and highly visible action, not to mention the way in which the drumbeat for war seems to lead immediately to the unification of society in collective solidarity at arms, is exceedingly difficult to recreate in non-warring ways. Even direct experience of the horrors of war and the lie of the myth of war, as we saw from the experience of the Post-World War I era in Europe, is not sufficient to deconstruct the power of these cultural tropes. Elshtain writes, 'What one strives for is war's generative powers without its destructiveness.'[103]

Other thinkers focus on the compelling lure of war as a kind of contagion, or disease. Barbara Ehrenreich compares the seemingly endless repetition of war in human societies and especially its operations in the twentieth century to a new kind of cultural virus with an inner dynamism of its own, not unlike that of living things, a 'meme.' In biological terms, genes are programmed internally to replicate endlessly through encounter with a variety of selective forces; in sociological terms, thinking about war as a 'meme' entails a similar analysis of the replicative energy of war, but instead of biological, this is a cultural investigation. To explore war as a 'meme' is to consider the patterns and possibilities that give rise over time and across context regarding the presence, even prevalence, of war in human existence. Why does war self-replicate with such ease across

101. James Hillman, *A Terrible Love of War* (New York: Penguin, 2004), p. 159.
102. Hillman, *A Terrible Love of War*, p. 158.
103. Jean Bethke Elshtain, *Women and War* (New York: Basic Books, 1987), p. 231.

so many human cultures? In many cases war begets yet more war. It survives the evolutionary forces of selection time after time. Is this because, as Richard Dawkins has asked, war is one of many cultural traits that has evolved, as genes do, in ways simply advantageous to its own survival?[104]

In comparison, Chris Hedges describes the repetitiveness of war as a form of 'chemotherapy.' In this understanding, war itself is preceded by social and political cancers of injustice, greed, hatred and mistrust. War as chemotherapy is the dubious yet inescapable 'treatment' that kills the very collective bodies it proclaims to try to heal through attacking the diseased cells within. War is a kind of poison that may be demanded given the ethics of responsibility in the face of immoral force.[105] At the same time, the idea that war provides the opportunity for the most sublime expressions of love is a bereft notion, according to Hedges. In fact, he claims, though war is the arena for comradeship, it never reaches the heights of true friendship; the 'collective rush of war' militates against the complex dynamics of friendship, which require time and a strong sense of self. Likewise, widely reported heightened sexual activity during war neither indicates sublime love or depth of relationship; on the contrary, the experience of increased eroticism during war grows in concert with the breakdown of prohibitions against violence, leading to a general breakdown of sexual, social and political norms. The end of a period of war results all too often to a general spiritual collapse of society.[106]

All the above lines of thinking with respect to the attractiveness and repetitiveness of war may be augmented by examination of the role of sacrifice, and the compelling energy it provides for war and war-culture. Though citizens of the United States might be horrified to hear such a statement, upon investigation it seems as though the state demands the violence of blood sacrifice as the necessary element required to unify and justify the nation itself. Just as in certain misguided interpretations of *imitatio Christi*, in which the veracity of Christian devotion to the faith is regularly measured by the willingness of the believer to go out as Jesus did and sacrifice her or

104. Barbara Ehrenreich, *Blood Rites: Origins and History of the Passions of War* (New York: Henry Holt and Co, 1997), pp. 232-33.

105. Hedges, *War is a Force*, p. 16.

106. Hedges, *War is a Force*, pp. 102, 116.

himself, so with the dynamics of state citizenship. The deepest and truest manifestations of citizenship and membership within the nation are revealed by the ultimate sign of the patriot who demonstrates willingness to sacrifice himself for the state [107]

For instance, the Oath of Allegiance taken by new citizens to the United States is a lesson in the ambiguity of citizenship. On one level, the oath certifies that citizenship is based in allegiance to the Constitution and laws of the United States. We might call this a 'textual commitment.' However, just a bit further the oath continues with the words that citizens promise to 'bear arms on behalf of the United States when required by law.'[108] In fact, in the United States (and other democratic nations as well), the idea of social and political unity through 'textual imagination' based in written formats such as the Constitution and systems of law hides a deeper and murkier reality. Lurking below this surface is the subconscious but widely held belief on the part of citizens that only violence through blood sacrifice produces enduring group unity and belonging – a Girardian understanding, to be sure. In this model it is the sacrifice of our own soldiers, such as the mind-boggling losses of the Civil War, or World War I or II, from which the deepest and truest national group identity is constructed. Lest this seem far-fetched, one only need recall the enduring trope in public school history textbooks of African American slaves proving the mettle of their citizenship by fighting and dying in the Civil War, or Japanese Americans doing

107. Carolyn Marvin, David W. Ingle, 'Blood Sacrifice and the Nation: Revisiting Civil Religion,' *Journal of the American Academy of Religion* 64.4 (winter, 1996). Also see Carolyn Marvin, and David W. Ingle, *Blood Sacrifice and the Nation: Totem Rituals and the American Flag* (Cambridge: University Press, 1999).

108. The Oath of Allegiance taken by naturalized citizens is as follows: 'I hereby declare, on oath, that I absolutely and entirely renounce and abjure all allegiance and fidelity to any foreign prince, potentate, state or sovereignty of whom or which I have heretofore been a subject or citizen; that I will support and defend the Constitution and laws of the United States of America against all enemies, foreign and domestic; that I will bear true faith and allegiance to the same; that I will bear arms on behalf of the united States when required by the law; that I will perform noncombatant service in the Armed forced of the United States when required by the law; that I will perform work of national importance under civilian direction when required by the law; and that I take this obligation freely without any mental reservation or purpose of evasion; so help me God.' U.S. Citizenship and Naturalization Services, http://www. uscis.gov/portal/site/uscis/, accessed 17 March 2009.

the same by fighting and dying in enormous numbers in World War II to quell suspicions about the depth of their commitment to the nation-state.[109] In both cases, as popularly understood, the veracity of citizenship was proven through fighting and dying for the nation-state.

Even today, one finds similar dynamics at work in terms of the naturalizing of non-citizens in the U.S. In 2009 the Army announced plans to enlist up to 890 non-citizens living in the United States, whose language and health-care skills can fill an important gap in the Army's ranks. 'Through service to the Army, those individuals may be able to earn citizenship.' This new initiative corresponds with older laws in the United States, 10 USC Sec. 504 and 8 USC Sec. 1440, that pave the way for non-citizens to earn citizenship by way of military service.[110] In an era in U.S. history in which walls have been constructed along parts of the U.S. border with Mexico to keep out non-citizens, an era in which the requirements for citizenship have multiplied and become much more stringent and costly, why do these military recruits merit the reward of citizenship? 'Communities of blood ... unite their members sacrificially.'[111] According to this understanding, the most important, unifying and constituting memories of the nation-state are linked to its most recent successful blood sacrifice. The supposed 'logic' above is encoded in the rituals of war-culture that demand the blood and energy of millions of people, while at the same time, as rituals, they are relatively protected from serious analysis or question. Ritual operates by way of a 'sub-lingual, even subliminal' language, and as a result

109. One sees such cultural tropes presented in unexamined ways especially in Hollywood films, such as *Glory*, the filmic portrayal of a black Union Army regiment and its white leader, Colonel Robert Gould Shaw. See Robert Burgoyne, 'Race and Nation in *Glory*,' in Robert Eberwein (ed.), *The War Film* (New Brunswick, NJ: Rutgers University Press, 2006). *Glory*, Edward Zwick, TriStar Pictures, 2007.

110. C. Todd Lopez, 'Army Seeks Language, Medical Skills from Non-Citizens,' www.Army.mil, 23 February 2009, http://www.army.mil/-news/2009/02/23/17328-army-seeks-language-medical-skills-from-non-citizens/, accessed 14 March 2009. At the end of 2010, the Senate Democrats withdrew 'The Dream Act' that would have made it possible for alien immigrant students in the U.S. to earn citizenship through military service or higher education. See Carl Hulse, 'Senate Democrats put "Dream Act" on Hold,' *The New York Times*, 9 December 2010.

111. Marvin and Ingle, 'Blood Sacrifice and the Nation', p. 4

achieves a remarkable kind of power through its very imperviousness to conscious awareness.[112] Thus, even in an era in U.S. history when the ability to achieve citizenship has become exceedingly difficult, expensive and time-consuming for many, fewer qualms are raised about conferring citizenship when the question pertains to those who offer their bodies for this sacrificial purpose.

The same dynamics profoundly impact the way U.S. presidents have understood and lived out their role. In a nation described by Glen Greenwald as 'a nation permanently at war,' all presidents are 'war presidents.' At least since World War II, American presidents have 'felt a need to demonstrate their willingness to shed blood.' And every U.S. president acted in the belief that the American political culture required them to show the world promptly that they carried big sticks. Thus, it is a disingenuous, though relatively uncontested media construct that 'war presidents' are deserving of special powers, secrecy and leeway in cases of 'urgent necessity'. Greenwald writes,

> Nothing excites our media stars more than saluting and fetishizing the President as a "War President" and "Commander-in-Chief." [For instance, columnist David Broder wrote,] "Obama is continuing, with minor modifications, the policies and practices of his Republican predecessor ... Obama's liberal critics are right. He is a different man now. He has learned what it means to be commander in chief."[113]

All these dynamics of blood sacrifice through which the nation is represented, unified and justified, call out for a more profound examination of idolatry of the nation itself. To borrow from theologian Paul Tillich, the state never may rise to the level of human beings' 'ultimate concern.' Idolatry occurs when we elevate finite realities to the rank of ultimacy, defined by Tillich as 'the unconditional, the absolute, the infinite.[114] Human beings regularly and mistakenly place their ultimate concern in things and places that

112. Wesley J. Bergen, *Reading Ritual: Leviticus in Postmodern Culture* (New York: T & T Clark International, 2005), pp. 73–74.

113. Glen Greenwald, 'Hailing the Leader as a War President and the Powers that Go along with it,' *Salon*, 21 May 2009, http://www.salon.com/src/pass/sitepass/spon/sitepass_website.html, accessed 26 May 2009.

114. Paul Tillich, *Dynamics of Faith* (New York: Perennial Classics, 1957), p. 10.

lead to failure. Financial success, religious institutions, family ties, ethnicity, and one's nation become destructive when elevated to the level of ultimate concern, because none of these realities is truly ultimate. Tillich uses his own experience from World War II Germany and the experience of German nationalism to demonstrate the perils of placing outsized ultimacy in any human configuration. In the twentieth century, he emphasizes, 'extreme nationalisms' presented a laboratory for examination of the ways in which nations made the life and growth of the nation itself an ultimate concern, demoting along the way all other concerns, including economic well-being, health and life, family, aesthetic and cognitive truth, justice and humanity. Idolatry is diagnosed by Tillich as those instances in which humans attempt to raise to the level of ultimate concern anything that properly cannot bear the weight, meaning and infinity of ultimacy; cases such as these represent instances in which human beings 'have given away their personal center without having a chance to regain it.'[115]

How shall we evaluate the relations of the United States populace and the state with respect to these dynamics of idolatry? Detranscendentalizing the nation means re-examining the processes by which the state has been raised to the level of ultimate concern, and reappraising the roots of those basic elements of the nation-state: sovereignty and citizenship.

In earlier centuries in the Western world, notions of sovereignty were based on peoples' relationship to a wholly sovereign God, who ruled through the earthly emperor/king/monarch/lord. However, these understandings gradually gave way to different interpretations of authority, such that, over time, sovereignty less and less was identified with the body of the ruler(s) and more in the texts of laws, constitutions and courts. As a consequence, people began to shift away from practices of submission to an absolute sovereign, to ideas of mutual governance in the development of modern republics and democracies.

In the early history of the United States, the colonists were painfully familiar with the overextension of monarchical and parliamentary sovereignty, and so endeavored to put specific limits on sovereignty within the American constitutional system. According

---

115. Tillich, *Dynamics*, p. 20.

to Jean Bethke Elshtain, in the United States, 'sovereignty can never be above the law but, instead, must always be of the law.'[116]

At the same time, certain tensions remained, suggesting that older manifestations of sovereignty had not entirely devolved. The word, 'sovereignty' was used to describe the jurisdiction of the United States within its own territory; and ultimately, the impetus of the sovereignty of the nation had to do with protecting and furthering the nation's own 'perpetuity.' As Abraham Lincoln said in his First Inaugural Address: 'It is safe to assert that no government proper ever had a provision in its organic law for its own termination ... I hold that in contemplation of *universal law* and of the Constitution the Union of these States is *perpetual*' (italics mine).[117] This is a fascinating statement by Lincoln, indicating a trace of something more, something beyond the 'textual' meaning of this relationship, this social compact between citizens and the state. It is as if the state has a life of its own, a right to its own 'perpetuity,' mandated by a kind of quasi-religious universal law.

And indeed, though overall the trajectory historians trace has to do with diminishing notions of sovereignty located in human rulers and God, nevertheless a 'strong sovereignty has sneaked through in the American experience.'[118] However, this is not an overt sovereignty, but must be traced beneath the surface. It operates in covert, less conscious ways; in fact, we might call it a 'subterranean sovereignty.' Moreover, subterranean sovereignty is most visible with respect to 'the exigencies of the effective use of force.' The strongest sense of national sovereignty in the United States is exemplified by the assumption of presidential powers in wartime. On the one hand, we may be frank regarding the possibility of overreach and error on the part of presidential powers during war-time urgencies. For this reason, the Supreme Court is the final arbiter of sovereignty's application in action. Nevertheless, on the other hand, historians such as Elshtain have concluded that in the United States, surprisingly, 'sovereignty takes on [as Lincoln implied] a metaphysical status'.[119]

An ambiguity is revealed here that is similar to the citizen's oath. On the one hand, the sovereignty of the United States is decidedly

116. Jean Bethke Elshtain, *Sovereignty: God, State, and Self* (New York: Basic Books, 2008), p. 153.

117. As quoted in Elshtain, *Sovereignty*, p. 155.

118. Elshtain, *Sovereignty*, p. 155.

119. Elshtain, *Sovereignty*, p. 155.

'textual,' that is, within the laws, constitution and the application of state documents through the system of the judiciary. Modern democracies such as the United States exemplify a 'chastened version of sovereignty' that makes possible criticism of one's own state, its leaders and other states.[120] On the other hand, especially given this study of war-culture and sacrifice, we must follow up on the ambiguity of sovereignty, in particular sovereignty related to 'periods of exigency.'[121]

The rise of 'textual imagination' manifested through the development of democratic law and constitutions *does not* necessarily mean the disappearance of other practices of sovereignty revealed in the dynamics of the nation and its citizens. In fact, this book has traced the reality of submerged sovereignty in U.S. War-culture that is expressed in the sacred operations of the military, the characterizing of the United States primarily by way of its outsized military force, the normalized interpenetrations of war-culture in economics, education, popular culture, religion, etc., and the powers and processes involved in the action of war itself. Moreover, all these characteristics are transcendentalized through Christian emphasis on the sacred status of sacrificial relations. The dynamism of these characteristics does not exist at the periphery of the United States' sovereignty, but is at the heart of the matter.

Additionally, submerged sovereignty is all the more dangerous because of its relative invisibility. It operates in ritual ways, through ceremony, memorialization, in coded rhetoric and other sublingual and subliminal forms. Though we live in a time in which the 'autonomous self' has risen to new heights in U.S. culture and politics, nevertheless those same selves remain captive to the manipulations of this submerged sovereignty, even as citizens at the same time tacitly encourage and willingly go along with its operations. Thus, the demands of U.S. sovereignty are more pernicious because they operate beneath the surface, and therefore are invisible and more impervious to active analysis and awareness.

As we have seen, the claim may be made that sacrificial relations are at the basis of the rise of the modern nation-state itself. The birth of 'popular sovereignty' at the beginning of U.S. history was experienced as a religious awakening, or religious revelation. 'We the

120. Elshtain, *Sovereignty*, p. 157.
121. Elshtain, *Sovereignty*, p. 156.

people,' the new sovereign, the state under the rule of law, rose to the level of a new civic religion that 'offers generations of Americans a common core of belief and an ultimate meaning for which they are willing to sacrifice themselves. [122]

Political theorist, Paul W. Kahn, analyzes the history of American politics as a distinctly religious experience, in which the popular sovereign ('the people') achieved an ultimate meaning for individual citizens. Rhetoric and practices of sacrifice slipped easily from formerly religious domains and understandings into the political and civic realms. In the end, sacrifice became a new form of political patriotism.[123] Our assumptions about the dominance of liberalism in U.S. politics, and its focus on social contract and rational deliberation, mislead us from recognizing the continuity of what Kahn calls 'the paradigmatic political act,' *sacrific* , through which citizenship and sovereignty are enacted:

> Citizenship [is experienced] as willingness to respond to the demand for sacrifice for the continued existence of the state – an ultimate meaning of life for each individual within the nation-state; a point of reference from which all else can gain meaning, family, church, nature.[124]

Thus, in this symbolic universe, the state becomes an ultimate value to be defended at any cost, and citizenship is revealed by its totalizing idolatrous character. Through our secular faith as U.S. citizens, our identity is affirmed by way of those who sacrifice   themselves for the conception and maintenance of the nation. In addition, through ongoing sacrifice (with war as the apotheosis), citizens are linked to 'the organic body that is the mystical corpus of the state.'[125] This, too, is submerged sovereignty. It operates as a subconscious awareness, and so it does not require reason to explain or justify it – it is political faith that functions alongside other, more conscious symbolic realities of social contract, liberalism, and textual commitments to law and the Constitution.

122. Paul W. Kahn, *Putting Liberalism in its Place* (Princeton, NJ: Princeton University Press, 2005), p. 110. Also see William G. McLoughlin, *Revivals, Awakenings, and Reform,* especially Chapters One and Two, 'Awakenings as Revitalizations of Culture,' and 'The Puritan Awakening and the Culture Core.'

123. Kahn, *Putting Liberalism in its Place*, p. 91.
124. Kahn, *Putting Liberalism in its Place*, p. 279.
125. Kahn, *Putting Liberalism in its Place*, p. 274.

In fact, according to the diagnosis of political theorist Sheldon S. Wolin, sovereignty in the post-9/11 period of the United States, more than anything else, demonstrates tendencies toward 'inverted totalitarianism.' In this political system, total power was wielded, but without any of the obvious elements that characterize traditional totalitarian states: there were no mass concentration camps, no visible enforcement of ideological unity, no forcible suppression of dissidents, nor clarion calls for massive sacrificial efforts on the part of the citizenry as a whole for 'a better future.' Inverted totalitarianism is detached from its identity. It utilizes a 'managed democracy,' in which governments are legitimated by elections they have succeeded in controlling (as with the first election of George W. Bush to the presidency), while the citizenry is depoliticized from forms of active engagement. Wolin writes,

> When a constitutionally limited government utilizes weapons of horrendous destructive power, subsidizes their development, and becomes the world's largest arms dealer, the Constitution is conscripted to serve as power's apprentice rather than as its conscience.[126]

If sacrificial operations and relations co-exist alongside textual constitutional, liberal and legal orders within the United States, submerged sovereignty also is manifested by the reality of the technology of power. Thus, while in theory, the Constitution prescribes and identifies the purposes for the legitimate use of power, in practice, the slow and deliberate routine of constitutional process cannot keep up with the operations of the actual means of power in war-culture. This has distinct consequences for the most basic of democratic values:

> Freedom and democracy are clearly subservient to free enterprise, a relationship that, by providing "cover" for the political incorporation of the corporation, assumes great significance in light of the fact that the economic structures defining free enterprise are inherently autocratic, hierarchical, and primed for expansion.[127]

These operations of submerged sovereignty in the United States manifest a form of idolatry. This is the militarized state raised to a level of ultimacy; it defines citizenship sacrificially, while glorifying

126. Sheldon S. Wolin, *Democracy Incorporated*, p. 99.
127. Wolin, *Democracy Incorporated*, p. 91.

and spotlighting military sacrifice so as to mitigate against civilian protest. It foists sacrificial mandates on the lives of its citizens (though such mandates are unequally distributed, and largely directed toward the least wealthy and powerful), and requires that they sacrifice the lives of others for its 'perpetuity.' But this ultimacy is hidden from view; submerged sovereignty functions by way of dense and normalized interpenetrations of the culture and institutions of war in economics, corporate structures, popular culture, education, religion and other institutions. The relative invisibility of submerged sovereignty is one part of the dynamics of empire that have been analyzed by many theologians and other thinkers. As Joerg Rieger notes, 'empire is not simply a remnant of early modern conquests but continues in milder modern colonialism and in mutant form, in postcolonial postmodernity. Asymmetrical distributions of power, based in economic structures, obviate the need for political top-down structures that were required to various degrees in order to maintain control.'[128] Though we move away from more explicit and so-called 'hard' expressions of the dynamics of empire such as those during the George W. Bush presidency, the continuing existence of the same operations in 'softer' format represents an even greater danger, since citizens relax their awareness and alarm. Such a softer version was on display at the first State of the Union Speech given by President Barack Obama to the two houses of Congress in March 2009. Perhaps the longest of many standing ovations during the speech came when the president addressed his continued support of the military:

> As we meet here tonight, our men and women in uniform stand watch abroad and more are readying to deploy. To each and every one of them, and to the families who bear the quiet burden of their absence, Americans are united in sending one message: we honor your service, we are inspired by your sacrifice, and you have our unyielding support.[129]

Here was an explicit ceremonial moment for just the kind of submerged sovereignty this book has explored. Watching the speech on

128. Rieger, *Christ and Empire*, p. 286.
129. 'Remarks of President Barack Obama: Address to the Joint Session of Congress,' 24 February 2009, The White House, http://www.whitehouse. gov/the_press_office/remarks-of-president-barack-obama-address- o-joint-session-of-congress/, accessed 30 March 2009.

YouTube, we see the ritual moment unfold as the applause mounts, and the television camera slowly pans across an entire row of military officers in their formal dress, accentuated by rows and rows of medals across their chests. Meanwhile, the choreographed ceremonial moment continues as the civilians in the hall turn and specifically direct their applause to the members of the military.[130] One need look no further to see the quasi-religious worship service of American civil religion, with the dynamics of sacrificial sovereignty at its very center.

In 1987 Wendell Berry emphasized the greatest danger we face as U.S. citizens: the 'lack of defensive alternative to this sort of hollow patriotic passion and its inevitable expression in nuclear warheads.'[131] For Berry and for others, resistance to the idolatry of sacrificial sovereignty involves the search for a sound national defense based on something other than sacrifice. This way forward is linked with a theology or philosophy of local economies and cycles of labor free from the processes of alienation and utility. Following Berry further, three changes would begin to dismantle the interpenetrations

130. 'Obama's Speech to Congress, Parts 1–6,' *You.tube.com*, http://www.youtube.com/watch?v=2A8AYa5JqmU, accessed 30 March 2009.

131. Wendell Berry, 'Property, Patriotism and National Defense,' *Home Economics* (San Francisco, CA: North Point Press, 1987), p. 108. In April 2009, President Barack Obama announced he would work to eliminate all nuclear weapons, but would not commit the United States to giving them up while other states retain them. In this respect he joined Presidents Jimmy Carter and Ronald Reagan in proposing to rid the world of nuclear weapons. However, Carter, during the Iran hostage crisis, threatened to use 'any means necessary' to halt Soviet moves into the Persian Gulf; and Reagan, despite his proposal to eliminate nuclear weapons, promoted a massive nuclear buildup. See Alexander Mooney, 'Obama Says Time to Rid World of Nuclear Weapons,' *CNNPolitics.com*, 6 April 6 2009, http://www.cnn.com/2008/POLITICS/07/16/obama.speech/index.html, accessed 4 August 2009; and Gregg Mitchell, and Robert Jay Lifton, *Hiroshima in America: A Half-Century of Denial* (New York: Avon, 1995), pp. 220–21. In fact, Lifton and Mitchell demonstrate that every U.S. president since the first use of nuclear weapons has threatened to use them. Though, as John Howard Yoder has written, there is fairly unified agreement across Christian ethics regarding the impermissibility of 'all-out nuclear war,' nevertheless the question remains regarding the ethics of 'threatening to do what you may not morally do.' What are the ethical ramifications of such 'bluffs?' See John Howard Yoder, *The War of the Lamb: The Ethics of Nonviolence and Peacemaking*, Glen Stassen, Mark Thiessen Nation, and Matt Hamsher (eds), (Grand Rapids, MI: Brazos Press, 2009), pp. 100–101.

of war-culture and the sacrificial dynamics that energize it. First, end every possibility that anyone could get rich from any military enterprise or industry. 'If all are asked to sacrifice their lives, why should not a few be asked to sacrifice their profits? [132] Second, acknowledge that *any* outbreak of armed force represents a failure of government, at the level of individual nations as well as at the level of the community of nations. Third, require everyone who is ablebodied to serve, both old and young, and beginning with all those who have orchestrated the war.[133]

Chapter One explored 'redistributive militarism' and its destructive consequences in the last decades in the United States. Indeed, economist Ismael Hossein-Zadeh wonders just how long the beneficiaries of militarism and war dividends can continue their (thus far) effective strategies to ever-increase Pentagon budgets at the expense of ordinary Americans. Those who overwhelming bear the brunt of war and militarism are 'the low income, poor and working people who shoulder most of the burden of war and militarism that costs them blood at the war front and social safety net programs at home.'[134] Can big business and the wealthy be coerced to share the rising costs of military expenditures? We need increased awareness regarding the nonmilitary public spending cuts that are used to finance military spending; and pressure must be applied to resist the practices of deficit financing for war and militarism. As Hossein-Zadeh writes,

> the combination of these two measures will force the rich and powerful interests to either pay their "fair" share of taxes, that is to roll back some of the enormous tax breaks they have enjoyed since the early 1980s, to finance their imperialistic wars, or to curtail further military expansion.[135]

Meanwhile, Berry's second admonition, which labels armed violence as a failure of government, is parallel with a variety of Christian ethical frameworks that declare any use of armed force, even that which meet the criteria of Just War tradition, as evidence

132. Berry, *Home Economics*, p. 102.

133. Berry's ironic tone nevertheless reveals the inequality of the way war's costs are distributed in the United States.

134. Ismael Hossein-Zadeh, *The Political Economy of U.S. Militarism* (New York: Palgrave, 2006), p. 252.

135. Hossein-Zadeh, *The Political Economy of U.S. Militarism*, p. 256.

of sin.[136] Among other examples, the social statement adopted by the Evangelical Lutheran Church in America strongly makes this point:

> Wars, both between and within states, represent a horrendous failure of politics. The evil of war is especially evident in the number of children and other noncombatants who suffer and die. We lament that the Church has blessed crusades and wars in the name of Jesus Christ. We recognize with sorrow that too often people formed in the Lutheran tradition have passively accepted their government's call-to-arms or have too readily endorsed war to resolve conflicts [137]

Moreover, seeing the use of armed force as a failure means a decisive change in the meanings we assign to the deaths of soldiers in armed combat. Instead of framing these deaths as 'a necessary sacrifice' for the salvation of the nation, instead of glorifying military action, instead of the dangerous lapse into 'the Myth of War Experience,' these losses fall under a different heading altogether. The deaths of soldiers are a tragedy, a consequence of the failure of politics for which all citizens are responsible and accountable. Once again, the appropriate reaction is a deep and reflective grief with the goal of rehumanization of all who are involved – soldiers, combatants, 'enemies' (including those named as 'terrorists'), civilians, etc. We repent, lament, hope and work toward a better politics that can provide the grounding in which people cooperate to search for solutions for a more just and peaceful world, a world that recognizes the precariousness of all life and works to support life for all.

136. See Stanley Hauerwas' reflections regarding Dietrich Bonhoeffer's offer to be the person to assassinate Hitler. According to Hauerwas, we will never for certain know just how Bonhoeffer understood his role in the assassination attempt; however, he writes, 'I remain unconvinced ... that Bonhoeffer thought this aspect of his life could be justified even if he did, as [ethicist Larry] Rasmussen suggests, think in terms of just war considerations.' *Performing the Faith: Bonhoeffer and the Practice of Nonviolence* (Grand Rapids, MI: Brazos Press, 2004), p. 36.

137. 'Deciding about Wars,' *For Peace in God's World*, Section 4.B, Social statement of the Evangelical Lutheran Church in America by the fourth Churchwide Assembly on 20 August 1995, at Minneapolis, MN, Evangelical Lutheran Church in America, http://www.elca.org/What-We-Believe/Social-Issues/Social-Statements/Peace.aspx, accessed 2 December 2009. This statement includes both advocacy of Just War theory as a resource for ethical deliberation about war, and this very strong statement about the nature of war as a failure and evil.

Perhaps most important, Berry insists, is that we first ask 'what kind of country is defensible?' Ultimately, the soundest national defense lies in 'widespread, settled, thriving local communities ... who defend the country daily and hourly in all their acts by taking care of it, by causing it to thrive, by giving it the health and the satisfactions that make it worth defending, and by teaching these things to the young.' Berry writes as a citizen worried about the destructive mechanisms of our war-culture, and in support of a more real and honest national defense based in the land and in human communities. This means challenging the idolatry of the nation. 'People who are concerned with the work of what I have called the real national defense will necessarily have observed that it must be carried out often against our own national government, and unremittingly against our present national economy.'[138]

Earlier in this chapter I suggested that given the intertwining nature of war-culture and sacrifice in the U.S. context, Christian followers have a decided responsibility to de-center sacrificial constructions and practices, and search for ways outside of sacrifice to live out the meaning of Christian following. Politically speaking, given the same reality of war-culture and sacrifice, and in contrast to the earlier struggles to achieve democracy in the United States, largely based in the attempt to achieve and encompass more in an economics of scarcity, today the challenge that faces the United States is to become more self-conscious regarding the need to recover the elements of democracy that have been lost. Political theorists such as Wolin have clear ideas about what needs to take place: political institutions and practices must be wrested from oligarchic/ corporate centers of control and returned to the people. The growth of presidential power must be reined in by restoring the Congress to a larger seat of power and activity, and the 'stranglehold of lobbyists' must be addressed, along with imposing an 'austere system of campaign finance.' Obstacles to third parties must be eliminated.

At the same time, Wolin emphasizes, all this can and will take place only to the extent that the citizens reinsert themselves as political agents even in a political system such as ours that has become thoroughly enmeshed with corporate and military power.[139]

138. Berry, *Home Economics*, p. 110.
139. Wolin, *Democracy Incorporated*, p. 258. Also see Jeffrey Sachs, 'Rethinking Foreign Policy,' *Common Wealth: Economics for a Crowded Planet* (New York: Penguin, 2008), in which Sachs outlines a series of points that would address

Only significant pressure from below can set the brake on unending military expansion. In addition, in the case of each of these suggested transformations of American culture and politics, the continuation of the insidious danger of war-culture, and its sacrificial relations in submerged U.S. sovereignty, play a strong role in preventing change. Thus, most important of all is the urgent task of expanding our level of *thought* with respect to questions of sacrifice, Christianity, U.S. War-culture, citizenship and sovereignty. The unconscious and ubiquitous operations of submerged sacrificial sovereignty in the U.S. have been formed by and have contributed to a war-like, sacrificially-based, exchanged-oriented soteriology in Christianity. This must be challenged, critiqued and rejected. Not only a rehumanization of the social, political and economic orders is called for, but a return to a deeply rehumanized Christology and soteriology equally is important, one that rejects the ecclesial sadomasochistic tendencies that are prevalent in so many theologies, and that instead uses Jesus' own particular humanity as a starting point for strategizing about how to *work* on suffering to affirm and extend life.

This book already concluded that the right to security ought not to be brokered through requiring citizens' unquestioning submission to the masculinized security regime. Here I add: neither should the perpetuity of the nation be brokered on the demand for sacrifice. Citizenship should not be bargained or defined by requiring the sacrifice of citizens, or through the framing of violence toward others as 'the necessary sacrifice' for the perpetuity of the nation. Moreover, the very definition of 'perpetuity' itself needs to be contested. Today the functional reality of national perpetuity is more and more separated from democracy and constitutionalism, instead being found in 'Superpower' and 'empire,' in dangerously submerged forms of national sovereignty based on notions of sacrificial exchange. We will have to act and speak our way into different frameworks for state sovereignty and citizenship. This means challenging and resisting current frames of war-culture energized by sacrificial norms and assumptions, and struggling toward new mediations. Or, to use Judith Butler's words, our work is to

the interpenetration and saturation of war-culture with a saner foreign policy based more strongly on diplomacy and international co-operation, much along the lines of just peacemaking thinkers.

overcome the differential ways through which grievability is allocated and a life is regarded as living, or indeed, as a living life. It is also to struggle against those notions of the political subject that assume that permeability and injurability can be monopolized at one site and fully refused at another.[140]

Can those who follow Christianity allow for more open-ended and ambiguous constructions of Christian salvation? Can willingness be summoned to more exacting examination of the difficult and dangerous relations between religious ideas and practices and their impact in U.S. War-culture? Do the possibilities for rehumanization have a chance over against the strength of binary and sacrificial exchange constructions that are so deeply embedded in the American subconscious? I harbor few doubts regarding the arduousness of the work ahead. But I remain utterly convinced that this is good work, work worth dedicating ourselves to, and work that is at the very heart of becoming more deeply human. Lastly, as a Christian, I also remain convinced regarding the moral imperative of this work for members of Christian communities who want to understand more profoundly just how we are involved in the traumas of others, how our very spiritual convictions involve us in violence, and who want to do something about it.[141]

At the end of writing this book, I found myself returning to a website I began to visit regularly over the course of this project. Confronted with so many national and international examples of the memorialization and sanctification of war and war-culture based on and mystified through sacrificial imagery and logic, I began to search for examples of memorializing peace. One of the most extensive examples of this kind of memorialization is the 'Peace Memorial Park' and 'Peace Memorial Museum' located at the hypocenter of the atomic bomb blast in Hiroshima, Japan. Of the dozens of exhibits and monuments, two in particular stand out. One is the grove of 24 'Phoenix Trees' (China Parasol Trees), located about 1.3 kilometers from the epicenter of the blast. These trees took the full hit of the atomic bomb and were stripped of all their branches and leaves; some were burned out at the center of their trunks. Though

---

140. Judith Butler, 'The Claim of Non-Violence,' in *Frames for War* (London: Verso, 2009), p. 183.

141. Tom Beaudoin, *Witness to Dispossession: The Vocation of a Post-modern Theologian* (Maryknoll, NY: Orbis Books, 2008), p. 34.

they were believed to be dead, the spring after the blast they put out new buds. The exhibit explanation on the Hiroshima Peace Park website reads, 'Seeing this new life, people dazed by the tumultuous aftermath of the atomic bombing and the war took courage.' Seeds from the Phoenix trees have been given to many in Japan and throughout the world, 'offspring of these trees thriving around the world.'

A second exhibit on the website simply lists photographs and 'messages for peace' from visitors of many nations of the world to the park. It seems that only one U.S. president, Jimmy Carter, took the time to leave a brief message. Kenzaburo Oe, the 1995 Nobel Prize Laureate in Literature, also left a message. With hope that we will find the courage to name and reject the practices and logic of 'the necessity of sacrifice'; and with desire that the seeds of rehumanized vision may lead us to the good work of building a more authentic, lasting and flourishing life, I close with Oe's words

> I have been to this memorial museum on many occasions. Today, I visited here once again with some of the world's most prominent and influential intellectuals, and reconsidered my way of living.[142]

142. Hiroshima Peace Site and Hiroshima Peace Museum: The Official Homepage of Hiroshima Peace Memorial Museum, http://www.pcf.city.hiroshima.jp/top_e.html, accessed 4 June 2009.

Appendix

JUST THIS ONCE
by Coleman Barks

President Bush, before you order airstrikes,
imagine the first cruis
missile as a direct hit on your closest friend.

That might be Laura. Then twenty-five othe
family and friends.
There are no survivors. Now imagine some

other way to do it. Quadruple the inspectors.
Put a thousand and one
U.N. people in. Then call for peace activists

to volunteer to go to Iraq for two weeks each.
Flood that country with
well-meaning tourists, people curious about

the land that produced the great saints, Gilani,
Hallaj, and Rabia.
Set up hostels near those tombs. Encourage peace

people to spend a bunch of money in shops, to bring
rugs home and samovars
by the bushel. Send an Arabic translator with

every four peace activists. The U.S. government will pay
for the translators and for
building and staffing the hostels, one hostel fo

every twenty visitors and five translators. Centra
air and heat are state of the art,
and the hostels belong to the Iraqis at the end

of this experiment. Pilgrims with carpentry skills
will add studios, porches,
ramadas, meditations cribs on the roof, clerestories,

and lots of subtle color. Jimmy Carter, Nelson
Mandela, and my friend,
Jonathan Granoff at the U.N., will be the core

organization team. Abdul Aziz Said too has got
to be in on this, who
grew up in a Bedouin tent four hundred miles

east of Damascus. He didn't see a table until
he was fourteen. Shamans
from various traditions, Martin Prechtal,

Bly, and many powerful women, Sima Simar,
Debra, Naomi, Jane.
I offer these exalted services without having

asked anybody. No one knows what might come
of such potlatch, potluck.
Maybe nothing, or maybe it would show some

of the world that we really do not wish to kill
anybody, and that we
truly are not out to appropriate oil reserves.

We're working on building a hydrogen vehicle
as fast as we can, aren't we?
Put no limit on the number of activists from all

over that might want to hang out and explore Iraq
for two weeks. Is anything
left of Babylon? There could be informal courses

for college credit and pickup soccer games every
evening at five. Long
leisurely, late suppers. Chefs will come for cookouts.

The U. S. government furnishes air transportation,
that is, hires airliners from
the country of origin and back for each peace tourist,

who must carry and spend the equivalent of $1001
U.S. inside Iraq. Keep part
of the invasion force nearby as police, but let those

who claim to deeply detest war try something else
just this once, for one year.
Call our bluff. Medical services, transportation

inside Iraq, along with many other ideas that
will be thought of later
during the course of this innocently, blatantly

foolish project will all also be funded by
the U.S. Government. But what
if terrible unforeseen disaster rains down

because of this spontaneous, unthought-out
hippie notion? One
never knows. Surely it wouldn't be worse

than the *shock and awe* display we have planned
for the first forty-eight hours
But we must always suspect intentionally good

deeds. Consider this more of a lark, a skylark.
Look. There is
a practice known as *sema*, the deep listening

to poetry and music, with sometimes movement
involved. Unpremeditated
art and ease. We could experiment with whole

nights of that, staying up until dawn, sleeping
in tents during the day.
Good musicians will be lured with more than

modest fees. Cellos, banjos, oboes, ouds,
French horns. Hundreds
of harmonicae and the entire University

of North Carolina undergraduate gospel choir.
Thus, instead of war,
there is a much relaxed, improvisational festivity

from March 2003 through February 2004. It could be
as though war had already
happened, as it has. Now we're in the giddy,

brokenopen aftertime. So let slip the pastel
minivans of peace and whoa
be they who cry surcease. I'll be the first t

volunteer for two weeks of wandering winter desert,
reading Hallaj, Abdul Qadir
Gilani, dear Rabia, and Scheherazade's life-prolonging

thousand and one *Arabian Nights*. I am Coleman Barks,
retired English professor eee-
meritus, living in Athens, Georgia, and I don't

really consider this proposal foolish. More brash
and hopeful for the bunch
I come along with, those born from the mid-1920s

until the mid-1940s, that before we die or lose
our energy, we might,
with help from tablas, sitar, waterwheeling

sixteen-strings, and the pulsing voices of seventy
black-church-bred students push away
from terrorism and cruise missile terrorism

and the video-techno-laser, loveless, unerotic-
idiotic, bio-chem atom-toys,
and decide not to study war so much no more.

Never denying we have the tendencies built-in,
a cold murderous
aggression, a who-cares-it's-all-bullshit-

anyway turning away from those in pain.
March 15th, 2003, and I am
not quite yet weary enough of words not to try

to say the taste of this failure we sponsor
with our tax dollars,
but after the stupidity starts, I might be.[1]

1. Coleman Barks, 'Just this Once,' *Winter Sky: New and Selected Poems, 1968–2008* (Athens, GA: University of Georgia Press, 2008), pp. 33–37. Reprinted with permission from Coleman Barks.

BIBLIOGRAPHY

American Anthropological Association, 'Annual Report: American Anthro-
    pological Association: Anthropology, Democracy, Inclusiveness, Trans-
    parency' 2009. http://www.aaanet.org/about/Annual_Reports/upload/
    AAA-2009-Annual-Report.pdf
American Institute of Aeronautics and Astronautics, Inc., 'Inside Aero08
    Report: Working Together to Build the Aerospace Workforce of Tomorrow.'
    Inside Aerospace: An International Forum for Aviation and Space Leaders, 14
    May 2008. http://www.aiaa.org/pdf/public/Inside_Aero08_Report_and_
    Recommendations.pdf
American Academy of Religion, History of Christianity Section and North
    American Religions Section, 'War and Religion in North America.' Pro-
    ceedings, November 2007, San Diego, CA.
Ana, Julio De Santa, Robin Gurney, Heidi Hadsell and Lewis S. Mudge, *Beyond
    Idealism: A Way Ahead for Ecumenical Social Ethics* (Grand Rapids, MI: Wm. B.
    Eerdmans Co., 2006).
Anselm of Canterbury, '*Cur Deus Homo* (Why God Became Man),' *A Scholastic
    Miscellany: Anselm to Ockham,* in Eugene R. Fairweather (ed.), (Philadelphia,
    PA: Westminster Press, 1956).
Arendt, Hannah, with Introduction by Margaret Canovan, *The Human Condition*
    (Chicago, IL: University of Chicago Press, 1998).
Armitage, John, 'Beyond Hypermodern Militarized Knowledge Factories,'
    Review of Education, Pedagogy, and Cultural Studies v27 n3 (2005): 212–39.
Army, Department of, *Soldier's Handbook* (Alexandria, VA: Bryyd Enterprises,
    1998).
Artz, Lee, and Yahya R. Kamalipour (eds.), *Bring Em On: Media and Politics in
    the Iraq War* (New York: Rowman & Littlefield, 2005).
Augustine, Bishop of Hippo, *City of God* (trans. Henry Bettenson; Baltimore,
    MD: Penguin Books, 1972).
Babcock, William S. (ed.), *The Ethics of St. Augustine* (Atlanta, GA: Scholars
    Press, 1991).
Bacevich, Andrew, *The New American Militarism* (New York: Oxford University
    Press, 2005).

— The *Limits of Power: The End to American Exceptionalism* (New York: Metropolitan, 2008).

Baker, Dori Grinenko, *Doing Girlfriend Theology: God-Talk with Young Women* (Cleveland, OH: The Pilgrim Press, 2005).

Barks, Coleman, *Winter Sky: New and Selected Poems, 1968–2008* (Athens, GA: University of Georgia Press, 2008).

Barstow, David, 'Behind TV's Analysts, Pentagon's Hidden Hand.' *The New York Times*, 20 April 2008.

Beaudoin, Tom, *Witness to Dispossession: The Vocation of a Post-modern Theologian* (Maryknoll, NY: Orbis Books, 2008).

Beckerman, Gal, 'Why Don't Journalists Get Religion? A Tenuous Bridge to Believers,' *Columbia Journalism Review* 3 May/June 2004. http://www.cjr.org/issues/2004/3/beckerman-faith.asp

Bellah, Robert Neelly, *The Broken Covenant: American Civil Religion in Time of Trial* (Chicago, IL: Chicago University Press, 1992).

Bergen, Wesley J., *Reading Ritual: Leviticus in Postmodern Culture* (New York: T & T Clark International, 2005).

Berrigan, Frida, 'The Pentagon Takes Over.' *TomDispatch*. 27 May 2008. http://www.tomdispatch.com/post/174936/frida_berrigan_the_pentagon_takes_over

Berrigan, Frida, 'Entrenched, Embedded and Here to Stay: The Pentagon's Expansion Will be Bush's Lasting Legacy.' *TomDispatch*, 27 May 2008. http://www.tomdispatch.com/post/174936/frida_berrigan_the_pentagon_takes_over

Berry, Wendell, *Home Economics* (San Francisco, CA: North Point, 1987).

Bilmes, Linda and Joseph E. Stiglitz, *The Three Trillion Dollar War: The True Cost of the Iraq Conflic* (New York: W.W. Norton and Company, 2008).

Biviano, Erin Loathes, *The Paradox of Christian Sacrifice: Self-Gift and Self-Love* (New York: Herder & Herder, 2007).

Boren Awards for International Study, 'David L. Boren Scholarships and Fellowships Program,' http://www.borenawards.org/boren_scholarship/basics.html

Brainard, Jeffrey and J. J. Hermes, 'Colleges' Earmarks Grow, Amid Criticism' *The Chronicle of Higher Education* (28 March 2008). http://chronicle.com/free/v54/i29/29a00101.html

Brauer, Jurgen and John Tepper Marlin, 'Defining Peace Industries and Calculating the Potential Size of a Peace Gross World Product by Country and by Economic Sector: Confidential Report for Economists for Peace and Security.' *Vision of Humanity: The Global 2010 Peace Index (April 2009)*. http://www.visionofhumanity.org/

Brock, Rita Nakashima, and Rebecca Ann Parker, *Proverbs to Ashes: Violence, Redemptive Suffering and the Search for What Saves Us* (Boston, MA: Beacon Press, 2001).

— *Saving Paradise: How Christianity Traded Love of This World for Crucifixion and Empire* (Boston, MA: Beacon, 2008).

Brower, George D., 'Re: FYI-Chinook Helicopter to Land in Quad Thursday/ Transport LV ROTC Cadets to Training.' 23 April 2008. E-mail.

Brubaker, Pamela K., Glen H. Stassen, and Janet L. Parker, 'A Critique of Jean Bethke Elshtain's Just War Against Terror and Advocacy of a Constructive Alternative,' *Journal of Religion, Conflict and Peac* 2.1 (Fall 2008).

Buffton, Deborah D., 'Memorialization and Selling War,' *Peace Review: A Journal of Social Justice* 17.1 (2005): 25–31.

Burkeman, Oliver, 'Obama Administration says Goodbye to "war on terror"?' *The Guardian*, 25 March 2009. http://www.guardian.co.uk/world/2009/ mar/25/obama-war-terror-overseas-contingency-operations

Burnham, Gilbert, Shannon Doocy, Elizabeth Dzeng, Rihadh Lafta, and Les Roberts, 'Human Cost of the War in Iraq: A Mortality Study, 2002–2006,' Bloomberg School of Public Health, Johns Hopkins University, School of Medicine, Al Mustansiriya University, Center for International Studies, Massachusetts Institute of Technology, Cambridge, Massachusetts, Baghdad, Iraq. http://i.a.cnn.net/cnn2006/images10/11/human.cost.of.war.pdf

Burgoyne, Robert, 'Race and Nation in Glory,' in Robert Eberwein (ed.), *The War Film* (New Brunswick, NJ: Rutgers University Press, 2006).

Burns, Robert, 'Admiral Says War Veterans Will Suffer for Years,' *Common Dreams* 3 April 2009. http://www.commondreams.org/headline/2009/ 04/03-2

Bush, George W., and Karen Armstrong, *A Charge to Keep: My Journey to the Whitehouse* (New York: Morrow, 1999).

Bush, George W., 'President Addresses the Nation,' Welcome to the White House. 7 September 2003. http://georgewbush-whitehouse.archives.gov/ news/releases/2003/09/20030907-1.html

— 'President Addresses Military Families, Discusses War on Terror,' Welcome to the White House. 24 August 2005. http://georgewbush-whitehouse.archives.gov/news/releases/2005/08/20050824.html

— 'National Strategy for Victory in Iraq,' Welcome to the White House. 30 November 2005. http://georgewbush-whitehouse.archives.gov/news/ releases/2005/11/20051130-2.html

— 'Fact Sheet: The Fifth Anniversary of September 11, 2001,' Welcome to the White House. 11 September 2006. http://georgewbush-whitehouse.archives.gov/news/releases/2006/09/20060911-2.html

— 'President's Address to the Nation,' Welcome to the White House. 10 January 2007. http://georgewbush-whitehouse.archives.gov/news/releases/2007/ 01/20070110-7.html

— 'President's Radio Address, Easter 2008.' The White House: President George W. Bush, 2 April 2008. http://georgewbush-whitehouse.archives.gov/news/ releases/2008/03/20080322.html

— 'President's Radio Address,' Welcome to the White House. 22 March 2008. http://georgewbush-whitehouse.archives.gov/news/releases/2008/03/ 20080322.html

Bush, Perry, 'Violence, Nonviolence and the Search for Answers in History,' in J. Denny Weaver and Gerald Beisecker-Mast (eds), *Teaching Peace: Nonviolence and the Liberal Arts* (New York: Rowan and Littlefield, 2003)

Butler, Judith, *Precarious Life: The Power of Mourning and Violence* (New York: Verso, 2004).

— *Frames of War* (London: Verso, 2009).

Cady, Linell Elizabeth, 'Identity, Feminist Theory and Theology,' in Rebecca S. Chopp and Sheila Greeve Davaney (eds), *Horizons in Feminist Theology: Identity, Tradition and Norms* (Minneapolis, MN: Fortress Press, 1997).

Cahill, Lisa Sowle, *Love Your Enemies: Discipleship, Pacifism, and Just War Theory* (Minneapolis, MN: Fortress Press, 1994).

— 'Just Peacemaking: Theory, Practice and Prospects.' *Journal of the Society of Christian Ethics* 23.1 (2003): 195–212.

Carnahan, Burrus M., 'Lincoln, Lieber and the Laws of War: The Origins and Limits of the Principle of Military Necessity,' *The American Journal of International Law* 92 (1992): 213–31.

Carter, Jeffrey (ed.), *Understanding Religious Sacrifice: A Reader* (New York: Continuum, 2003).

Castilli, Elizabeth A. (ed.), *Women, Gender, Religion: A Reader* (New York: Palgrave, 2001).

Cavanaugh, William T., *The Myth of Religious Violence: Secular Ideology and the Roots of Modern Conflic* (Oxford: Oxford University Press, 2009).

Chilton, Bruce, *The Temple of Jesus: His Sacrificial Program Within a Cultural History of Sacrific* (University Park, PA: Pennsylvania University Press, 1992).

— 'Sacrificial Mimesis.' *Religion* 27 (1997): 225–30.

— *Abraham's Curse: The Roots of Violence in Judaism, Christianity, and Islam* (New York: Doubleday Religious Group, 2008).

Ciralsky, Adam, 'Tycoon, Contractor, Soldier, Spy.' *Vanity Fair.* January 2010. http://www.vanityfair.com/politics/features/2010/01/blackwater-201001

Clough, David L., and Brian Stiltner, *Faith and Force: A Christian Debate About War* (Georgetown, WA: Georgetown University Press, 2007).

Coalition Against Militarism in Our Schools, 'California Federation of Teachers Resolution 27,' *The Coalition Against Militarization in Our Schools. CAMS Homepage.* http://www.militaryfreeschools.org/pdffiles.htm

Cole, Alyson M., 'The Other V-word: The Politics of Victimhood Fueling George W. Bush's War Machine,' in Robin L. Riley, Chandra Talpade Mohanty, Minnie Bruce Pratt (eds), *Feminism and War: Confronting U.S. Imperialism* (London: Zed Books, 2008).

Commission on Wartime Contracting, 'At What Cost? Contingency Contracting In Iraq and Afghanistan' 10 June 2009. http://www.wartimecontracting. gov/nr4-wartime-contracting-concerns.html

Condren, Mary, 'To Bear Children for the Fatherland: Mothers and Militarism,' in Elisabeth Schüssler Fiorenza (ed.), *The Power of Naming: A Concilium Reader in Feminist Liberation Theology* (New York: Orbis Books, 1996).

Cowen, Tyler, 'The New Deal Didn't Always Work, Either.' *The New York Times*, 23 November 2008.

CNN, 'Bush Says it is Time for Action,' *CNN.com*. 6 November 2001. http://archives.cnn.com/2001/US/11/06/ret.bush.coalition/index.html

Daly, Robert J., *Sacrifice Unveiled: The True Meaning of Sacrific* (London: T & T Clark International, 2009).

David, Deborah, 'News & Culture in America: Immigrants and Armed Forces Recruitment,' *Metroactive: Metro Newspaper Silicon Valley: News, Events, Movies, Clubs*. 9 September 2007. http://www.metroactive.com/metro/09.19.07/news-0738.html

Denton-Borhaug, Kelly, 'A Bloodthirsty Salvation: Behind the Popular Polarized Reaction to Gibson's *The Passion*,' *Journal of Religion and Film* 9.1 (2005).

DeYoung, Karen, and Michael Abromowitz, 'Bush Says War's Outcome "Will Merit the Sacrifice"' *The Washington Post*, 25 March 2008.

Domke, David, and Kevin Coe, *The God Strategy: How Religion Became a Political Weapon in America* (Oxford: Oxford University Press, Updated Version 2010).

Drew, Christopher, 'Obama Wins Crucial Senate Vote on F-22.' *The New York Times*, 21 July 2009.

Dumas, Lloyd J., 'University Research, Industrial Innovation, and the Pentagon.' *Uwatch.org*. http://utwatch.org/war/militarizeduniveresearch.html

Dyer, Gwynne, *War* (New York: Crown, 1985).

— *War: The New Edition* (Toronto, Ontario Canada: Vintage Canada, 2005).

Eberwein, Robert (ed.), *The War Film* (New Brunswick, NJ: Rutgers University Press, 2006).

Ehrenreich, Barbara, *Blood Rites: Origins and History of the Passions of War* (New York: Henry Holt & Co., 1997).

Ehrman, Bart D., *The New Testament: A Historical Introduction To The Early Christian Writings* (New York: Oxford University Press, 2008).

Eisenhower, Dwight, 'Eisenhower's Farewell Address to the Nation,' *Eisenhower Presidential Library and Museum Homepage*. 17 January 1961. http://www.eisenhower.archives.gov/All_About_Ike/Speeches/Farewell_Address.pdf

Eisenstein, Zillah, 'Resexing Militarism for the Globe,' in Robin L. Riley, Chandra Talpade Mohanty, Minnie Bruce Pratt (eds), *Feminism and War: Confronting U.S. Imperialism* (London: Zed Books, 2008).

Elshtain, Jean Bethke, *Women and War* (New York: Basic Books, 1987).

— 'Sovereignty, Identity and Sacrifice,' in V. Spike Peterson (ed.), *Gendered States: Feminist (re)Visions of International Relations Theory* (London: Lynne Rienner Publishers, 1992).

— *Augustine and the Limits of Politics* (Notre Dame, IN: University of Notre Dame Press, 1995).

— *Just War Against Terror* (New York: Basic Books, 2003).

— *Sovereignty: God, State, and Self* (New York: Basic Books, 2008).

Enloe, Cynthia, *Nimo's War, Emma's War: Making Feminist Sense of the Iraq War* (Ewing, NJ: University of California Press, 2010).

Entman, Robert M., 'Cascading Activation: Contesting the White House's Frame after 9/11.' *Political Communication* 20.4 (Oct–Dec 2003): 415–33.

Evangelical Lutheran Church in America, 'Deciding about Wars,' *For Peace in God's World*, Section 4.B., Social Statement. 20 August, 1995. http://www. elca.org/What-We-Believe/Social-Issues/Social-Statements/Peace.aspx

Fairweather, Eugene R. (ed.), *A Scholastic Miscellany Anselm to Ockham* (New York: Westminster John Knox, 1982).

Falk, Richard, 'Renouncing Wars of Choice,' in David Ray Griffin, John B. Cobb Jr, Richard A. Falk, and Catherine Keller (eds), *The American Empire and the Commonwealth of God* (Louisville, KY: Westminster, 2006), 69–85.

Faludi, Susan, 'Let Us Prey.' Review. *The Nation*, 12 May 1997.

Faust, Drew Gilpin, *This Republic of Suffering: Death and the American Civil War* (New York: Knopf, 2008).

Feaver, Peter, 'Casualties are the First Truth of War.' *Weekly Standard* 7 April 2003.

Fehrenbacher, Don E. (ed.), *Abraham Lincoln: A Documentary Portrait through His Speeches and Writings* (New York: Signet, 1964).

Fiddes, Paul, *Past Event and Present Salvation: The Christian Idea of Atonement* (Louisville, KY: Westminster, 1989).

Fluri, Jennifer L., '"Rallying Public Opinion" and Other Misuses of Feminism,' in Robin L. Riley, Chandra Talpade Mohanty, Minnie Bruce Pratt (eds), *Feminism and War: Confronting U.S. Imperialism* (London: Zed Books, 2008), 143–57.

Fox, Matthew, *The Reinvention of Work: A New Vision of Livelihood for Our Time* (New York: Harper Collins, 1995).

French, Shannon E., *The Code of the Warrior: Exploring Warrior Values Past and Present* (New York: Rowman & Littlefield, 2003).

Friesen, Ronald L., 'War and Peace in Economic Terms,' in J. Denny Weaver and Gerald Beisecker-Mast (eds), *Teaching Peace: Nonviolence and the Liberal Arts* (New York: Rowan and Littlefield, 2003)

Fulford, Ben, 'Saved From Sacrifice: A Theology of the Cross.' *Modern Theology* 24.2 (April 2008): 311–13.

Giroux, Henry A., *University in Chains: Confronting the Military-Industrial-Academic Complex* (Boulder, CO: Paradigm, 2007).

Glanz, James, 'Senators Accuse Pentagon of Delay in Recovering Millions.' *The New York Times*, 4 May 2009.

Glenn, David, 'A Policy on Torture Roils Psychologists' Annual Meeting,' *Chronicle of Higher Education*, 7 September 2007.

— 'Congressional Panel Weighs Social Science's Role in Warfare,' *The Chronicle of Higher Education*, 25 April 2008. http://chronicle.com/daily/2008/04/2633n. htlm

— 'New Details of "Minerva" Project Emerge, as Social Scientists Weigh Pentagon Ties,' *The Chronicle of Higher Education*, 12 May 2008. http://chronicle.com/news/article/4467/new-details-of-minerva-project-emerge-as-social-scientists-weigh-pentagon-ties

Goodman, Peter S., 'Despite Signs of Recovery, Chronic Joblessness Rises,' *The New York Times*, 21 February 2010.

Goudzwaard, Bob and Julio de Santa Ana, 'The Modern Roots of Economic Globalization,' in Julio de Santa Ana (ed), *Beyond Idealism: A Way Ahead for Ecumenical Social Ethics* (Grand Rapids, MI: Eerdmans, 2006).

Green, Joel B., 'Jesus on the Mount of Olives (Luke 22: 39-46): Tradition and Theology,' *Journal for the Study of the New Testament* 26 (1986): 29–28.

— *Recovering the Scandal of the Cross: Atonement in New Testament and Contemporary Contexts* (Downers Grove, IL: Intervarsity, 2000).

Green, Joel B., and Jon Carroll, *The Death of Jesus in Early Christianity* (Peabody, MA: Hendrickson, 1995).

Greenwald, Glen, 'Hailing the Leader as a War President and the Powers that Go Along with It.' *Salon.com.* http://www.salon.com/src/pass/sitepass/spon/sitepass_website.html

Gregory, Eric, *Politics and the Order of Love: An Augustinian Ethic of Democratic Citizenship* (Chicago, IL: University of Chicago Press, 2008).

Grensted, L.W., *A Short History of the Doctrine of the Atonement* (Manchester: Manchester University Press, 1920).

Grills, Matt, 'Death, Not in Vain.' *American Legion,* May 2007.

Grossman, Dave, *On Killing: The Psychological Cost of Learning to Kill in War and Society* (New York: Little Brown and Company, 1995).

Gudorf, Christine, *Victimization: Examining Christian Complicity* (Philadelphia, PA: Trinity International, 1992).

Guth, James L., John C. Green, Lyman K. Kellsted, and Corwin E. Emidt, 'Faith and Foreign Policy: A View from the Pews,' *Faith and International Affairs* 3.2 (2005): 5–6.

Hall, Douglas John, *The Cross in Our Context: Jesus and the Suffering World* (Minneapolis, MN: Fortress Press, 2003).

Hampson, Daphne, *After Christianity* (Valley Forge, PA: Trinity, 1996).

Hauerwas, Stanley, *Performing the Faith: Bonhoeffer and the Practice of Nonviolence* (Grand Rapids, MI: Brazos, 2004).

— 'Sacrificing the Sacrifices of War.' *Criswell Theological Review* n.s.4/2 (Spring 2007): 77–96.

Hedges, Chris, *War Is a Force that Gives Us Meaning* (New York: Anchor Books, 2002).

Heim, S. Mark, *Saved from Sacrifice: A Theology of the Cross* (Grand Rapids, MI: Wm. B. Eerdmans Co., 2006).

Herbert, Bob, 'An Army Ready to Snap,' *The New York Times,* 10 November 2005, A29.

Higgs, Robert, *Depression, War, and Cold War Studies in Political Economy* (Oakland, CA: Independent Institute, 2006).

Higgs, Robert, 'Military Keynesianism to the Rescue?' *The Independent Institute,* 2 January 2009. http://www.independent.org/newsroom/article.asp?id=2399

Hillman, James, *A Terrible Love of War* (New York: Penguin, 2004).

Hinkelammert, Franz J., *Sacrificios Humanos y Sociedad Occidental* (San Jose, Costa Rica: Editorial Departamento Ecumenico de Investigaciones, 1991).

Hiroshima Peace Site, The Official Homepage of Hiroshima Peace Memorial Museum, http://www.pcf.city.hiroshima.jp/top_e.html.

Hossein-Zadeh, Ismael, *The Political Economy of U.S. Militarism* (New York: Palgrave, 2006).

Hsiao-Rei Hicks, Madelyn, Hamit Dardagan, Gabriela Guerrero Serdán, Peter M. Bagnall, John A. Sloboda, and Michael Spagat, 'The Weapons That Kill Civilians: Deaths of Children and Noncombatants in Iraq, 2003–2008,' *The New England Journal of Medicine* 360 (2009): 1585–588.

Hughes, John, *The End of Work: Theological Critiques of Capitalism* (Victoria, Australia: Blackwell, 2007).

Hulse, Carl, 'Senate Democrats put "Dream Act" on Hold,' *The New York Times*, 9 December 2010.

Hultgren, Arland J., 'The Gnostic Gospels and Current Popular Views of Jesus,' *Reformed Review* 59.3 (2006): 283–91.

Hynes, Patricia H., 'On the Battlefield of Women's Bodies: An Overview of the Harm of War to Women,' *Women's Studies International Forum* 27 (2004): 431–45.

International Day of Peace. http://www.internationaldayofpeace.org/

Ivies, Robert L., *Dissent from War* (Bloomfield, CT: Kumarian, 2007).

— 'Images of Savagery in American Justifications for War,' *Communications Monographs* 47 (1980): 281.

Ingersoll, Julie, 'Is It Finished? *The Passion of the Christ* and the Fault Lines in American Christianity,' in Michael Berenbaum (ed.), *After the Passion is Gone* (Lanham, MD: Altamira Press, 2004), pp. 75–87.

Jacobs, Jack, and Douglas Century, *If Not Now, When? Duty and Sacrifice in America's Time of Need* (New York: Berkeley Caliber, 2008).

Jantzen, Grace M., *Violence to Eternity*, Jeremy Carette and Morny Joy (eds), (London: Routledge, 2009).

Jarecki, Eugene (Director), *Why We Fight*. Sony Pictures, 2006.

Jay, Nancy, *Throughout Your Generations Forever: Sacrifice, Religion, and Paternity* (Chicago, IL: University of Chicago Press, 1992).

— 'Sacrifice as Remedy for Having Been Born of Woman,' in Elizabeth A. Castelli (ed.), *Women, Gender Religion: A Reader* (New York: Palgrave, 2001).

Jefferson, Thomas, 'Sidebar – Tree of Liberty Letter,' *The Atlantic*, October 1996. http://www.theatlantic.com/issues/96oct/obrien/blood.htm

Jensen, David H., *Responsive Labor: A Theology of Work* (Louisville, KY: Westminster John Knox, 2006).

Jersak, Brad, and Michael Hardin, (eds), *Stricken by God? Nonviolent Identification and the Victory of Christ* (Grand Rapids, MI: Wm. B. Eerdmans Co., 2007).

Johnson, Chalmers, *Sorrows of Empire* (New York: Metropolitan, 2004).

— *Nemesis: The Last Days of the American Republic* (New York: Metropolitan, 2006).

— 'America's Unwelcome Advances,' *Mother Jones*, 22 August 2008. http://www.motherjones.com/print/15574

Johnson, George S., 'Was Jesus Subversive? Considering the "Other" Reason Jesus Died on the Cross,' *The Lutheran* (March 2008): 28–29.

Juhi, Bushra, 'Iraq Museum Reclaims 700 Stolen Artifacts,' *National Geographic News*, 28 April 2008. http://news.nationalgeographic.com/news/2008/04/080428-AP-iraq.html

Kahn, Paul W., *Putting Liberalism In Its Place* (Princeton, NJ: Princeton, 2005).

Kohler, Judith, and Colleen Slevin, 'Will War Protesters "Recreate 68?"' Associated Press 25 August 2008. *Themorningcall.com*. http://www.mcall.com/news/local/all-a1_cvnprotests.6560317aug25,0,1932893.story

Koizumi, K., 'Chap. 5 – R & D in the FY 2009 Department of Defense Budget.' *AAAS – The World's Largest General Scientific Society*, 7 March 2008. http://www.aaas.org/spp/rd/09pch5.htm

Lakoff, George, *Moral Politics: How Liberals and Conservatives Think* (Chicago, IL: University of Chicago Press, 2002).

Landres, J. Shawn and Michael Berenbaum (eds), *After the Passion Is Gone: American Religious Consequences* (New York: Altamira, 2004).

Langan, John, S.J., 'The Elements of St. Augustine's Just War Theory,' in William S. Babcock (ed.), *The Ethics of St. Augustine* (Atlanta, GA: Scholars Press, 1991).

Larry King Live, 'Interview with George Tenent.' *CNN.com*. 30 April 2007. http://www.cnn.com/CNN/Programs/larry.king.live/

Lawrence, Bruce B., and Aisha Karim (eds), *On Violence: A Reader* (Durham, NC: Duke University Press, 2007).

Lenoir, Tim, 'All but War Is Simulation: The Military-Entertainment Complex,' *Configurations* Johns Hopkins University Press and the Society for Literature and Science, 2008, 289–334.

Leshan, Lawrence, *The Psychology of War: Comprehending Its Mystique and Its Madness* (Chicago, IL: Noble Inc., 1992).

Lictblau, Eric, 'Senate Approves Bill to Widen Wiretap Powers,' *The New York Times*, 10 July 2008.

Lincoln, Bruce, *Holy Terrors: Thinking about Religion after September 11* (Chicago, IL: University of Chicago Press, 2003).

— 'Bush's God Talk: Analyzing the President's Theology,' *Christian Century* 121, no. 20 (2004): 22–29.

Lopez, C. Todd, 'Army Seeks Language, Medical Skills from Non-Citizens,' *Army Mil/News*. 14 March 2009. http://www.army.mil/-news/2009/02/23/17328-army-seeks-language-medical-skills-from-non-citizens/

Lowell, Robert, 'On the Gettysburg Address,' in Allan Nevins (ed.), *Lincoln and the Gettysburg Address* (Urbana, IL: University of Illinois Press, 1964).

Lutz, Catherine, 'Making War at Home in the United States: Militarization and the Current Crisis,' *American Anthropologist* 104.3 (2002): 723–36.

— *The Bases of Empire: The Global Struggle Against U.S. Military Posts* (New York: New York University Press, 2009).

Lynch, Gordon, *Understanding Theology and Popular Culture* (Oxford: Blackwell, 2005).

Maguen, Shira, Barbara A. Lucenko, Mark A. Reger, Gregory A. Gahm, Brett T. Litz, Karen H. Seal, Sara J. Knight and Charles R. Marmar, 'The Impact of Reported Direct and Indirect killing on Mental Health Symptoms in Iraq War Veterans, *Journal of Traumatic Stress*, February 23.1 (2010): 86–90.

Marcuse, Herbert, *An Essay on Liberation* (Boston, MA: Beacon Press, 1969).

Markus, R.A., 'Augustine's Views on the Just War,' in W.J. Shiels (ed), *The Church and War: Papers Read at the Twenty-first Summer Meeting and the Twenty-second Winter Meeting of the Ecclesiastical History Society* (Great Britain: Ecclesiastical History Society, 1983).

Marvin, Carolyn, and David W. Ingle, 'Blood Sacrifice and the Nation: Revisiting Civil Religion,' *Journal of the American Academy of Religion* 64.4 (1996).

— *Blood Sacrifice and the Nation: Totem Rituals and the American Flag* (Cambridge: University Press, 1999).

May, Larry (ed.), *War: Essays in Political Philosophy* (Cambridge: Cambridge University Press, 2008).

McDonald, H.D., *The Atonement of the Death of Christ in Faith, Revelation and History* (Grand Rapids, MI: Baker Book House, 1985).

McLeroy, Carrey, 'Army Center Experience Opens in Philadelphia,' *Army Mil/News*, 2 September 2008. www.army.mil/-news/2008/09/02/12072

McLoughlin, William G., *Revivals, Awakenings and Reform: An Essay on Religion and Social Change in America, 1607–1977* (Chicago, IL: Chicago University Press, 1978).

Meredith, Catherine, 'Soldier from Quakertown Killed in Iraq,' *The Morning Call*, 23 February 2009. www.themorningcall.com

Merton, Thomas, *The Nonviolent Alternative*, Gordon C. Zahn (ed.), (New York: Farrar, Straus and Giroux, 1971, rev. ed. 1980).

'Military Helicopter Picks up Lehigh Valley ROTC Cadets,' *WFMZ-TV 69News Online*. Web. 8 August 2008. http://www.wfmz.com/

Miller, Arthur G. (ed.), *The Social Psychology of Good and Evil* (New York: Guilford, 2004).

Mitchell, Greg and Robert Jay Lifton, *Hiroshima in America: A Half-Century of Denial* (New York: Avon, 1995).

Moltmann, Jürgen, 'The Cross as a Military Symbol for Sacrifice,' in Marit Trelstad (ed.), *Cross Examinations: Readings on the Meaning of the Cross Today* (Minneapolis, MN: Augsburg Fortress, 2006), p. 262.

Mooney, Alexander, 'Obama says time to rid world of nuclear weapons,' *CNN.com*. 8 April 2009. http://www.cnn.com/2008/POLITICS/07/16/obama.speech/index.html

Mosse, George L., *Fallen Soldiers: Reshaping the Memory of the World Wars* (New York: Oxford University Press, USA, 1990).

— *Confronting the Nation: Jewish and Western Nationalism* (Hanover, NY: Brandeis University Press, 1993).

Myers, Ched, *Binding the Strong Man: A Political Reading of Mark's Story of Jesus* (Maryknoll, NY: Orbis Books, 1988).

National World War II Memorial, http://www.wwiimemorial.com/default.asp?page=facts.asp&subpage=intro

National Commission on Terrorist Attacks, 9/11 Commission Report, National Commission on Terrorist Attacks upon the United States, 21 August 2004, http://www.9-11commission.gov/

National Commission on Terrorist Attacks upon the United States, 'Commission Report,' 11 October 2008. http://govinfo.library.unt.edu/911/report/index.htm

Nelson-Pallmeyer, Jack, *Jesus Against Christianity: Reclaiming the Missing Jesus* (New York: Trinity International, 2001).

— *Is Religion Killing Us? Violence in the Bible and the Quran* (New York: Continuum, 2003).

Ness, Cindy D., 'The Rise in Female Violence,' *Daedalus* (2007): 86–97.

Nevins, Allan (ed.), *Lincoln and the Gettysburg Address* (Urbana, Ill: University of Illinois Press, 1964).

Niebuhr, Reinhold, *Moral Man and Immoral Society* (New York: Scribner's Sons, 1960).

Noll, Mark A., and Luke E. Harlow (eds.), *Religion and American Politics From the Colonial Period to the Present* (New York: Oxford, 2007).

Obama, Barack, 'Remarks of Senator Barack Obama on the Iraq War,' 2 April 2008, http://obama.senate.gov/speech/070321-remarks_of_sena_11/

— 'Obama Speech to Congress Part 1/6' *YouTube,* 24 February 2009, http://www.youtube.com/watch?v=2A8AYa5JqmU

— 'Remarks of President Barack Obama – Address to Joint Session of Congress.' The White House, 24 February 2009, http://www.whitehouse.gov/the_press_office/remarks-of-president-barack-obama-address-to-joint-session-of-congress/

— 'The Transcript of Obama's Remarks on Airline Security and Terror Watch Lists.' *Washington Post,* 28 December 2009, http://voices.washingtonpost.com/44/2009/12/obama-remarks-on-airline-secur.html

O'Connell, Mary Ellen, 'Unlawful Killing with Combat Drones: A Case Study of Pakistan, 2004–2009,' in Simon Bronitt (ed.) *Shooting to Kill: The Law Governing Lethal Force in Context.* Forthcoming, Notre Dame Legal Studies Paper No. 09–43.

Okuda, Sadako Teiko, *A Dimly Burning Wick: Memoir from the Ruins of Hiroshima* (trans. Pamela Bea Wilson Vergun; New York: Algora Publishing, 2008).

Olson, Gary L., 'The Rich Are Very Different from You and Me.' *Z Communications,* 1 January 2007. http://www.zmag.org

— 'Re: FYI – Chinook Helicopter to Land in Quad Thursday/Transport LV ROTC Cadets to Training,' 23 April 2008. E-mail.

Pagels, Elaine, *Beyond Belief: The Secret Gospel of Thomas* (New York: Random House, 2003).

Pahl, Jon, *Empire of Sacrifice: The Religious Origins of American Violence* (New York: New York University, 2010).

— 'Shifting Sacrifices: Christians, War and Peace in America,' in Catherine Brekus and W. Clark Gilpin (eds), *American Christianities* (Chapel Hill, NC: University of North Carolina Press, 2011).

Perry, Tony, 'Judge Allows Blackwater to Resume Work on San Diego Facility' *Los Angeles Times*, 5 June 2008. *CommonDreams.org*. See http://www.commondreams.org/archive/2008/06/05/9432/

Peterson, Spike (ed.), *Gendered States: Feminist (re)Visions of International Relations Theory* (London: Lynne Rienner, 1992).

Perkins, Judith, *The Suffering Self: Pain and Narrative Representation in the Early Christian Era* (London: Routledge, 1995).

Pew Forum, 'Iraq and Just War: A Symposium.' *Pew Forum on Religion & Public Life*. 30 September 2002. See http://pewforum.org/events/?EventID=36

Pilisuk, Marc with Jennifer Achord Rountree, *Who Benefits from Global Violence and War: Uncovering a Destructive System* (Westport, CT: Praeger Security International, 2008).

Pincus, Walter, 'Obama Administration Looks to Colleges for Future Spies,' *Washingtonpost.com* 20 June 2009. http://www.washingtonpost.com/wp-dyn/content/article/2009/06/19/AR2009061903501.html?referrer=emailarticle

Pollin, Robert and Heidi Garrett-Peltier, 'The U.S. Employment Effects of Military and Domestic Spending Priorities: An Updated Analysis,' *Political Economy Research Institute* (Amherst, MA: University of Massachusetts Amherst, 2009).

Priest, Dana and William M. Arkin, 'Top Secret America: A Hidden World, Growing Out of Control,' *The Washington Post*, 19 July 2010.

PRISP, *Pat Roberts Intelligence Scholars Program*, https://www.cia.gov/careers/jobs/view-all-jobs/pat-roberts-intelligence-scholars-program-p

PsySR, 'I Approve This Resolution.' *Psychologists for Social Responsibility*, http://www.psysr.org/voteyes

Purcell, Sarah J., *Sealed With Blood: War, Sacrifice, And Memory in Revolutionary America* (Philadelphia, PA: University of Pennsylvania Press, 2007).

Rabie, Dina, 'Militarizing Anthropology,' *IslamOnline.net*. 18 October 2007. http://www.islamonline.net/

Rasmussen, Larry, 'In the Face of War.' *Sojourners: Christians for Justice and Peace*. 34.1 (January 2005):12–17.

Redpill.8.blogspot.com, 'The Army Center Experience: The Future of Recruiting,' Web log post 20 February 2009. http://redpill8.blogspot.com/2009/02/army-experience-center-marketing.html

Reed, Jay, 'UT Military: Toward a 21st Century Peace Movement.' 12 September 2001. *UT Watch on the Web*, http://utwatch.org/war/ut_military.html

Reisman, W. Michael and Douglas L. Stevick, 'The Applicability of International Law Standards to United Nations Economic Sanctions Programs' *European Journal of International Law* 9 (1998): 86–141.

Rejali, Darius, *Torture and Democracy* (Princeton, NJ: Princeton University Press, 2007).

Rich, Frank, 'Obama Can't Turn the Page on Bush,' *The New York Times*, 17 May 2009.

— 'The Swift-Boating of Cindy Sheehan,' *The New York Times*, 21 August 2005.

Richey, Russell E., and Donald G. Jones (eds.), *American Civil Religion* (New York: Harper and Row, 1974).

Rieger, Joerg, *Christ & Empire: From Paul to Postcolonial Times* (Minneapolis, MN: Fortress Press, 2007).

— *No Rising Tide: Theology, Economics, and the Future* (Minneapolis, MN: Fortress Press, 2009).

Riley, Robin L., Chandra Talpade Mohanty, and Minnie Bruce Pratt (eds), *Feminism and War: Confronting U.S. Imperialism* (London: Zed, 2008).

Rist, John M., *Augustine: Ancient Thought Baptized* (Cambridge: Cambridge University Press, 1994).

Rohde, David, 'Army Enlists Anthropology in War Zones,' *The New York Times*, 5 October 2007. http://query.nytimes.com/gst/fullpage.html

Rossing, Barbara R., *The Rapture Exposed: The Message of Hope in the Book of Revelation* (New York: Basic Books, 2004).

Rubin, Elizabeth, 'Battle Company is Out There,' *The New York Times*, 24 February 2008.

Ruether, Rosemary Radford, *America, Amerikkka: Elect Nation And Imperial Violence* (London: Equinox Publishing, 2007a).

— 'Sexuality, Gender and Women' in Judith Chelius Stark (ed.), *Feminist Interpretations of Augustine* (University Park, PA: Pennsylvania State University Press, 2007b).

Schachtman, Noah, 'Army Sets Up New Office of Videogames,' *Wired*, 12 December 2007. http://blog.wired.com/defense/2007/12/armys-new-offic html

Sachs, Jeffrey D., *Common Wealth: Economics for a Crowded Planet* (New York: Penguin, 2008).

Salaheddin, Sinan, 'Iraq Bars Blackwater, Tarnished by Civilian Deaths.' *CommonDreams.org.* 29 January 2009. http://www.commondreams.org/headline/2009/01/29

— 'Iraqi Shoe Thrower Speaks Out,' *AOL News*, 19 February 2009. http://news.aol.com/article/iraqi-police-bomb-kills-4-wounds-11-in/342834?icid=sphere_newsaol_inpage

Scahill, Jeremy, *Blackwater: The Rise of the World's Most Powerful Mercenary Army* (New York: Nation Books, 2007).

Schaff, Philip, and Henry Wace (eds), *Nicene and Post-Nicene Fathers*, Vol. 5 (Peabody, MA: Hendrickson, 1994).

Scheer, Robert, *Pornography of Power: How Defense Hawks Hijacked 9/11 and Weakened America* (New York: Twelve, 2008).

Schell, Johnathan, and Robert S. Boynton, 'People's Power Vs. Nuclear Power: A Conversation.' *Daedalus* (Winter 2007): 28–29.

Schmitt, Eric and Robert F. Worth, 'US Widens Terror War to Yemen, a Qaeda Bastion,' *The New York Times*, 27 December 2009.

Schüssler Fiorenza, Elisabeth, 'Ties that Bind: Domestic Violence Against Women,' in Elisabeth Schüssler Fiorenza (ed.), *Women Resisting Violence: Spirituality for Life* (Maryknoll, NY: Orbis Books, 1996).

Schüssler Fiorenza, Elisabeth, and Hermann Haring (eds), *The Non-Ordination of Women and the Politics of Power* (Maryknoll, NY: Orbis Books, 1999).

Shane, Scott, 'Bush's Speech on Iraq War Echoes Voice of an Analyst,' *The New York Times*, 5 December 2005.

Shanker, Thom, 'Despite Slump, U.S. Role as Top Arms Supplier Grows,' *The New York Times*, 6 September 2009.

Sheehan, Cindy, 'Good Riddance, Attention Whore,' *Daily Kos: State of the Nation*, 28 May 2007. http://www.dailykos.com/storyonly/2007/5/28/12530/1525

Sherman, Daniel J., *The Construction of Memory in Interwar France* (Chicago, IL: University of Chicago Press, 1999).

Shiels W.J. (ed.), *The Church and War: Papers Read at the Twenty-first Summer Meeting and Twenty-second Winter Meeting of the Ecclesiastical History Society* (Oxford: Blackwell, 1983).

Simpson, Gary M., *War, Peace and God: Rethinking the Just-war Tradition* (Minneapolis, MN: Augsburg Fortress, 2007).

Sobrino, Jon, *Christology at the Crossroads* (trans. John Drury; MaryKnoll, NY: Orbis Books, 1985).

— *Jesus the Liberator: A Historical-Theological Reading of Jesus of Nazareth* (trans. Paul Burns and Francis McDonagh; Maryknoll, NY: Orbis Books, 1993).

— *Where is God? Earthquake, Terrorism, Barbarity, and Hope* (trans. Margaret Wild; Maryknoll, NY: Orbis Books, 2004).

Soelle, Dorothee, *Suffering* (trans. Everett Kalin; Minneapolis, MN: Fortress Press, 1975).

Soelle, Dorothee, and Shirley A. Cloyes, *To Work and to Love: A Theology of Creation* (Philadelphia, PA: Fortress Press, 1984).

Spiro, Ellen and Phil Donahue, *Body of War*, Docudrama Films and New Video, 2007.

Stark, Judith Chelius, 'Augustine on Women,' in Judith Chelius Stark (ed.), *Feminist Interpretations of Augustine* (University Park, PA: Pennsylvania State University Press, 2007).

Stassen, Glen (ed.), *Just Peacemaking: Ten Practices for Abolishing War* (Cleveland, OH: The Pilgrim Press, 1998).

— 'The Unity, Realism, and Obligatoriness of Just Peacemaking Theory,' *Journal of the Society of Christian Ethics* 23.1 (Spring/Summer 2003): 171–94.

Stassen, Glen and Michael Westmoreland-White, 'Defining Violence and Nonviolence,' in J. Denny Weaver and Gerald Beisecker-Mast (eds), *Teaching Peace: Nonviolence and the Liberal Arts* (New York: Rowman & Littlefield, 2003).

Sterling, Greg, '*Mors Philosophi*: The Death of Jesus in Luke,' *Harvard Theological Review* 90.4 (2001): 383–402.

Stewart, Robert B. (ed.), *The Resurrection of Jesus: John Dominic Crossan and N.T. Wright in Dialogue* (Minneapolis, MN: Augsburg, 2006).

Stockholm International Peace Research Institute, 'Recent Trends in Military Expenditure,' *Stockholm International Peace Research Institute Report*, 21 October 2009. http://www.sipri.org/research/armaments/milex/resultoutput/trends

Stout, Jeffrey, *Democracy and Tradition* (Princeton, NJ: Princeton University Press, 2004).

Sung, J.M., *Desire, Market and Religion* (New York: SCM Press, 2007).

Sylva, Dennis D., 'The Temple Curtain and Jesus: Death in the Gospel of Luke,' *Journal of Biblical Literature* 105.2 (1986): 239–50.

Tamez, Elsa, *The Amnesty of Grace: Justification by Faith from a Latin American Perspective* (trans. Sharon H. Ringe; Nashville, TN: Abingdon, 1993).

Tanner, Kathryn, 'Incarnation, Cross, and Sacrifice,' *Anglican Theological Review* 86.1 (2004): 35–56.

Taylor, J.R. Stuart Jr., 'How Bush Can Save International Law, Not Sacrifice It,' *National Journal* 35.16 (2003): 1207–209.

Taylor, Mark Lewis, *Religion, Politics, and the Christian Right: Post-9/11 Powers and American Empire* (Minneapolis, MN: Fortress Press, 2005).

— 'American Torture and the Body of Christ: Making and Remaking Worlds,' in Marit Trelstad (ed.), *Cross Examinations: Readings on the Meaning of the Cross Today* (Minneapolis, MN: Fortress Press, 2006).

Taylor, Robert, 'Senate Puts the Finishing Touches on Obama's $636 Billion "Defense" Budget,' *Philadelphia Examiner,* 20 December 2009.

TeSelle, Eugene, 'Toward an Augustinian Politics,' in William S. Babcock (ed.), *The Ethics of St. Augustine* (Atlanta, GA: Scholars Press, 1991).

Tenent, George, *At the Center of the Storm: My Years at the CIA* (New York, NY: HarperCollins, 2007).

Terrell, JoAnne Marie, *Power in the Blood? The Cross in African American Experience* (Maryknoll, NY: Orbis Books, 1998).

— '"Our Mothers" Gardens: Rethinking Sacrifice,' in Marit Trelstad (ed.), *Cross Examinations: Readings on the Meaning of the Cross Today* (Minneapolis: MN: Fortress Press, 2006).

Thornton, Sharon, *Broken Yet Beloved: A Pastoral Theology of the Cross* (St. Louis, MO: Chalice, 2002).

Tillich, Paul, *Dynamics of Faith* (New York: Perennial Classics, 1957).

Trelstad, Marit (ed.), *Cross Examinations: Readings on the Meaning of the Cross Today* (Minneapolis, MN: Augsburg Fortress, 2006).

Trudeau, Gary, 'Doonesbury.' Cartoon, *The New York Times,* 9 October 2005.

Turse, Nick, *The Complex: How The Military Invades Our Everyday Lives* (New York: Metropolitan, 2008).

— 'The 700 Military Bases of Afghanistan: Black Sites in the Empire of Bases,' *TomDispatch.com,* 9 February 2010. http://www.tomdispatch.com/dialogs/print/?id=175204

UK Political Studies Association Women and Politics Annual Conference Ethics, 'Feminist Politics and the States We're In: Critical Reflections in Uncertain Times,' Proceedings, University of Edinburgh, 2006.

United Press International, 'U.S. Arms Sales Increase,' *UPI.com* 14 September 2008. http://www.upi.com/Top_News/2008/09/14/US-arms-sales-increase/UPI-70641221429321/

University of Southern California Institute for Creative Technologies, *ICT.USC. edu. See,* http://ict.usc.edu/

US Citizen and Immigration Services, *UCIS.gov*. http://www.uscis.gov/portal/site/uscis/

Vine, David, 'Enabling the Kill Chain,' *Chronicle of Higher Education*, 30 November 2007, Vol 54.14, B9–B10.

Walzer, Michael, *Arguing About War* (New York: Yale University Press, 2004).

Warner, W. Lloyd, 'An American Sacred Ceremony,' in Russell E. Richey and Donald G. Jones (eds.), *American Civil Religion*, (New York: Harper and Row, 1974).

Watt, Alan J., 'Which Approach? Late Twentieth-Century Interpretations of Augustine's Views on War,' *Journal of Church and State* 46.1 (Winter 2004).

Weaver, J. Denny. *The Nonviolent Atonement* (Grand Rapids, MI: Wm. B. Eerdmans Company, 2001).

— 'The Nonviolent Atonement: Human Violence, Discipleship and God,' in Brad Jersak and Michael Hardin (eds), *Stricken by God? Nonviolent Identification and the Victory of Chris* (Grand Rapids, MI: Eerdmans, 2007).

— 'Responding to September 11: Which Religion Shall We Follow?' *Conrad Grebel Review* 20.2 (2002): 79–100.

Weaver, J. Denny and Gerald Beisecker-Mast (eds), *Teaching Peace: Nonviolence and the Liberal Arts* (New York: Rowan & Littlefield, 2003)

Weil, Simone, *Waiting for God* (New York: Harper, 1951).

Weiser, Benjamen, 'Appeals Court Hears Case of Canadian Citizen Sent by U.S. to Syria,' *The New York Times*, 9 December 2008.

Wellman Jr, James K., 'Is War Normal for American Evangelical Religion?' in James K. Wellman, Jr (ed.), *Belief and Bloodshed* (New York: Rowman & Littlefield, 2007).

West, Traci C., *Disruptive Christian Ethics: When Racism and Women's Lives Matter* (Louisville, KY: Westminster John Knox, 2006).

Whitney, Helen (Producer), *Faith and Doubt at Ground Zero*, Frontline, PBS, 2002.

Williams, Delores S., 'Black Women's Surrogacy Experience and the Christian Notion of Redemption' in Marit Trelstad (ed.), *Cross Examinations: Readings on the Meaning of the Cross Today* (Minneapolis, MN: Fortress Press, 2006).

— *Sisters in the Wilderness: The Challenge of Womanist God-Talk* (New York: Orbis Books, 1995).

Williams, Rowan, *Writing in the Dust: After September 11* (Grand Rapids, MI: Eerdmans, 2002).

Wilson, Michael, 'FYI-Chinook Helicopter to Land in Quad Thursday/Transport LV ROTC Cadets to Training.' 24 April 2008. E-mail.

Wink, Walter, *Engaging the Powers: Discernment and Resistance in a World of Domination* (Minneapolis, MN: Fortress Press, 1992).

Wolin, Sheldon S., *Democracy Incorporated: Managed Democracy and the Specter of Inverted Totalitarianism* (Princeton, NJ: Princeton University Press, 2008).

Yoder, John Howard, *The War of the Lamb: The Ethics of Nonviolence and Peacemaking*, Glen Stassen, Mark Thiessen Nation, and Matt Hamsher (eds), (Grand Rapids, MI: Brazos Press, 2009).

Young, Marion Iris, 'Feminist Reactions to the Contemporary Security Regime,' *Hypatia* 18.1 (2003).

Zimbardo, Phillip G., 'A Situationist Perspective on the Psychology of Evil: Understanding How Good People are Transformed into Perpetrators,' in A.G. Miller (ed.), *The Social Psychology of Good and Evil* (New York: The Guilford Press, 2004).

Zwerdling, Daniel, 'Peace Department Proposal Rattles Small Town,' *Weekend Edition, National Public Radio*, 24 March 2007. http://www.npr.org/templates/story/story.php?storyId=9083208.

Zwick, Edward (Director), *Glory*. TriStar Pictures, 2007.

Subject Index

Afghanistan (*see* Iraq and
  Afghanistan)
alienation, in theologies of work
  208–11, 213, 241
America
  as an empire 27, 51, 67, 95, 176,
    240
  as exceptional 3, 66–7, 173
  as the new Israel 178
American
  Anthropological Association 46
  Civil War 132–3, 177–80, 232
  dream 59
  Psychological Association 42
  Revolutionary War 59, 131
  wealth-gap 95
anthropology
  militarizing 42–6
  of sacrifice 79–80, 128, 159–6
  of war 135–8
arms trade (*see* weapons industry)
atomic bombs 19, 170–2, 246–7
atonement, Christian
  as sacrament 54
  theories/metaphors (salvation
    images)
      penal substitution 76–7,
        80–3, 156, 185–6, 189
      ransom 186–8
      satisfaction 76, 185–7,
      sacrificial 76–7, 83, 101, 18
      christus victor 76–7, 80–1,
        83, 88, 155

images 80
theologies of 118, 146, 155–6, 183

budgets
  black 19
  military (*see* military budget)
Bush, George H.W. 197
Bush, George W.
  and 'shoe' protest (*see* protest)
  and 'victory' in Iraq 86, 88
  constitutional changes under 21
  military expansion under 18,
    29, 63
  policy makers 26
  rationale for war in Iraq 111,
    122
  religious language of 65–7
  response to 9/11 (*see* 9/11)
  sacrificial language of *see* sacri-
    ficial language

Carter, Jimmy 65, 228, 241, 247
Cheney, Richard 20
Christian
  doctrines, challenging 54
  ethics 219, 241–2
  evangelism 65, 182–3
  forms of sacrifice, distinguis -
    ing 125
  images of paradise 191
  pastoral care 119
  Right 65–7
  ritualized ethos 67

Author Index

Made in the USA
Middletown, DE
22 September 2021